Christine Faber

The guardian's mystery

Rejected for conscience's sake

`

Christine Faber

The guardian's mystery
Rejected for conscience's sake

ISBN/EAN: 9783741140181

Manufactured in Europe, USA, Canada, Australia, Japa

Cover: Foto ©Andreas Hilbeck / pixelio.de

Manufactured and distributed by brebook publishing software
(www.brebook.com)

Christine Faber

The guardian's mystery

THE GUARDIAN'S MYSTERY;

or,

REJECTED FOR CONSCIENCES' SAKE.

BY

CHRISTINE FABER.

AUTHOR OF "A MOTHER'S SACRIFICE," "CARROLL O'DONOHUE," etc.

P. J. KENEDY AND SONS

3 AND 5 BARCLAY STREET NEW YORK

THE GUARDIAN'S MYSTERY;

OR,

REJECTED FOR CONSCIENCE'S SAKE.

I.

"WHY doesn't he come? I declare it is too bad—but it will be just like him, the old bear, to disappoint me. And he knows Florence will *have* to go to-morrow, and that I want to go with her. I do not see why people will be so disagreeable just to please themselves."

All this is a soliloquy tearfully delivered by a young girl in one of the study-rooms of the Sacred Heart Convent at Manhattanville. She has been impatiently waiting from the moment of the announcement of the first visitor for her own summons to the parlor, and now it is within the last half hour of the time allotted to the friends of the pupils, and no message has come for her. Her impatience is augmented by the fact that on the morrow there will be the final parting of a dozen of the pupils, these being the honored few who have borne the triumphs of graduation. She and her dear friend, Florence Wilbur, are part of the dozen, and some relatives of Florence have invited her to accompany that young lady on a visit to them; but, in order to complete her acceptance of the invitation, it is necessary to see this expected visitor who does not come: and as the minutes wear on she grows more impatient and more tearful. She wrings her white hands in vexation, and even gives a little wrathful twitch to the blue ribbon she wears for good conduct, as if that meritorious badge has something to do with her disappointment.

She is tall enough to look graceful, and erect and slender enough to suggest pretty comparisons, and her black uniform makes her complexion look fairer than it is, while just a tinge of color in her cheeks caused by her impatience, sets off to immense advantage a broad, full brow, large heavily-lashed hazel eyes, and wavy dark hair.

As the minutes pass, leaving but a bare quarter of an hour, her disappointment becomes keener, and at length it culminates in a passionate burst of tears; but at that very instant, "Miss Hammond," is summoned to the parlor.

She dries her eyes, rubbing them so vigorously that the story of her tears is apparent at a glance, and hastily descends.

Many of the visitors lingering until the last minute, the reception parlors seem to be crowded as Miss Hammond hurries from one to another in search of *her* caller. She sees him at length in a corner—he always takes a corner—his dark, green cotton umbrella held stiffly before him, and his clothes looking as if each separate garment had been chosen for its grotesque appearance and its misfit. As he rises to greet the young lady no stranger figure can be well imagined. Displaying an unusual amount of shirt bosom he has made the display still more conspicuous by exceedingly large and brilliant studs; his coat while of the clerical cut, departs in great degree from the clerical color, and his pantaloons, though sober enough in hue and design, lose their appropriateness when one regards their length. Evidently their owner was parsimoneous about the quantity, and thought that as he had been lavish in the matter of his coat, he must atone for it by the size of his unmentionables;

they are four inches above his low-cut shoes and give ample view of large, bony ankles snugly encased in white, woolen stockings. His hat that he holds in his hand is a low crown, brown felt, but with a brim broad enough to suggest a Mexican sombrero. He has red hair, red, grizzled hair, plentifully mixed with gray, a florid face, and brown eyes capable of a great variety of expressions. His age is difficult to guess, though most observers would place it well in the forties. Being somewhat above the medium height and inclined to portliness, his grotesque figure always attracts attention just as it is doing now while Miss Hammond is greeting him.

"I thought you did not intend to come, Mr. Mallaby," she says, her indignation not yet spent, and consequently showing itself in her voice. She is aware that everybody is looking at them, and that conversations are suspended in order to give them more attention, but she is accustomed to that, having experienced it on every occasion of Mr. Mallaby's visit, and she is also indifferent to it. Her indifference arises partly from the fact that Matthias Mallaby is no relative—only a friend of her deceased father to whom has been intrusted her fortune until she shall become of age—and partly to an independence and willfulness of character which make her rather defiant of the opinion of others.

"I was detained, my dear," replies Mr. Mallaby in a deep voice, "and now that I am here I suppose you want me to proceed to business at once."

"If you please, Mr. Mallaby."

The tone of the young lady indicates her estimation of her guardian; he is her guardian, and nothing more.

"Well, my dear;" the brown eyes have assumed a very kindly expression, and looked at without regard to the apparent oddity of their owner, they are exceedingly winning.

"An income is assured to you for the present; it will amount to—"

Before he can name the sum she, struck alone by the first part of his remark, exclaims with alarm:

"*For the present*—what do you mean? Am I not *always* to have an income? Did not papa leave fortune enough?"

"Softly, my dear; don't get so excited. Your papa's fortune was hardly as large as it was thought to be, and speculations made just before his death have not turned out so well. But you will not want, and, as I was saying, your income for the present will be six hundred a year."

"Only *six hundred a year*," she exclaims in dismay; "why that will not buy much more than shoes and gloves, and I shall want ever so many things."

He does not reply, but settles his big, freckled, ungloved hands more firmly on the horn handle of his umbrella.

"Six hundred a year," she repeats, and then as if with sudden resignation, she says quickly:

"Well, I must only practise economy. But I shall want all the money for which I wrote to you, because while making my visit to Miss Wilbur's friends, I expect to buy a good many things; we have both arranged to make several purchases."

"A sensible way to begin the practice of economy," says Mr. Mallaby; then, fumbling in one of his breast-pockets, he continues:

"You have not written much about this Miss Wilbur in your letters—what kind of a place is she going to take you to? Is she—" suddenly hesitating, and his hesitation increases as the big hazel eyes begin to express a most indignant wonder; but at length he brings, or rather blurts out:

"Is she the right kind of a person for you to be invited by?"

"*Mr. Mallaby!*"

Miss Hammond's tone expresses astonishment, anger, reproach, and so many other emotions that Mr. Mallaby takes his hand out of his bosom without producing anything, and clasps it with the other hand on the handle of the umbrella; then he unclasps and clasps them both alternately a number of times, while Miss Hammond in that same tone relentlessly continues:

"Miss Wilbur is a young lady of excellent family; she is quite rich, her income being ten times the amount of my paltry six hundred. I am honored by her friendship and her invitation."

"Perhaps you are, and perhaps she is more honored by yours; but I must ask a few other questions, my dear."

As if to brace himself, he rises, putting the umbrella under his arm in such a manner that it adds very much to his comical appearance.

"Who constitutes this family where Miss Wilbur is going to visit? Are they of the male, or female gender, and are they Catholics, Protestants, Jews or heathens?"

Miss Hammond is too indignant to see any humor in this question, and she having also arisen, draws herself up while she answers:

"Her mother is abroad for health. Her father like my own is dead. She is an only child. The people we are going to visit are her father's brother and sister who live on Hubert Street in New York. They are Protestants as was also her father until his marriage. Her mother was always a Catholic. Three months from this date she is going abroad to join her mother. Now having given you the essential part of her history, have you any more questions to ask, Mr. Mallaby?"

"No, my dear; I shall take the rest on trust, entirely on trust, and hope that you will enjoy your visit. Let me know in time before you end it so that

Mrs. Denner will be ready for you.   And here is the money—'' again fumbling in his breast and this time drawing forth a wallet which he places in Miss Hammond's hand.

"Be careful of it, and good-bye!" as the signal for the departure of all visitors just then sounds.

He extends his hand looking as if he would very much like to linger over the limp passive fingers she lays within his grasp for a moment; but her cool, dignified manner abashes him, and he goes forth, his cotton umbrella perched ludicrously under his arm, and his long, clerically-cut coat, and his short pantaloons making a figure so grotesque and comical that Miss Hammond is fain to hasten from the sight.

II.

HUBERT STREET was a short street, and it had little distinctive character, but, in some of the days prior to elevated roads and telephones, it contained the abodes of well-to-do, and eminently respectable families. Exciting business had not then thrust itself up to its very doors, as it did in latter years, and the sober blocks about it bore an equally quiet, and genteel air. It had also the additional advantage of being near St. John's Park, a local attraction which enhanced the value of property and determined the claim to aristocracy of the neighboring inhabitants; for admission to the park was obtained only by key, and the ownership of a key marked at once the wealth and pedigree of the owner. The houses on Hubert Street were built mostly after the same pattern, and all of their occupants with two exceptions, were staid, slow-going people to whom the stirring events of subsequent years might have seemed like sacriligious innovations upon nature's own progress. The exceptions were a brother and sister who dwelt in one of the corner houses that fronted on Hubert Street, and who, because of their long residence in that particular abode, were well known to the whole neighborhood. In that house both had been born, and in that house both of their parents had died.

The brother was known to be a scholar, thoroughly collegebred and accomplished by travel, devoted to books, and averse to society; the sister was equally famed for her devotion to her brother, her sharp tongue, and her strong and generally wrong opinions upon every subject.

She was forty years old, but ten years older looking because of her fretful disposition, and from that same cause she was somewhat unprepossessing in appearance. Her forehead having taken naturally to knotting itself when she was a baby, had formed on its high, bald surface, so many knots since, that even her smile when she actually yielded to one, was gloomily overshadowed by them, and her sharp, puckered face was made still more so by small, deeply set, intensely black eyes. Some attempts to detract from the height of her forehead was apparent in the fringe of thin, straggling little spit-curls which surmounted it. She was petite in size and so light and noiseless in her movements, that Anne, the servant of all work frequently experienced no little secret wrath to find Miss Wilbur at her shoulder when a few moments before she had left that lady busily occupied in the extreme upper part of the house.

Miss Wilbur was mistress and housekeeper, and her sole charge was her scholarly, and retiring brother. He was four years her junior, utterly unlike her in appearance, and while she fretted and made herself old, he derived comfort from his books, his pen, and a certain philosophy born of his very reflections. Her worriments were greatly argumented on the day that she received a letter from her niece, Florence Wilbur, announcing not only an intended visit of that young lady to the Wilbur homestead, but that she actually had taken the liberty of inviting for the two months of her own stay, her dear, and intimate friend and classmate, Agnes Hammond. Not alone was Miss Wilbur worried by that news, but she became very angry, and she burst upon her brother in his study, with a tirade against women in general, but against her niece, Florence, in particular.

"Does she suppose we keep open house here, that she should take it upon herself to invite this person —how dare she assume such a liberty?"

Her little black eyes snapped, and the knots in her forehead protruded.

The young man whom she addressed, beyond lifting his eyes for a moment from the page of foolscap on which he was writing when she entered, took no further notice of her; her presence, nor her tirade did not seem to cause him the least disturbance, for his pen held firmly between white, well-shaped fingers, moved as rapidly òver the paper as it could have done prior to her entrance.

"Are you deaf, Sydney Wilbur, that you can go on writing in the face of what I tell you? Is it nothing to *you* that these two girls are coming here—two, mind you, and one a total stranger?

Continuing to approach him as she spoke, her last words were uttered as she stood directly in front of his desk, and she shook poor Florence's letter almost in his face, an action that compelled him to drop his pen and look at her. But it was a very pleasant look he gave; his mouth curved into a smile that partly showed very white, even teeth under his slight brown mustache. His eyes, large, brown ones they were, had a laughing look also; indeed, with his Grecian features, dark hair, and complexion clear as a girl's, he made so handsome and pleasant a sight it seemed a wonder how his sister could maintain her anger in its presence; but she did not soften a jot; not even when he pleasantly replied:

"You are inconsistent, Deborah—how often have you reproached me for not cultivating at least the society of our own neighborhood, and especially of that ridiculous friend of yours, Miss Liscome? And now that there is an opportunity of my cultivating society within our very doors you are angry."

"Cultivating the society of the neighborhood is a very different thing from having two hoydenish girls on a visit," pushing back her little spit-curls until her large forehead was revealed in all its baldness, "and

Miss Liscome is a sensible person, and what is more, she is not a Catholic. It is bad enough to have one Catholic coming in the person of Florence, but two are too much for human nature to bear. I shall write immediately and tell Florence to retract her invitation."

"You will do nothing of the kind." The change in the tone and appearance of the speaker was startling. Every trace of his recent smile had disappeared leaving in his place only the expression of an inflexible determination; even the handsome brown eyes seem to have grown hard, and to emit flashes of a temper that it would be hardly well to encounter.

Miss Wilbur cowered a little, and she retreated a pace as she saw her brother rise from his chair and give it an angry fling behind him. He was above the medium height and somewhat slender but with strong and compact muscles. He carried himself very erect, on occasions holding his head so well up that it gave to his appearance an air of great haughtiness; he was holding himself in that manner now, and looking down upon his sister with such an expression as he had never turned upon her but twice before in his whole life.

"Florence Wilbur is *my* niece as well as yours, and as I am of age, and the master of this house, you will write and tell her that not alone is she to make our house *her* home for the two months of her stay before she goes to Europe, but the home for so long a period as she chooses, of any friend, or friends she may care to invite. You will write that letter immediately, please, and write it here, at my dictation."

He had placed, while he was speaking, paper into position for her, returned to its place the chair he had flung behind him, and stepped courteously aside that she might seat herself at the desk.

The knots in Miss Wilbur's forehead were growing

slightly purple from impotent rage. Remembering the two former occasions on which her brother had shown just such determination, she knew how vain would be any attempt to oppose him; still, she could not and she would not yield without a further effort for the mastery.

"Just let me reason with you," she said, her thin voice raised to its shrillest pitch.

"Write;" he commanded, dipping the pen into the ink, and extending it to her.

She persisted;

"We don't know anything of this person—she may—"

"Write!" he interrupted, still extending the pen to her.

"She will be falling in love with you, and trying to make you go against the terms of that awful will."

This time her words were fairly screamed.

"Write," he repeated, and striding toward her, he grasped her shoulder with a hold like a vise, actually lifting her from the floor with that single grasp, and setting her down in the chair at the desk.

"Write!" he again commanded, putting the pen between her fingers, "write what I dictate. 'My dear Florence, both Sydney and I extend to your young friend, Miss Hammond—'

"You're a mean, hateful, savage, cruel, unreasonable, horrible, tyrannical fellow," interrupted Miss Wilbur, who, knowing she would have to obey, was determined to temper her obedience by a few uncomplimentary adjectives.

But she wrote the letter, and wrote it at Sydney's dictation, even being compelled to add that Sydney himself would escort Florence and her friend from the convent. And it was the reception of that letter containing so cordial an invitation from "Aunt Deb," that made Florence Wilbur most urgently repeat her invitation to Agnes Hammond.

III.

THE journey in those days, comparatively recent as they were, from Manhattanville to the lower part of the city, was neither the rapid nor the easy one that it is at present. Its length was sufficient to set the hearts of the two ladies who were to make it quite aglow with pleasurable anticipation. Both might be compared to fledglings who know not how to fly, for both had been placed in the convent in their very tender years and save for infrequent and very brief visits neither had been in the great city.

Their trunks had been already dispatched, and they themselves were but waiting the advent of Mr. Wilbur to say their final adieus. They had hung about their favorite Madames all the morning, listening tearfully to loving admonitions, and promising on their part to be true and constant to the numerous lessons of piety they had received. For Florence perhaps, the gentle *religieuse* felt there was not so much to fear, as the girl was naturally sensible and so prone to humor that she probably would be spared many of the temptations which beset more imaginative and ardent temperaments.

Then, also, while exceedingly pleasant-looking, there was nothing about her to distinguish her from a host of equally good but common-place girls. She was short in stature and inclined to be stout; and she had a freckled face in which not a single feature could lay claim to beauty save a set of exquisite teeth; these were often revealed because of the constant disposition to laughter of the mouth which inclosed them. Her hair was light and so were her eyes, but the color of the latter seemed to be redeemed by their mirthful twinkle: altogether, she was so good-natured, affectionate, and disposed to see the humorous in even vexatious incidents, that she won her way to hearts without effort, and once known, no one thought about her looks.

The affectionate intimacy which from their first acquaintance had existed between herself and Agnes Hammond gave no little wonder to the other pupils—Agnes being so different from Florence. She was reticent, thougthful, dignified, independent almost to defiance, and beautiful, besides being much more ambitious, studying even in recreation times, and reading the most solid works. But that their affection was deep and constant was evinced in many ways, and at no time perhaps more than on this morning, when their eyes humid from the tears of parting with the beloved Madames, often sought each other with an expression that seemed to say:

"The agony of these farewells could hardly be borne but that *we* shall be together."

Mr. Wilbur arrived, and while the girls at the announcement of his name flew to don their out-door garments, he was taken in charge by the sweet-faced, low-voiced, and courtly superioress. It was his first visit to a Catholic institution of the kind, and how shocked his righteous, and prejudiced sister would have been could she have witnessed the charming grace with which he received the kindly attentions of Madame H———.

Had Miss Deborah Wilbur been in his place she would have deemed it her sacred duty to maintain a most rigid exterior in order to show the evil one by her stiff dignity that her accidental entrance to a Romish institution was no sign that she was going to succumb to any Romish blandishment. Fortunately for her peace of mind she did not see the gracious manner of her brother, and still more fortunately for the benefit of her sleep and appetite, she did not behold his meeting with Miss Hammond. He kissed his niece, Florence, when she entered, and then he was presented to Agnes.

She had never looked lovelier; her dark, becoming costume fitting her like a riding habit, and her Grecian face from anticipation, timidity and some embarrassment, wearing the brightest of blushes. The very plainness of Florence seemed to act as an admirable foil to the beauty of her friend; but the generous-hearted girl without a thought of herself, was rejoicing at the favorable impression made by her friend and she looked with affectionate delight at the cordial way in which her young and handsome uncle continued to hold Miss Hammond's hand, while he told the pleasure it gave him to take to his home so charming a guest.

The old-fashioned, but comfortable carriage of the Wilbur's waited at the door, and when the very last farewell had been said, intermitted with vehement promises of frequent letters from the two girls, the three slowly bowled out of the picturesque grounds, both Florence and Agnes continuing to look back and to wave their handkerchiefs to some of the remaining pupils who had come out a little distance to see them quite off. Then Miss Hammond's hand sought a little pearl rosary in her pocket, the parting gift of Madame H———, and her lips formed involuntarily the little ejaculation to the Mother of God that she had been taught to repeat in the convent.

How faithful she meant to be to all the lessons of piety which had been instilled during her school life; how heroic in the fulfillment of every duty, and just at that stage of her fervent thoughts she looked up and across at Wilbur. He was looking at her, and though she had not been aware of it, he had been doing so for some time. Now, however, that he was observed, he withdrew his eyes instantly, but when the carriage had bowled out of the old convent road and was speeding to what is now known as the western Boulevard, he began so interesting an account of the improvements already projected for that locality that she found herself delightedly listening, and even meeting his eyes quite as if she had known him a long time. Not once during the journey did her interest flag, the gentlemanly escort being so full of information and possessed of so much grace and tact in imparting it. She even found herself as they got well into the precincts of of the city proper, imparting bits of her own little family history—her mother's death when she was an infant; her father's shortly after; her own consignment to the convent at a tender age; her annual two days' visit to the home of Mrs. Denner who kept a boarding-house near the central part of the city, and where lived Mr. Mallaby, her father's executor and her own guardian.

"Mallaby!" repeated Mr. Wilbur. "Is it Matthias Mallaby, and does he dress somewhat oddly?"

"Yes;" answered Agnes, "do you know him?" her tone indicating no little surprise, while Florence laughing heartily, said:

"Dress oddly? if you have never seen him, Uncle Sydney, then there is a treat in store for you, for I mean to have Agnes invite him to Aunt Deb's. I saw him once accidently and I expected Agnes to scold me the way I laughed, but she didn't. I thought I should have convulsions at the sight of his pantaloons. I dreamed of them, and the big, bony ankles, below them dancing a jig in the study-hall—fancy the scene, Anges," and in the indulgence of her mirthful imagination, she leaned back in the carriage and laughed immoderately.

Agnes laughed also, and Wilbur smiled; then he replied to Miss Hammond's question.

"I do not know Mr. Mallaby. I never saw him, but I have heard of him; I have heard that though he is extremely odd, he is a man of great integrity."

He may or may not have added the latter part of his remark for the purpose of tempering the fun which his niece was disposed to make of Mr. Mallaby, but if he thought that by so doing he was sparing Miss Hammond's feelings, he was not to know, for that young lady betrayed no sign of either pleasure or displeasure. He was not aware that her indifference arose from the fact that Mr. Mallaby was no relation of hers.

By the time they had arrived at the homestead on Hubert Street, Miss Hammond felt as if she knew Mr. Wilbur quite well, and knowing him so favorably she looked forward with pleasure to meeting his sister, " Aunt Deb."

But Aunt Deb did not see them immediately; Anne, the domestic who admitted them, said that Miss Wilbur had gone to Miss Liscome's to bring that lady to spend the evening with the company. Sydney frowned on receiving the information, but as his sister had completed her preparations for the guests, and Anne had an appetizing repast ready, the absence of the lady of the house did not make much difference.

The girls were to room together; so Anne informed them, when on the conclusion of the repast, Florence desired to know where they were going to sleep that she and Agnes might fortify themselves by a nap for the festivity of the evening. The room to which Anne conducted them was a very large one, containing a great double bed, an immense wardrobe, and the other accessories of a sleeping-chamber, all of equally substantial size. With a view perhaps to banishing the effect of any Romish incantation her young guests might be inclined to perform, Aunt Deb had liberally supplied the apartment with script-

ural texts. She herself had fashioned them out of
huge pieces of bright-colored pasteboard. and glued
them to the walls, to the utter exclusion of every
picture that had at any time adorned the room. She
seemed to have chosen the texts because of their
special warning against idolatry, as if she thought
that was the danger most to be feared from the religion of her guests. The texts looked incongruous
and ridiculous against the pure white walls and they
caused Florence such a fit of laughter that she was
fain to throw herself into the nearest chair and let
her mirth have its way. In Agnes they only caused
wonder. Anne, not knowing at what the young
lady was laughing, but feeling it incumbent upon
her to make some remark since the hostess was not
present, said:

"Miss Wilbur was awful anxious to have this
room fixed for you. She spent all day yesterday
making them letters—" indicating with a sweep of
her arm the brilliantly colored texts—"and hanging them up, and taking down the pictures."

"I think she must have, and spent the night too,"
answered Florence, recovering sufficiently from her
mirth to speak, and then she shook herself out of the
chair, and dismissing the would-be voluble Anne,
turned to Agnes with:

"Aunt Deb was determined to supply us with
scriptural food, but did you ever see anything so
funny? I declare that, 'Make to thyself no false
Gods,' the way it is pasted to the wall has a rollicking air; and as for, 'Make to thyself no graven image,'
it looks as if it were leering at the other texts. But,
seriously, Agnes, as soon as we doff our dresses,
get into our loose gowns, and are comfortably lying
down, I shall tell you what perhaps I ought to have
told you before about Aunt Deb."

Agnes lost little time in getting into the proposed
attire and climbing into the high, wide bed where she

was speedily joined by Florence, and with her arms
arouud Florence's neck she listened while Florence
told the following:

"You know that I have maternal uncles and aunts
to whom I might have gone for these couple of
months before I join my mother in Europe, but with
them I would not have the accommodation afforded
here; then also when I came on occasional visits here
with my mother I liked Uncle Sydney so much.   He
knows how to please, and though he is as strict in his
religious principles as Aunt Deb is, he never obtrudes
them upon others as she does.   She is dreadfully
prejudiced—could never forgive my father for marrying my Catholic mother, and particularly for allowing me to be brought up a Catholic.   For that
reason she has never quite liked either my mother or
me, and perhaps I should have hesitated about coming
here if it were not for the fear that this might be my
last opportunity of seeing Uncle Sydney, my mother,
thinking, as you know, of making a permanent home
abroad.   For the sake of Uncle Sydney's company I
can endure Aunt Deborah, and for the sake of my company I think you also will be willing to endure her; at
all events you saw ner warm letter of invitation, so that
you may feel, no matter what her oddities are, you
are welcome.   I did not tell you about her prejudice
before, lest it might make you hesitate to accept
any invitation to the house.   But you are willing,
dear, to endure a little that we may be together for
a while yet, are you not?"

"Willing to endure a great deal, Florence, for the
sake of being with you," and the rounded arms about
Florence's neck pressed that young lady very tightly.

IV.

THE meeting of Aunt Deb and Miss Hammond had taken place leaving with each a most unfavorable impression of the other. Aunt Deb conceived at once a fierce hatred for her guest because of her beauty and its probable effect upon her brother, while Miss Hammond could not repress an inward shivering at the piercing little bead-like black eyes, and the cold, thin, shrill voice. But Florence was by her side to reassure her with a covert pinch, and Sydney was before her to make amends with his warm smile and pleasant voice for the sharp coldness of his sister's greeting. Miss Hammond also met Miss Liscome. Miss Liscome was a lady of very uncertain age in a very elaborate toilet, her dress being a combination of pea-green silk and white lace, and so scanty, or rather fashionably made, that it had only shoulder knots for sleeves, and the merest pretense for a waist. Her face was not ill-looking, but its natural comeliness was destroyed by the heavy coat of rouge on her cheeks, and the affected simper of her mouth. She was unusually tall and thin, and whenever she stood, having a habit of thrusting her head out before her, she made one think of some scraggy animal looking over a fence. Unlike her friend Deborah Wilbur, she had neither been born nor bred in that neighborhood of Hubert Street; she was even a comparatively recent comer; her residence in the vicinity dating but five years back. She supervised the housekeeping of a partially invalided married sister, and it was while out on marketing duties that she had made the acquaintance of Miss Wilbur who also personally attended to such cares. Whether it was that each intuitively discovered in the other affinities of character, or that they were attracted, by a mutual sympathy because of their trying domestic anxieties they became almost instant friends and confidants calling each other Prudence and Deborah, and pouring regularly and faithfully into each other's ears their own affairs and whatever they might ascertain of the affairs of the neighborhood.

Prudence Liscome did not belie her name; she prudently sought to turn everything to her own interest, and had she not overreached herself in the matter of her beloved virtue she might not have arrived at her present mature age without having entered the matrimonial state. Perseverance, however, in that respect was her axiom, and when she met Deborah Wilbur, and found that lady had a brother whose chivalrous manhood made him polite to every woman, and for his sister's sake attentive to his sister's guests, she took fresh heart in her pursuit of a husband. Her resolution received new vigor from the fact that Miss Wilbur had once in a confidential outburst declared she would be delighted should her brother marry Miss Liscome, avowing as her reasons for her satisfaction, Miss Liscome's sensible age and amiable disposition, (Prudence was always careful not to express a thought unless she was sure it would be approved by her dear friend Deborah.)

Thus the reader may be certain of the full confidence which Miss Liscome had received relative to the coming of Aunt Deb's guests.

Her appearance gave so much mirth to Florence, the girl was in an agony trying to repress it, and at length, in order not to disgrace herself, she began to tell funny stories that they might afford her a pretense for laughing. Her uncle penetrating her *ruse* assisted her, and even Miss Liscome joined in the merriment, not dreaming that the hearty mirth of Sydney and his niece, and her friend, was caused by her a great deal more than by the comical anecdotes.

Aunt Deb was somewhat sharper; she suspected the occasion of the laughter, and she could have strangled both Florence and Agnes. After the first story at which she smiled—she was never known to laugh at anything —she showed her disapproval by looking very solemn and stern, and when she found there was little probability of the pleasantries coming to an end, she unceremoniously interrupted them by requesting—it was more a command—Miss Liscome to sing.

Prudence would not dare to disobey; but she was nothing loth to grant the favor, having taken singing lessons in her youth, and fondly imagining that her voice was both strong and sweet.

Wilbur with perfect gravity, conducted her to the little old-fashioned piano, while his niece pinched herself until she felt the pain sharply in order to compose her face; but just as she had succeeded, Miss Liscome's song nearly sent both her and Agnes into another convulsion. Her voice had all the strength that she imagined it to possess, but as for sweetness it came out absolutely through her nose, and was quite regardless of pitch, or note. To add to its ludicrousness, she had chosen a most tender love song, and the endearing words were dwelt upon and repeated until Florence felt despite her pinching which she had vigorously recommenced, that she should explode, and right in the face of Aunt Deb who, instead of looking at the singer was threateningly watching both her and Agnes.

Even Agnes had far more self-control, for after the first violent disposition to laugh caused by the song, she had quite composed her countenance, and sat looking dignified and respectful enough and Sydney's control seemed marvellous. He had actually remained beside the creature, looking down upon her with an imperturbably grave countenance, and seem-

ing to be as attentive and interested as though his
ears must not have been split with the horrible dis-
cord.   And when she had finished he thanked
her and led her back to her seat into which she sank
looking heated from her exertion, but also looking
very much pleased with herself.

Then Mr. Wilbur would hear Miss Hammond.
Her voice was neither very loud, nor strong, but it
was a pure, sweet contralto of the kind to harmonize
exquisitely with sad, tender strains. Upon Wilbur
the effect was indescribable even to himself, and it required all that determination which was the keynote
of his character to prevent himself from falling then
and there madly in love with his beautiful guest.
As it was, he begged from her song after song until
Miss Liscome grew so pale from jealousy, her rouge
looked like hideous red daubs, and Aunt Deb, her
own knotted face red from anger, interposed sharply:

"I think, Sydney, you have troubled Miss Hammond quite enough.   Suppose you let us hear Florence's voice."

Florence on whom the low, sweet pathetic strains
had the effect of banishing her disposition to mirth,
immediately disclaimed;

"Hear *me*, Aunt Deb, after those exquisite songs—
the effect would be most uncomplimentary to me. I
must beg you to excuse me this evening."

That little speech seemed to enlighten Miss Liscome
with regard to her own musical performance, more
even then Miss Hammond's singing had done, and
she hated both speaker and singer as intensely as the
latter was hated by Aunt Deb.

In their room that night and before either had begun to remove her dress which, according to the modest convent fashion—in direct contrast to Miss Liscome's—was made extremely high in the neck and
long in the sleeves, the two girls were exchanging
merry confidences. But, as usual, Florence was much

the merrier, delivering it as her wise, but laughing opinion, that Agnes' singing had crushed completely Miss Liscome's hopes.

" And oh," she continued, " an idea has just struck me—won't you invite Mr. Mallaby for some evening when Miss Liscome is expected? I fancy now that I see the two together-oh-oh-oh!" and Florence laughed so wildly and violently that it was some seconds before she could recover herself; when she did, she repeated:

" Will you, Agnes?"

" Invite my guardian to your Aunt Deb's house when I am only hear myself on sufferance," replied Agnes in a very questioning tone.

"Fiddlesticks!" ejaculated Florence. Who cares for Aunt Deb when we have Uncle Sydney on our side, and any one can see you have him on your side. You don't know him. From my childhood I have heard about his firm will; that when he was a mere lad at school his firmness was the marvel and fear also, of many. When he wants a thing he'll move heaven and earth to get it, and when he does not want to yield no power short of the supernatural can make him do so. You would not think he had such a character under his affable exterior ; but he has, being passive and gentle until some one or something thwarts him ; then, beware ! not that he storms ; he just resolves, and that resolution is quietly, relentlessly executed. He is equally strong in his likes and dislikes. You look at me with those great eyes of yours as if you wondered where I obtained so much knowledge of him. My mother who admires and loves him used to tell me, and I confidentially acknowledge to you that he is quite my hero. If he were not my uncle I should hardly be answerable for my youthful affections. Neither would I be so sure of trusting you, dear sweet girl that you are, within the influence of such fascination, but that I know your great piety, and that you would never, never consent to make a mixed marriage. But, even though I am so confident of your being proof against his charms, I beg of you to be careful not to run counter to his will, lest you might feel the weight of his inflexible and terrible determination."

The last words were spoken as all the preceding words had been, playfully, and there certainly was no disposition, nor thought in the mind of the speaker, as to prophecy, but with their utterance an involuntary shudder passed over Agnes, and the admonition seemed to become a sort of fixture in her brain.

Florence beginning to yawn, looked at her watch.

"Half past eleven, as I am a sinner"—she exclaimed, springing up with a vigor that was laughable considering her previous indisposition to do anything but talk, "and Uncle Syd means to begin to-morrow morning to show us some of the city sights. Nice looking pair we shall be, losing our night's rest in this manner. I insist that you prepare for bed immediately, Agnes Hammond," using a very peremptory tone, and beginning a hasty disrobing of herself as she spoke.

"When I say my rosary," replied Miss Hammond, taking from her pocket the little pearl gift of the morning. It was enclosed in an odd-shaped case which had the name, Agnes, engraved on a tiny silver plate, and opening the case she drew from it the beads, and proceeded to kneel in a very straight, mortified manner in the middle of the room in order not to be tempted by the proximity of a chair to any reclining position.

"You uncanonized saint!" rejoined the irrepressible Florence, "I forgot that you never omit your rosary. I said part of mine at Mass this morning, and Blessed Mother will have to take the rest on credit. I am too tired and sleepy to do more than say my prayers now."

But tired and sleepy as she declared herself to be, she could not help watching her erectly-kneeling friend, and wondering at, and effectually envying the piety that made Agnes say such long prayers, and say them with such evident devotion and mortification; for herself, when she was ready to say her own prayers she could not resist the temptation of making a very comfortable *prieu-Dieu* out of the great easy chair, and she made her prayer very short: so short, that she was in bed and quite comfortably asleep when Miss Hammond crept in beside her and awoke her with a very warm goodnight kiss, at which she aroused herself sufficiently to say:

"You are such a good, pious girl, Agnes—surely God must love you very much."

And Agnes' heart responded to the praise by a secret, a very secret, but conscious throb of vanity at her superiority in the matter of piety to her friend. Alas! pride goeth before a fall.

V.

The next day, when Aunt Deb found herself not invited to make one of her brother's company into an interesting excursion about the city, she consoled herself by sending for Miss Liscome, and treating that lady to all she would like to have said to both Miss Hammond and her niece. And Miss Liscome, because of her jealousy, feeling equally indignant and revengeful, listened with a most deferential silence, or added by her remarks to the wrath of Miss Wilbur.

"But never you mind, Pru," (when Miss Wilbur was very confidential the Christian name of her friend was abbreviated) "there is one excellent thing to be remembered—the terms of the will I told you about, and in consequence of that, my brother could not, absolutely *could not* marry Miss Hammond, no matter how much her pretty face might win him."

"She has a pretty face, certainly," admitted Pru, "but don't you think Deb.—"(whenever Miss Wilbur got down to Pru, Miss Liscome in flattering imitation abbreviated to Deb) "that she is very forward; at least it so struck me last night, the way she kept on singing, and that, after I, mindful of the rest of the company, had sung only once."

"Forward! the creature is odiously so; but come up stairs and see the way I have fixed their room. They say that these Romanists never read the Bible, so I thought I'd make them take a few of its texts as folks are said to get small-pox, without any special effort."

And Miss Wilbur smiled at her little effort of wit, while Miss Liscome laughed, and rejoined that Deb's sayings were so good they ought positively to be kept in writing. And thus smiling, and laughing, and flattering, the two found themselves in the text-adorned bed chamber.

Miss Wilbur's quick eyes caught the sparkle of something on the dressing table.

"As I live, Prudence Liscome, if there isn't one of their Romish spells—don't touch it—" as Miss Liscome hurrying to the table, was about to lift the little case that partially open, disclosed the silver crucifix attached to Miss Hammond's pearl rosary.

"Don't touch the abomination," she repeated. "I shall get the duster and brush it to where it ought to be—these people even if one of them *is* my own niece have no right to turn a good Presbyterian house into a Romish institution."

And while she spoke she had taken a fancy feather duster from its place by the mantle, and brushed the little case with its contents from the dressing-table to the floor; then, triumphantly continuing her effort she swept it to the open brick fire-place, where the little case with its half revealed rosary fell into a cavity between two somewhat loose bricks and became utterly lost to view.

What events sometimes hang upon our trifling actions! Could Aunt Deb have foreseen that which would happen one day to the hated rosary, lost though it then seemed to be, she would have left it undisturbed on the dressing-table.

As it was, Miss Liscome could not refrain from saying:

"Will it not be missed, and inquired for?" To which Miss Wilbur savagely replied:

"And if it is, what difference will that make? I want it to be missed and inquired for, so that I may give *my* opinion about such things. I am not afraid, Prudence Liscome, to speak *my* mind; when truth and religion require it."

An assertion in which Prudence Liscome immediately and emphatically concurred.

In the midst of the sight-seeing which both girls enjoyed with a delight all the more refreshing to Wilbur, because of its simplicity and naturalness, Florence could not help recurring to her pet thought of inviting Mr. Mallaby.

"Beg Agnes to do it, "Uncle Syd," she said with exquisite persuasiveness, and Uncle Syd immediately turned upon his guest a most imploring look, while he entreated:

"Do, Miss Hammond! I assure you, it will afford me exceeding pleasure to meet your guardian."

There was a sincerity in his tones which his guest could not doubt, and to Florence's delight she promised to write to Mr. Mallaby that very evening, asking him to name the time of his visit.

And her friend did not permit her to forget her promise, for as soon as they were at home, and before even they had changed their street costumes, Florence was clamoring for the letter, saying as an apology for her haste,

"You say that he leaves the city frequently and sometimes for long periods, so that if you do not write immediately he may be absent when the invitation reaches him."

"Oh, I'll write it instantly," with a yawn, "to get rid of your importunities;" but tell me what to say, Florence, for I declare Mr. Mallaby seems to me such an odd, prosy, practical man, that I never write to him but when I am obliged to, and then, in the most brief manner."

"I'll dictate it," said Florence, and she did, so kind and warm and affectionate an epistle, that dignified Miss Hammond paused midway in sheer amazement.

"I never write to him like that," she said, looking almost reproachfully at her friend. "He is not any relative."

" Well, suppose he is not; he is your guardian, and that is akin to relationship. It is high time, Miss, that you condescend to put off a little of your dignity with odd Mr. Mallaby. I dare say if we could only see beneath all that eccentricity, we should find something to admire and to love."

Agnes shrugged her shoulders, not dreaming how one day those words would come back to her with a bitter force and truth.

"Anyway," continued Florence, "I want Mr. Mallaby to feel that he is wanted and looked for, in order to prevent any fear of the acceptance of our invitation. So, you will please, continue, Agnes."

Agnes obeyed, and when the note was written, addressed and sealed, and she was about to change her dress, she felt in her pocket for the little case containing her rosary, that she might transfer it to the pocket of the dress she was about to put on. With her action came also a little twinge of self-reproach for having been so wanting in recollection all day, remembering with a sigh that not once had she repeated her wonted daily little aspiration, and in her secret heart she felt that her neglect had been all owing to the charm which she experienced in Sydney Wilbur's company.

No matter into what recess of her pocket she thrust her fingers, she could not feel the little case, and at length, shaking forth her handkerchief and turning her pocket inside out without any better result, she exclaimed in dismay:

" Oh! Florence! I have lost it—the little pearl rosary with my name on its case that dear Madame H—— gave me just before we came away. What *shall* I do? I would not lose it for anything in this wide world! "

"Don't look so distressed, dear!" rejoined the practical Florence; " if it be really lost, you can say your rosary on your little brown beads, as you have been in the habit of doing. But you are not sure that it *is* lost. Perhaps you did not take it with you this morning, and that it is lying here somewhere in the room."

And she proceeded to look for it quite energetically.

" No; it is not in the room, for I am sure I put it into my pocket this morning the first thing. I wouldn't I couldn't forget it. I value it too highly."

But even while she so vehemently declared her recollection of it, her secret conscience was telling her how she lied, for that morning, the first thing, her thoughts had been full of Sydney Wilbur.

And when her search joined to that which Florence was making, revealed nothing of the missing treasure, tears of vexation and regret welled up in her eyes, and she said to herself:

"I deserve the loss: I have forgotten my pious resolution and the Blessed Virgin did not think I was worthy to retain dear Madame's gift."

A thought which made her feel not quite so much the superior in piety of Florence as she had done the previous night.

VI.

MATTHIAS MALLABY was the fixture, stand-by and oracle of Mrs. Denner's modest boarding-house. Nobody there thought of so much as smiling at his singular dress, for if they had done so, Mrs. Denner, Mr. Denner all the little Denners belonging to Mrs. Denner and Mr. Denner, and all the large Denners, belonging to Mr. Denner by a former spouse, would have gone in a body to smite the person so smiling. Indeed, the children not alone of the house, but of all the houses on that block, and of all the houses on the block adjoining made themselves a sort of **bodyguard** for Mr. Mallaby, for never was he seen going up the street or coming down the street, but that there was seen also a little army of children about him. They seemed to consider his hands, arms, and legs their's to hold, hug, twist, and pinch, if they would, and how their good-natured victim ever succeeded in reaching his own doorway was sometimes a matter of surprise even to himself. His business was the collection of bills, and for that avocation he seemed to have a very special and decided talent. No reluctant debtor who once encountered Matthias Mallaby would be willing to repeat the meeting. It was said that his eyes enforced the payment as much as ever did his tongue, and that, to get away from his peculiar, hard, persistent, following stare, a man would pay any bill no matter how unwilling he might be just then to meet it. It was also said that he enforced the presentation of his bill by a sort of threatening presentation of his green cotton umbrella, which he carried on all occasions,

and that when he met an unwilling or disput-
ing debtor, he was wont to accompany every word
he uttered with a s—i—r, which long drawn out,
and having the r very much trilled, produced a
most ludicrous effect. On one occasion he had even
tracked an escaping debtor, and had succeeded in
capturing him, to the disappointment and envy of
the detectives engaged in the pursuit, and to the
congratulations and delight of the firm by which he,
Mallaby, was employed. And his cleverness had
been made the subject of a long newspaper article in
which was included even an accurate description of
his own appearance; but Mallaby bore the printed
honor with great modesty.

That none of the pugnacious qualities which distinguished his daily avocation were suffered to appear in his leisure moments, was attested by the af'
traction which he had for children. They hailed his
coming and deplored his going, when, as it sometimes
happened he was obliged to go to somewhat distant
localities in the interest of his business.

From all this the reader will infer that he was
neither an obscure, nor unfamiliar figure in business
circles, and that it was not unlikely Sydney Wilbur
in his business intercourse—which even he, retired as
he lived, was sometimes obliged to hold—should
have heard of him.

Mrs. Denner loved the ground upon which he walked, and she frequently called him "that blessed
man," a term of praise that was hardly to be wondered at, as she being a very affectionate mother was
naturally touched by Mr. Mallaby's attention to her
offspring.

On the day that Miss Hammond's invitation arrived
by post for him there came by the same post, another
letter also for Mr. Mallaby, and as Mrs. Denner
placed them both in conspicuous position in his
room, while she smiled over one, recognizing Miss

Hammond's penmanship, she shook her head very dubiously over the other.

"That's one of the letters as always affects him so," she said quite aloud: and then she bent to it and examined very critically the clear, bold, handsome hand.

"He isn't quite himself for days after he gets one of these," she said quite aloud again, and then she started, for at that instant Mr. Mallaby's voice accompanied by the shrill treble of a quartet of her own boisterous little Denners, floated up to her from the entrance hall.

She hurried down calling him, even before she could see him:

"Two letters for you, Mr. Mallaby! One, I know by the handwriting is from that dear child, Miss Agnes."

She might have added, that though she did not know the writer of the other, she knew the handwriting quite well and dreaded for Mr. Mallaby's sake its coming to the house.

"Two," he repeated, and then he shook himself from the noisy little Denners and ran laughingly to his room.

Mrs. Denner was right about the effect of the letter which was not Miss Hammond's. One hasty perusal of it caused Mr. Mallaby to let it drop from his tremulous hand, and to sit staring straight before him with a very helpless and bewildered look, after which his lips compressed so tight in the effort to stifle some mental agony that a blue line formed about his mouth. For the space of an hour he retained that position looking straight before him, and with the letter lying open at his feet. Then Mrs. Denner, her anxiety aroused, (he had not responded to the dinner bell) knocked at the door saying very loudly at the same time:

"Mr. Mallaby; aru't you coming down, or would you like as a bit sent up to you?"

Mr. Mallaby started, picked up the letter, and hastily thrusting it into a drawer which he locked, answered:

"Yes; yes, Mrs. Denner, I'm coming down as soon as I read Miss Hammond's letter."

"As soon as he reads Miss Hammond's letter;" Mrs. Denner soliloquized. That statement simply and unsuspiciously made was proof that the letter had its usual effect, for instead of reading the dear child's letter he had taken the other one up and had brooded over it ever sinc, and the good woman felt almost as if she would be willing to give her right hand to know the contents of these mysterious letters; not through curiosity she assured herself, but just for the sake of "that blessed man."

While she was descending, Mr. Mallaby perused Miss Hammond's very warm note of invitation. It *was* so different from her wonted brief, cool manner of writing to him, that before he finished he looked at the signature to be sure it was written in her name: and then he read it again, and smiled a little, as if somewhat incredulous still, after which he put it away, not however, in the drawer with the other. Despite its warm tone he was a little doubtful about accepting the invitation. When however, he had his dinner, and in response to Mrs. Denner's inquiry for the dear child, Miss Agnes, he had acquainted her with the object of the note, Mrs. Denner so strongly pressed him to accept the invitation that his doubt was quite shaken, and when she added that it was his duty to accept it in order to see for himself something of the family with whom the dear child was staying, his doubt entirely disappeared; and before he went forth on the business of the afternoon, he dispatched in his stiff, old-fashioned hand, a characteristic reply to his ward, in which he named the next evening but one as the date on which he would give himself the extremely felicitous pleasure, &c. &c.

Florence Wilbur fairly screamed when Agnes, after a hasty and indifferent perusal of the note of acceptance, handed it to her to read. It was so precise, and contained so many dictionary words, as Florence called every word of more than three syllables, and it was so accurately dotted as to *i*'s crossed *t*s, and immense punctuation marks, that it was enough, as the merry girl said, to make a stoic laugh.

"And what a blessed thing it is, Agnes," she continued, "that you are not sensitive about him—else, where would my fun be? I say *my*, because all of his oddities do not seem to raise the ghost of a smile in you."

"Oh! I am used to him," replied Agnes. "All of his letters are like this one, models of composition and punctuation—and why should I be sensitive," opening her big eyes a little wider and placing them very earnestly on her friend, "when he is not my flesh and blood."

But Florence was in such haste to show the note to her uncle, and to get him to plan some way of having Miss Liscome present on the evening named by Mr. Mallaby, that she did not wait to reply to Agnes' last remark.

Sydney Wilbur seemed to enjoy the little epistle as much as his niece had done, for the smile with which he began its perusal, broke into a hearty laugh when he ended it.

"He *is* a character," he said when having folded the note, he handed it back to Florence.

"And what about Miss Liscome, Syd?"

On occasions, when she was mirthful and very eager, Florence dropped the term with which she usually prefaced Mr. Wilbur's Christian name.

"You know," she continued vivaciously, "that if *I* so much as hinted to Aunt Deb a wish for Miss Liscome's company on a particular evening she would immediately contrive that, that maiden lady should not stir one inch from her own domicile for twelve whole hours."

"And you expect me, I suppose, to coax, bully, force, hoodwink, or palaver, my respected sister into inviting her dear friend here to-morrow evening."

"Of course I do; just exert one iota of that awful will of yours, and your respected sister," absurdly mimicing his tone, "and everybody else's respected sisters will yield at once."

In pretended anger he hurled a sheet of foolscap at her, but she dodged it and was out of the study before it had well settled on the floor.

Aunt Deb was iu the dining-room sharply berating Aune for some trifling neglect in the appointment of the table. She had to berate some one as a sort of vent to the worry, indignation, and alarm caused by her guests. Anybody could see, as she had averred to her friend, Prudence, that horrid, doll-faced creature, Miss Hammond, was doing everything in her power to win Sydney Wilbur, and her own niece, Florence, she verily believed, was not a whit behind in the matter of helping her. The only hopeful thing about it, was that Florence was going to London in a couple of months, to stay there, and Miss Hammond, should she have the assurance to prolong her stay until then, would be obliged to depart also; but then what mischief might not be worked in those couple of months! her heart sank to think of it, and only for the fortunate terms of a certain will which *must* keep Sydney from marrying Miss Hammond, she declared she would die. Miss Liscome had spent days, and even a portion of some nights, wondering what could be the mysterious terms of that oft-mentioned will; but even so much as a hint at gratifying her curiosity was never vouchsafed: for, singularly enough, with all her intimacy, and confidence upon every other matter,

Miss Wilbur studiously refrained from imparting any information upon this one.

That, thus far, she had treated her guests with even ordinary politeness, was due to the strong will of her brother, and to her own care not to come into more frequent contact with them than was possible. Of course, she had to meet them at table, and her stiff, solemn demeanor there, while it made Agnes at times, feel very ill at ease, was generally provocative of more than one mirthful sally from Florence, who knowing that Uncle Sydney was on her side, had no fear or thought of any of Aunt Deb's peculiarities, or prejudices. It was the burning remembrance of all these things that made Miss Wilbur so sharp with Anne as to cause the poor girl to wonder whatever had come over her mistress. It is true the latter was always what domestics call "a driver," but never had she raised her voice, nor scolded so much as she had done since the young ladies had come. Since their advent, with little, or no provocation, she had often scolded as she was doing now in the dining room, her voice raised to such a high, shrill pitch, that her brother who had left his study to seek her, had no need of inquiring her whereabouts. He was going to her in the interest of Florence's little plan, but he paused just outside his study-door, in sheer anger and disgust at his sister's exhibition of temper. When, finally he conquered his feelings sufficiently to meet her, he went no further in his approach than to stand on the threshold of the dining-room and utter very severely:

"*Deborah!*"

Deborah wilted, while Anne, never quite able to overcome her awe of Mr. Wilbur, retreated rapidly to the kitchen.

Though Miss Wilbur had been giving such frequent and unrestrained way to her tongue, she had been doing so with the firm and comfortable assur-

ance that her brother, being either out with his guests
or secure in his study, did not hear her; she knew
his abhorrence of a scolding woman, indeed of any
loud-voiced female, and she dreaded at all times in-
curring from him censure in that respect.

His aspect now, positively frightened her, though
she was making a desperate effort not to appear so,
and she did manage to squeeze out what, compared
with her former higher tones, was a very softly-spok-
en:

"Well, what do you want?"

"That you would step this way please, and inform
me how often you employ that unwomanly voice."

Miss Wilbur thought it well to cover her fear by an
assumed irritability, and a sort of defiant disobe-
dience in the matter of not advancing more than a
step.

"If you had the cares of housekeeping, Sydney,
you might not be able to modulate your tones, either.
It's all very well for folks that have nothing to do
but be ladies and gentlemen, and go out with, and
be attentive to guests."

"I always supposed *you* held the position of a
lady. If not, to enable you to do so, it were better
you hired some housekeeper to attend to these trying duties. Should they continue, I am afraid our
guests will think bigotry and termagants are close
companions."

She shot a little quick glance at him from her
bead-like eyes, wondering for an instant if his last
words were meant as an indication of his knowledge,
of what she had done with Miss Hammond's little
case and its contents. But after that instant's fear
she felt assured that such could not be the case.
Did he know, her brother would not have hesitated
to take her to open task.

"I sought you," he resumed, without waiting for
her to reply, "in order to ask you to invite your

friend, Miss Liscome, here to-morrow evening. Mr. Mallaby, Miss Hammond's guardian, by my express desire is coming."

Having said which, he instantly turned, and ascended to his study, leaving his sister mute and motionless from amazement, anger, and some dismay. Her amazement rose from the fact of being requested to invite Miss Liscome—Sydney never before having expressed the hint of a desire to meet the lady,—her anger that any friend of Miss Hammond's should be invited, and her dismay lest her brother was indignant with her beyond forgiveness.

The last feeling however made her somewhat anxious to please him and as soon as she had recovered from her various emotions, she dispatched Anne with a little note of invitation to Miss Liscome, the note saying that Sydney especially wished her to come.

What the feelings of Prudence were on reading such unexpected lines, were portrayed in the very warm and grateful message, also written, which she returned by Anne, and in the way she soliloquized after Anne's departure:

"That dear, sensible Sydney! of course he could not help drawing forcible contrasts between that great-eyed chit of a girl and myself. He knows *she* would be no wife for him, even if that mysterious will of which his sister speaks so much, were not in the way. What kind of a wife would she make him? bah!"

And Miss Liscome glanced at herself in the glass to make sure that the crows' feet were not very apparent, and to wonder if she rouged her cheeks a little higher would it not tend to conceal them.

VII.

PUNCTUALLY at eight o'clock of the designated evening, Matthias Mallaby presented himself at the door of No. —— Hubert Street. He was the same figure which caused so much mirth to Florence, even down to the item of the cotton umbrella, though there was not a suspicion of a cloud in the august sky. But closer inspection revealed a difference in the matter of his shirt collar; usually wearing it low and turned down, on this occasion it was so high and stiff that it seemed like a sort of wedge to support his head, and it certainly prevented that member of his body from turning itself unless the whole body turned with it.

Even Anne, as she admitted him, stared a little, and she could not repress a sly laugh as she put his umbrella into the old-fashioned hall-stand preparatory to ushering him out of a little reception room back of the parlor, and taking his card to Miss Hammond. But before she had an opportunity for doing all this Florence came dancing into the parlor.

"Mr. Mallaby, is it not? I thought it must be, and I begged Agnes to let me have the privilege of meeting you first. I have heard so much about you, Mr. Mallaby, that I feel as if I knew you quite well."

And she grasped both of his hands and drew him into the parlor, all the while looking up into his brown eyes that the brightly-lighted hall lamp revealed very distinctly.

Surprised and delighted by this most unexpected welcome, the owner of the brown eyes permitted them to turn upon the good-natured girl with all that wonderfully winning softness of which they could be capable, and the longer Florence looked into them the more favorably impressed she became, and the more she forgot all her former disposition to laugh at his odd appearance.

His ward greeted him kindly but with an unmistakable dignity, and then Florence presented him to her uncle, who in turn introduced him to his sister and Miss Liscome.

And Mr. Mallaby with his *very* old-fashioned manner, insisted upon taking the hand of each lady, and saying as he made to each in turn, a most ludicrous bow: ·

"I am delighted ma'am to make your acquaintance —I hope I find you in the enjoyment of exceedingly good health, ma'am," and then his stiff shirt collar warning him to be careful how he turned his head, he held that member so exceedingly high, that, taken in connection with his odd costume, he looke l exactly like one of the absurdly grotesque sign figures, with which some store keepers draw attention to their wares.

But Florence, remembering his eyes was enabled to control herself, while Sydney, in neither manner nor expression showed anything save the gracious and kindly host.

Miss Hammond was a little bit annoyed. It was the first time that she had ever seen her guardian in company like the present, for on her brief visits to Mrs. Denner, Mr. Mallaby's deportment did not seem to be so out of place, and she regretted having been persuaded to give him the invitation. Her regret was rendered keener as she saw his reception by the two maiden ladies; Miss Wilbur had drawn back, indignant that he should have seized her hand without having it proffered to him, and her little black eyes twinkled wrathfully over his whole person, while Miss Liscome in servile imitation, had drawn back also, arching her thin, bare shoulders, and par-

tially hiding her rouged cheeks with her fan.
But Wilbur, with inimitable self-possession and
grace, managed to take the awkwardness out of it all
and to put Mr. Mallaby so much at his case, that in
a few moments he found himself seated between Agnes and Florence, and talking away to the latter as
if he knew her a great deal better than he did Agnes,
while Sydney, to keep matters very straight, devoted himself to Miss Liscome, putting that lady into
an ecstasy of delight, and fairly charming his sister.   Under its influence, Miss Wilbur relaxed, and
became actually gracious in the glances she threw at
Mr. Mallaby, a fact that made her brother redouble
his attentions to Miss Liscome. He even went so
far as to request that lady to sing, which request
she cordially granted, and as he led her to the piano,
Florence asked Mr. Mallaby if *he* ever sung.   "Not
much, my dear,   now-a-days,   though I used
to be quite a singer when I was a lad like your uncle there."

Hardly any one else looking at Sydney Wilbur's
well-matured manliness, would have termed him a
lad, and Florence treasured the speech as something
with which to tease her uncle the next day.

Miss Liscome had begun her song, the same very
tender ditty with which she had favored them on a
former occasion, and she sang it in the same nasal,
discordant manner.   Florence watched its effects on
Mr. Mallaby, but he seemed to listen to it with rapt
attention, sitting bold upright, with his head, owing
to his shirt collar, very rigidly in the air.

When the song was finished, with his antiquated
and exaggerated ideas of the attentions due to a
lady, he felt it incumbent upon him to both thank
and congratulate the fair singer, and jumping up, he
exclaimed:

"I'm obliged to you, ma'am. Your song was really
beautiful. It used to be one of my own songs long

ago, and it's a very hard one to get the proper pitch of."

The ludicrous surprise of his speech well-nigh overcame for an instant, even Sydney Wilbur, but he managed to recover his self-possession by bending very close to the music rack of the piano, as if to examine some spot on its rosewood surface, and consequently he was so close to Miss Liscome, she could almost feel his breath upon her cheek. Attributing his action to a sort of tenderness upon his part, she would not disturb it by attempting to leave her seat, nor even, by turning round to acknowledge Mr. Mallaby's complimentary speech.

Florence by dint of smiling broadly, managed to keep herself from laughing outright, and then she obeyed a sudden mischievous impulse:

"Mr. Mallaby won't you sing with Miss Liscome? she will not refuse to favor us again with that same song—her clear soprano will harmonize so well I know, with a male voice."

She was standing beside him, both of her hands clasped coaxingly round his arm, and looking with all her merry soul up into his face. She had already so won her way to his heart, that he could not find it in him to refuse, and he answered, giving a desperate twitch to his unyielding collar:

"If the lady isn't tired and wouldn't mind jining our voices," (the jining was unmistakably broad.) "I'm agreeable to your wish, Miss."

Florence led him to the piano, Sydney promptly giving way to him, and Miss Liscome was too surprised and indignant to do more than jump up and look about her helplessly.

"Oh, Miss Liscome; surely ou will not refuse. Uncle Sydney do entreat her," and Florence tried to pull the lady down to the piano stool, while she cast imploring eyes at her uncle, to which he responded after a moment by saying:

"*I* shall be obliged if Miss Liscome will favor us again."

The slight emphasis on the I, had the effect of making the lady as willing to yield, as she had before seemed reluctant and she seated herself immediately, her pea-green dress falling in ample folds on each side of her, and her long, bony, exposed arms held at very stiff angles to the piano.

Mr. Wilbur prudently seated himself near his sister, feeling that proximity to her sharp, serious face would naturally moderate his disposition to the fun that was in store for him, while Florence betook herself to a sofa in a remote corner, and got her handkerchief in readiness to cram into her mouth. Miss Hammond sat dignified, but flushed, next to the chair that her guardian had vacated.

The duet began; the fair soprano in her effort to be heard above the deep guttural voice that seemed to absorb every other sound, absolutely shrieking, regardless of time or tune, while Mr. Mallaby, hearing nothing but his own voice, pursued his own key, and his own notes without the slightest regard to those of his companion. In vain she thumped the accompaniment, and shrieked, until the perspiration threatened to interfere with her rouge, in order to bring Mr. Mallaby to some sense of his errors. Mr. Mallaby had struck exactly on the tune that suited him, and it made little difference that it contained not a note of the harmony or rather discordance which his companion sang, and to see them both, she thumping and shrieking, her shoulders going up to her ears with her efforts, and he standing beside her, with his short unmentionables, long coat, and grizzled head held very high in the air, was a sight that made even Miss Hammond hold her handkerchief before her face to hide her laughter. Sydney was biting his lips, and once or twice, when the shrieking efforts became very violent, he passed his hand over his face. His sister never moved a muscle. Florence, poor Florence, had audibly exploded, but the music caused such a din that nobody heard her, and she curled herself into a corner of the sofa and laughed until her cheeks were wet with tears and her sides ached.

Even Anne heard the racket (it could be called little less) and she stole up the stairs from the kitchen, to the parlor-door, through the keyhole of which she both looked and listened. When she returned to her domain, she was as thoroughly convulsed with laughter at the sight she had beheld, as was even Florence Wilbur.

When at length the violent musical performance was concluded, Mr. Mallaby thanked Miss Liscome, and offered her his arm to lead her from the piano. There was no help, but to take it, and the sight of the pair crossing the room together, the lady being quite as tall as her tall companion, was as mirth-provoking as when they had appeared at the instrument.

Then the gentleman thought it his duty in return for the agreeableness of Miss Liscome to devote himself to her, at least for a part of the evening, and that lady was favored with attentions from which she could not free herself until Miss Hammond at Mr. Wilbur's request went to the piano. Her plaintive exquisite singing had the effect of not only silencing Mr. Mallaby, but of changing totally the expression of his face. To Florence, who was more interested in watching him than even in listening to the voice of her friend, he seemed to grow extremely sad and wistful-looking as if the strains were painfully touching upon some hidden sorrow of his own. The heart of the sympathetic girl went out more and more to him, and she could not help wondering how Agnes Hammond *could* always be so cool and dignified to him. Was he *her* guardian, she felt she should love him, oddities and all.

But at this stage of her thoughts, Miss Hammond's song was finished, and Miss Hammond herself be ing led back to her seat, directly after which her uncle requested Florence to sing.

"Now, Uncle Sydney, how can you?" being obliged to rouse herself in order to answer, she had been so absorbed in her thoughts of Mr. Mallaby. "You know we Wilburs were never musical; were we Aunt Deb?" at which appeal Aunt Deb smiled grimly, but deigned no reply.

"And I declare," she resumed, when she found no response from her aunt, "if you insist upon my singing, Uncle, I shall retaliate by insisting on a display of *your* own voice." (She knew her uncle never by any possible chance could even whistle a tune.)

What rejoinder he might have made was prevented by Mr. Mallaby entreating:

"Do, Miss Florence, favor us."

And being unable to resist the accompanying entreaty of his eyes, she went to the piano, laughingly waving back Sydney's proffered escort.

"If you were somebody else, I might accept it, but an uncle is too ridiculously prosaic," shrugging her shoulders as if to emphasize her disgust.

Her voice lacked sweetness but it was true and not unpleasant, and as she had chosen a sort of rollicking song in which the very harmony was made to imitate a laugh, it pleased everybody even including her grim, curt aunt. As for Mr. Mallaby he could not express sufficiently his delight and his thanks.

Refreshments were served, consisting of cake and fruit with wine for the gentlemen and some effervescent, but strictly temperate beverage for the ladies; and by that time Miss Liscome was actually holding a conversation with Mr. Mallaby. Her condescension owed herself to two facts; the first and more im-

portant being the absence of Deborah, that lady
having to withdraw in order to supervise the proper
serving of her guests, and the second that her vanity had been fired by the continued attention of Mr.
Mallaby and his frequent little complimentary
speeches, and whether it was that the wine warmed
him to the toast, or that the lady herself did actually
inspire it, he said as he raised his glass to his lips
to finish its contents:

"Here is, ma'am, to your eyes; they are like wells
in which one may look back for miles, and discover
nothing but love in their depths."

And Miss Liscome actually seemed to accept the
ridiculous compliment, being so seated that she did
not see the faces of the rest of the company, nor did
they dream how she was wondering if Mr. Mallaby
were married, and why she should not improve her
present chances with him—the impression she was
endeavoring to make upon Sydney Wilbur was so
uncertain; these thoughts were in accordance with
her wonted prudence, and they made her almost
brave enough to defy Deborah in the matter of continuing her graciousness to Mr. Mallaby, when that
lady returned to the parlor.

At ten o'clock, Mr. Mallaby rose to take his
leave, that being the hour which in his old-fashioned
punctiliousness, he deemed the proper time for departure, and to the remonstrances of Mr. Wilbur and
Florence, (Aunt Deb was prudently silent) answered that he was exceedingly obliged, "but justice, and
right, and etiquette" demanded that he must go home;
and then he shook hands heartily with everybody,
and thanked everyone separately, even Miss Liscome, for the kindness shown to himself, and the
kindness shown to his ward!

His ward's cheeks were a very bright crimson from
all this effusion of gratitude on her behalf, and having responded briefly to his adieu, she was willingly

permitting Mr. Wilbur to attend him to the door, when Florence intervened:

"Agnes and I shall see Mr. Mallaby out, Uncle; *we*"—with an arch emphasis on the pronoun,—"may have something particular to say to him."

It was her own thought, that Agnes might have some private word for him, and might not have the courage to leave the parlor in order to say it, and to give her the opportunity she whispered as soon as they had reached the hall:

"I shall leave you with your guardian a moment; you may have something particular to say to him." But Agnes caught her as she was turning away, and said with some irritation in her tones:

"Don't be so foolish! what in the world should I have to say to him?"

All of which irritably-spoken speech Mr. Mallaby heard, but if he understood its import, he did not pretend to do so; he only stood when all three had reached the hall door and Florence had opened it, holding a hand of each of the girls, and looking down upon them with an indescribable expression of sadness and wistfulness in his own face. Florence saw it and Agnes saw it, for the rays from the street lamp opposite falling upon all three, revealed it very plainly, and though Agnes in her present dignity and indifference did not dream of such a thing, the day was approaching when that expression would recur to her like a blow from a powerful weapon.

"And how long are you going to make your visit, my dear?" he asked at length of Agnes.

Florence answered as if the question had been addressed to her:

"She is going to stay until I go to Europe which time is almost two months yet."

"Oh-o-oh," responded Mr. Mallaby, and then with another adieu he went away.

That evening, ludicrous as its incidents were, was to leave its memory upon the hearts of all three, and its remembrance was to twine itself with a sad fatality into a future made dark with mystery and pain.

VIII.

"FLORENCE, I am going to confession."

"Well, that it not so surprising considering you went every two weeks in the Convent; but come to think, having gone just before we left, a week ago to-day, what have you been doing that you want to unburden your conscience, now?"

"Doing? why I'm just succumbing to every temptation you put in my way—I'm growing lazy, and careless and lukewarm," and Miss Hammond threw herself back into the easy chair, as if the laziness against which she protested, was exceedingly comfortable.

"Lazy, and careless, and lukewarm," repeated Florence very slowly, and with an expression of most comical dismay. "Shades of the Saints deliver us! How dare you make such assertions when you have been in my company? And to contradict further your awful statements, have you not said your rosary faithfully every day, and made interminably long prayers with no end of pious reading? I am sure you devour pages of Father Faber to the lamentable exclusion of all those interesting novels in Uncle Sydney's library."

"Nevertheless I *am* guilty of all the things with which I have charged myself, and I am going to confession this afternoon, to-day being Saturday; and as I do not know the way to the nearest church you will have to accompany me and help me to find it."

"Which request means also, that I am to accompany you to confession, I suppose," said Florence making a very wry face.

"As you choose about that—I never attempt to force people's piety," and Miss Hammond drew herself slightly up.

"Never force people's piety," echoed Florence with pretended indignation. "As if the example of your long prayers, and your constant dignity, were not a very absolute forcing of one's piety, but, then, you dear girl"—imagining that she might have hurt Miss Hammond by such chafing—"it is such a delight to have you with me, that I should positively try to play croquet with my own head, if I thought it would please you, and so you may rest assured I shall accompany you anywhere; and as a proof of my words I shall go this minute to Uncle Sydney and tell him we want this afternoon absolutely to ourselves," and suiting the action to the word, she did go immediately to her uncle and tell him that she and Agnes were going to take a walk by themselves.

"Is Miss Hammond tired of my company?" he asked, arching his eye brows. "Of course I know it could not possibly be you, my dutiful niece, who would want to dispense with my escort."

"Mistaken lad!" she retorted playfully.

Having already teased him about the youthful term applied to him by Mr. Mallaby, he quite understood her use of it now, and he laughed heartily as she continued:

"You don't know anything about it, nor how Agnes and myself may want to exchange opinions about things in general, and you in particular."

The last words were spoken at random, and without a thought of their significance even after they had left her lips, and her uncle had shot at her one of the quick questioning glances that sometimes sent his sister's heart into her mouth.

He answered, however, as if her speech had caused no more thought in his mind than it had done in her own.

"And not having space enough within doors to discuss matters, you must needs go abroad. Is it to St. John's Park you are going, or to unexplored precincts beyond; and do you intend to be back before dark and shall I call for you at some appointed place?"

"You will please hold your tongue and not so much as dare to think where we are going!" and lest under cover of all that playfulness he might ask questions which would compel her to reveal the object of their afternoon walk, she left his study instantly.

Her haste to leave him was not that she was afraid, or ashamed to tell him any of her Catholic practices, but that, knowing the dreadful idea most Protestants, and he in particular (strict one that she knew him to be) had of confession she thought it as well not to let him know that the very first week of her rather self-invited stay at his house, both she and her friend were practising that mysterious and abhorred devotion.

That St. Peter's Church in Barclay Street, was the nearest, the girls speedily ascertained when they turned into Hudson Street, and inquired of the good-natured-looking keeper of an apple stand on one of the corners, and to St. Peter's they wended their rapid way. Never having been out unescorted before, the feeling was a little novel, and had even a slight touch of fear in it, causing them to keep their veils down very closely, and to hold each other's hands very tightly.

St. Peter's was not then quite the renovated edifice it is now with its roomy basement and Parochial School. It was much plainer, though perhaps as large, and confessions were heard in the basement chapel

Nor was the little crowd of penitents waiting about the two tribunals, such in appearance as might greet the eye at the present time. They were mostly women, (it being too early an hour for the men) whose plain, poor dress, rough hands, and coarse-featured faces told that they came from the lower walks of life. They seemed surprised at the advent among them of such ladies as our two heroines, (both of whom of course had thrown up their veils, and removed their gloves,) making instant way for them, and even indicating they might precede them. But both Agnes and Florence discountenanced any such injustice, and while they sweetly thanked the kind people, they dropped very humbly and very edifyingly on their knees at the end of one of the somewhat long lines of penitents.

Agnes was so seemingly devout, never once turning her eyes from the altar, and kneeling up so erect that her devotion, together with her beautiful face, attracted the admiring glances of everybody in her vicinity. Florence tried to follow her example, and for a while actually surprised herself by her fervor, until her sense of the humorous was aroused by the sight of an old man on one of the benches in front of her. He had a flaming red handkerchief tied round his neck, the end of it hanging down his back like a shawl, and a blue skull-cap on his head. From the constant clicking of something against the bench in front of him, he was evidently saying his beads, and the constant bobbing of his head seemed to suggest the idea that he was keeping time to every Hail Mary he uttered. In vain Florence tried not to look at him; do what she would, his ludicrous appearance was constantly attracting her, and when at length, it seemed from the unusual depth to which his head descended in its bobbing motion that he was dropping asleep, she could not turn her eyes from him. Indeed, there might seem to be an excuse for attention to him and even anxious attention, for his swaying movement, became at last so much in a forward direction that he threatened to

go quite over the bench. He caught himself however just in time to prevent the catastrophe, and
Florence drew a freer breath, and made an Act of
Contrition for the mirth that rose within her at the
thought of such an event. She even stole a glance
at Agnes to see how she regarded the situation, but
apparently, Agnes did not even see the old man; her
eyes were riveted upon the altar. Then she covertly
looked at the other penitents; they also seemed to
be watching Miss Hammond, or devoutly absorbed
in their prayers. Not the attention of a single soul
beside herself appeared to be drawn to the ridiculous creature, and with another Act of Contrition,
and a desperate determination not to look at him,
she did manage for a little to fix her thoughts
and her eyes upon the altar. But it was only for a
little; involuntarily her eyes turned upon the comical figure before her. He was asleep again, and
swaying so much forward that he was in the same
imminent danger as before. Florence could not
take her eyes from him; indeed, in anticipation she
seemed to be just holding her breath. Over, over,
he was going—would he recover himself as he did before? In an instant her mental question was answered; the old man had turned a complete somersault
over the low bench, evidently striking on his head,
the way that his feet were elevated; and as the latter were encased in immense rough calfskin shoes,
the effect was all the more ludicrous. The shock
awoke him, and probably, his slumber having banished all recollection of his locality, his present re-
versed position frightened him all the more. He
screamed lustily, causing several of the women to
rush to him, and the two Confessors to open the
doors of their confessionals and look out.

The efforts of the women to pull the old man out
of his narrow quarters were almost as ludicrous as
his fall had been, and Florence to shut out the sight

had clasped both hands tightly over her face, but she was shaking with suppressed laughter.

In vain, Agnes who had not even smiled, pulled her and whispered to her to control herself; Florence but shook the more, drawing upon herself at length the loud-spoken censure of an old woman near.

"Do you know it's in the house of God, you are? you disrespectful snip! Get off your knees and go outside, and don't be desecrating this holy place with your presence."

A command that Florence gladly obeyed, waiting only to bless herself hastily, and make as hasty a genuflection. Agnes extremely mortified, and not a little angry with her friend, followed.

Out on the porch, Miss Wilbur gave unrestrained way to her mirth.

"Scold as much as you like, Agnes; I know I deserve it all; but I must laugh," and laugh she did until as usual, her cheeks were wet with tears.

"Don't look so horrified, dearest—I shall confess every bit of it, and tell my Confessor into the bargain all about Miss Liscome and Mr. Mallaby; and I shall ask him if it is my fault to laugh, when God sends such ridiculous people in my way, and he will say:

'Bless you my child, you have committed no sin, for God loves a merry heart.' "

"Florence Wilbur you will bring some dreadful judgment upon yourself if you continue in this way. Just think of all you have been guilty of this afternoon; disedifying those poor people in there: besides making me angry."

And Miss Hammond looked so thoroughly in earnest, that, as usual, Miss Wilbur became affrighted and penitent, and hastened to say:

"I really am sorry, Agnes, and I wish I could control myself like you do, but it is no use, I cannot. You go back to your place, like a dear good girl, and say a prayer for me, and by that time I think that old woman whom I so terribly disedified has gone, I shall go in also. Until then, I'll walk up and down here, and examine my conscience, and make fervent Acts of Contrition.''

Miss Hammond obeyed the request, the woman looking at her respectfully and admiringly, for her dignity, contrasted with the levity of her companion, had very much edified them.

Poor Florence stole back when she thought she had certainly waited a sufficient length of time for the old woman to be at least safely within the confessional; but she had miscalculated, for there was the same old person with actually three to be heard before it should be her turn, and only Agnes kneeling below her. And as she very gravely and humbly took her place she tried not to see the scowling look with which the old woman raised her eyes from her beads to look at her.

Whatever could Agnes have to tell to keep her in the confessional so long, thought Florence; and actually, her cheeks were wet with tears when she came out, and her whole face wore a most touchingly sorrowful look, as she went to the altar to make her thanksgiving; but Florence did not have much time for conjecture, her own turn came so speedily.

Her confession was, like her prayers, short, and it did not seem to call for much advice from the Confessor; so, even before Miss Hammond had finished the petition she was fervently making Miss Wilbur was kneeling beside her, praying with all her guileless, affectionate heart to be made as pious as was her beloved friend.

All the way home, Miss Hammond was unusually silent, and Florence thinking, with a little pang of generous envy, that her silence was due to the recollection she desired to maintain in preparation for the Communion of the morrow, forbore to interrupting it. Only, as they neared Hubert Street, under

the influence of a sudden thought she exclaimed :
"There! we forgot to inquire the hour of the Masses
on Sundays."

"I did not," responded Agnes, in a sort of preoccupied manner. I asked the priest who heard our
confession, and he told me the first Mass would be
at six o'clock."

"Oh, Agnes; how I envy and admire you," burst
from generous-hearted Florence, "you forget nothing
pertaining to spiritual interests—now poor me, I
never thought until this moment of the hour of going to Mass. Oh! dear Lord! forgive me, and make
me better."

And the little prayer was put up from a most hum-
ble and earnest heart, while in the heart of her beautiful companion was a repetition of that throb of
vanity which made her on an occasion before, rejoice in the superiority of *her* piety to that of her
friend.

On the stoop of the house Florence paused to
say:

"We can manage very well about going out so
early in the morning, for as breakfast is not until
nine, on week days, it is probably much later on
Sundays, and consequently the rising of my respected
uncle and aunt must be late in accordance. I shall
find out from Anne, the mechanism of the fastening
of the front door, so that we shall have no difficulty
about egress, and certainly none about our ingress,
for I shall contrive to smuggle a latch-key." But,
with all her precautions—precautions so cleverly
managed, that Anne thought the information about
the fastening of the door was only desired by Miss
Florence in a spirit of mischief, and Sydney did not
know his niece had secretly appropriated his latch
key—the next morning, when she and Agnes bon
neted and closely veiled, stole down to the hall-door
so noiselessly that not even an occasional creak was

caused by their footsteps, neither could open it.
Either Anne had not explained fully the mechanism
of the lock, or an extra catch had been put on after
they had retired. In vain they tugged at the great
key; in the way that Anno had shown, it seemed to
turn, but no effect was produced, and in blank and
wretched dismay they looked at each other.

"What shall we do?" whispered Florence, throwing back her veil, and preparing for another attempt.
Agnes threw back her veil, and stood by, red from ex
citement and even fear, lest the clicking noise made
by the key should awaken somebody. Not that
there was anybody in reach of its sound save Sydney,
and he could hardly be expected to hear it, sleeping
in a sort of extension at the rear of that floor. Aunt
Deb occupied a room directly over that of her guests',
and Anne an apartment next to Aunt Deb's. But for
the latter fact, Florence would have gone to Anne to
relieve them from their difficulty, and have bribed
her to secrecy.

At length, both girls in nervous desperation began
to tug together at the key, some evidence having
been given that if it could be turned in a certain
direction the desired effect might be produced.

"Say a Hail Mary," whispered Agnes, in a perspiration, and just as Florence had begun to obey the
request, the key under their united efforts, turned
in the lock with a tremendous thud; it startled them
both, and penetrated to Sydney Wilbur, light sleeper that he was. In an instant he had donned slip-
pers and dressing-gown, and was out in the hall confronting the dismayed girls.

His stern demeanor, and his sternly asked:
"What is the meaning of this?" frightened them
both for an instant; then Florence, recovering her
self-possession, approached him, drawing Agnes with
her, and when she reached him she whispered, lest
the sound of her voice might awaken Aunt Deb:

"Come into the parlor, Uncle Sydney, and I shall explain; if I did so here, Aunt Deb might be aroused."

He allowed himself to be drawn unresistingly into the partially darkened parlor, and he listened very patiently to her account of how she and Agnes came to be in their present unpleasant predicament. Of course her account had to include a very special and extended reference to that which she had been so anxious on the previous day, to conceal, confession, but she also explained to him how all her secrecy had been to spare his feelings.

"Thinking I was such a bigot, that even in my character of host I could not tolerate the devout practices of my guests, I suppose," he answered, when she had finished.

"I am much obliged to you, my dear niece, for your tolerant opinion, and as a punishment for the same, I command that you both wait for me to dress in order to accompany you."

"Uncle Sydney!" exclaimed Florence in absolute dismay, "*You* to accompany us to *Mass!*"

"Do you want me to be guilty of the unmanliness of suffering you two girls to go forth unescorted, at this early hour. I shall be ready in a very few moments."

And before Florence could reply again, he had gone from the room, leaving Agnes and her gazing at each other in dumb amazement. Then Agnes recovered sufficiently to whisper:

"We shall be late—it must be almost six o'clock now."

To which Florence in the same low tone reassuringly rejoined:

"Well, if we are, dear, it will not matter so much, for we intend, you know, to get back to the High-Mass."

And directly after those whispered remarks, Mr.

Wilbur returned, looking, despite the incredibly short space of time he seemed to have taken, as neatly and faultlessly attired as ever he did when he accompanied the girls on their daily excursions. As Agnes glanced at him, when having gained the street, he took his place between her and Florence, she thought his face with its clear, dark complexion and fine eyes, looked unusually handsome. And then she took herself to severe task for having had such a worldly thought in the midst of the recollection she was endeavoring to maintain, and she drew her veil closer, and murmured behind it very fervent Acts of Contrition, at the same time remembering with a great deal of pain what the Confessor of the previous day had replied to her troubled admission regarding this same Mr. Wilbur.

By the time they arrived at the church, the first gospel was nearly over, and the congregation was so scattered about that there were many vacant pews especially in the middle aisle. To one of these Florence, finding there was no usher, boldly piloted her companions, sending Agnes into the pew in advance and leaving Sydney to follow them.

When abroad, Wilbur had visited Catholic churches because of his interest in architecture, or painting, but he had never been present at any Catholic service, and now while the two girls knelt, and bowed their faces into their hands, he leaned back in his seat (an attitude that immediately stamped him as a Protestant to everybody in his vicinity) and looked at the altar with its vested priest, and two little acolytes with an air of keen curiosity. He was too well-bred to look openly about him, but he seized occasional opportunities—as when the people knelt or bowed their heads—to do so, and he was, it must be confessed, a little disgusted that his companions should be thrust, for even a short time among such coarse, vulgar-looking people.

The congregation, at that early hour, was similar in caste to the penitents of the day before, the only difference being that there were more men among them; a good many of the latter being old men as ridiculous-looking as the old man who had so excited the mirth of Florence.

The bell rang for the Elevation, and Wilbur was absolutely startled by the sudden and simultaneous kneeling of everybody in the church but himself—Florence and Agnes were almost prostrate in the ardor of their devotion.

There was no one to observe him now did he look about him; he might do so as rudely as he wished to, and he did, feeling in spite of himself an awe as he saw the prostrate forms, and then turned his eyes back to the altar where the priest was making his own deep genuflection.

When the time for giving Communion to the people came, he was further startled by the bustle about him; every pew seeming to give up one or more of its occupants to the line of people moving toward the altar; even his companions arose for the purpose, and as he stepped into the aisle to permit them to pass, he felt within him a sort of savage protest that Miss Hammond should be placed in such vulgar contact. Singularly enough, the protest did not then include his niece; perchance, because there did not appear to be such a vast difference between plain-looking, undersized Florence, and the plebian crowd, as between the latter, and beautiful Miss Hammond. He watched Agnes as she gently urged her way, her slender, willowy figure showing an admirable contrast to the flabby, dowdy forms about her, and the thick coil of her abundant dark hair disclosing itself beneath the back of her bonnet.

When she returned to her seat, her countenance attracted him still more. It reminded him with its rapt, devout look, of an exquisite painting he had

seen abroad, and he found himself despite all his
efforts to the contrary, looking at her constantly,
and wishing that she would take her hands from
her face so that he might see at least its profile.

But Agnes did not gratify his wish until the Mass
was finished, the priest had retired from the altar, and
Florence had gently touched her as a hint that it was
time for her departure.   Then she arose quickly and
accompanied them out, hardly conscious that many
of the congregation had waited about the church
door in order to have a better look at the elegant
Protestant gentleman, and his Catholic companions.

The three were unusually silent on their way home;
Wilbur because of a rush of strange, and impetuous
feelings relative to Miss Hammond; Miss Hammond,
owing to the fervor of certain resolutions which she
had made, and considerate little Florence because
she would not interrupt what she felt to be the pious
silence of her friend.

Not even Anne was stirring when they reached the
house, and Sydney searching in his pockets, had
just began to deplore the absence of his latch-key,
when Florence with a laugh produced it.

"Some good spirit, I think," she said, "made you
leave it on your study-table yesterday and I seized
it."

"Thus adding pilfering to the rest of your
virtues, my exemplary niece," he retorted playfully,
as he opened the door, when he stole a look at Agnes.   But that young lady did not return it; she was
evidently very much occupied with her own
thoughts.

He looked at his watch when they were in the
hall.   It wanted a quarter of eight, and as he put
it back, he said in a whisper:

As breakfast will not be until half past nine, I
think you two had better go to bed for an hour,

or else, Florence, you might awaken Anne, and have her make you some coffee immediately."

That speech aroused Miss Hammond. "Please do nothing of the kind for me. I assure you I am not in the least need of it. Indeed, both Florence and I have fasted quite as long in the Convent; have we not, Florence?"

Florence yawningly nodded. "Well get up stairs, then, or Deborah may find us."

And he turned to go to his own room.

The girls had begun to ascend, and had mounted a step, or two, when Agnes, as if prompted by some extremely sudden impulse turned, and darting past her companion, ran lightly to Mr. Wilbur, overtaking him just as he had reached the threshold of his apartment.

"I have been so wanting in gratitude, in courtesy," she whispered breathlessly, "I have not yet once thanked you for your kindness of this morning." I "—she stopped abruptly, being a little abashed by her own boldness, and by the penetrating, though kindly look of his eyes.

He retorted playfully:

"Are you sure that you are really grateful?" and then for one instant he flashed involuntarily upon her a look that told even to her, that deep regard in which he held her.

She turned from him, her heart beating wildly, and her cheeks so brightly blushing, that Florence who had waited for her, inquired curiously:

"Whatever have you two been saying? your cheeks are like peonies."

"Oh! I was just thanking your uncle for his escort," replied Agnes half pettishly, and when the two had gained their room, and Florence announcing her intention of taking her uncle's advice with regard to going to bed for an hour, had begun to disrobe. Agnes having removed only her bonnet, threw herself into the easy chair and sat staring before her with the air of one in deep mental trouble.

"Agnes Hammond!" ejaculated Florence, when she had watched her for a few minutes, "is it your devotional meditation that gives you such an expression? if it is, I shall not have a word to say—though, even in that case I do not see why devotion should make you so sad-looking. If it is not the case, do say what *is* the matter, and whether you are coming to bed, like a respectable Christian, or if you intend to sit there looking as if you saw the ghost of somebody."

For reply to which speech, Miss Hammond suddenly burst into a fit of uncontrollable weeping.

"Agnes! dearest, darling Agnes; what *is* the matter? Have *I* said anything to hurt you? Has Uncle Sydney said anything?"

And Florence in the act of doffing her dress by lifting it over her head, rushed to her friend, leaving the garment hanging most uncomfortably about her neck, the consequences of which was that Miss Hammond being forcibly embraced was wrapped smotheringly in its folds. Indeed, the effort to free herself, and to regain her struggling breath, did no little toward stopping her tears, and enabling her to answer:

"No, Florence; it is nothing you have said, or done, and nothing your kind uncle has said or done; it is—it is that I should be so recreant to graces which I feel have been given to me; that I should be so weak in the matter of resolution."

And Miss Hammond looked very earnestly and very pitifully at her friend.

She had certainly told the truth, but she had told it in such an enigmatical way, that it was most likely her simple, trusting, unsuspicious companion would never dream of the facts that prompted such a confession; and she was right; poor little Florence saw

In it all only another proof of the ardent piety of her friend, and she exclaimed in her generosity:

"Agnes, you are *so* good, I really think you are intended for a religious. Oh, dearest Lord! how much ashamed I ought to be of *myself*. Do, Agnes, love, pray for me, that I may become like you."

And Florence, with her dress still hanging ludicrously about her, sat herself upon the floor, and looked up into Miss Hammond's face with a most woe-begone expression.

To do Miss Hammond justice, she did shrink a little this time from the compliment of her friend. "Intended for a religieuse!" Never had there been a bigger or drearier mistake.

Could Miss Deborah Wilbur, at that instant bestirring herself from her morning slumber, have looked in upon her guests, and then have glanced down into her brother's room, where he, instead of seeking any repose was sitting at his dressing table, his face bowed upon his hand, and his whole attitude expressive of deep and painful thought, her temper would have taken a more than usually acid turn, and was it given to her to know the object of her brother's troubled cogitation, not alone upon Anne would she have vented her wrath, but upon her guests as well.

Her wrath, however, received sudden kindling at the breakfast table.

Her brother asked with seeming carelessness, whether she would attend the morning or afternoon service.

"The afternoon," she answered somewhat snappishly, "having so much housekeeping to attend to,"— darting a little spiteful look at Miss Hammond— "I can't get the time some folks can for going abroad."

Sydney gave her a warning glance; then he said again in his apparently careless way:

"Then, since you are not going until the afternoon, I shall attend our young ladies to their church."

--

"To their church—a Romish church?" Her aston-ishment and indignation made her lose all guard.

"Yes; to their church, a *Romish* church," answer-ed her brother with exasperating coolness.

"And do you intend, Sydney Wilbur, to enter that church— to be present at their Romish service?"

"I do intend so doing, and Deborah," his voice chang-ed to an appalling sternness of accent, "I desire and insist that you no longer insult our guests by the use of that word Romish —you will please employ the term Catholic."

His reproof administered in the presence of her hated guest made her so angry, that it inspired her with a very unusual and sort of desperate courage. She absolutely jerked herself from the table, saying as she did so:

"When Sydney Wilbur forgets for the sake of his guests, the consideration due to his sister, it is time that his sister should retire.

And she bounced from the room leaving the guests looking a little frightened, but Wilbur without a ruffle in his countenance touched the handbell for Anne, and desired her to remove Miss Wilbur's plate.

IX.

ѺYDNEY WILBUR went to church with his guests a second time that Sunday, and at the second service his fastidiousness was not quite so much offended by the coarse appearance of the congregation. The latter contained many evident ladies and gentlemen, and there was a polite usher to show him and his companions to desirable seats, but his preoccupied mind kept him from feeling the same curiosity he had experienced in the morning; kept him indeed from doing anything but watch Miss Hammond, when he could do so unobserved. To all appearance Miss Hammond was intent alone upon her devotions, her eyes turning only from her prayerbook to the altar, and during the sermon she seemed to pay the most rapt attention.

The preacher spoke entirely upon self-sacrifice, a virtue that he glowingly depicted, and the practice of which he enforced in vigorous and almost startling language. His words sank into Miss Hammond's soul and for the time made her strong in all that she felt she ought to do. Upon Sydney Wilbur the impression of the forceful words was a little peculiar. It brought to his mind what he once accidently read but thoroughly disbelieved, of the sacrifices in the life of a Catholic saint, and he could not help linking that account with the ascetic appearance of the present speaker. And then, oddly enough, his thoughts wandered to the female saints of the Catholic Church, and from that to the religious orders of both sexes, and at length, with a jump to the fact that Miss Hammond, in her piety, might be thinking about joining one of those religious Or-

ders. He absolutely shuddered at the thought of
shutting under one of those hideousbonnets(his mind
reverting to the Sisters of Charity, whom he had
sometimes met in the street,) Agnes' beautiful face;
and turning his eyes from the preacher to her—
he could only see her exquisite profile—he shut his
teeth hard together, and then and there made up his
mind to do that about which he had been in such
painful hesitation all the morning.

Florence seated between her uncle and her friend,
and trying to be as attentive as the latter, was nevertheless, wishing a little that the long sermon would
come to an end. Despite what Agnes had said of
the harmlessness of their fast, either that, or the concern produced by Miss Hammond's extraordinary
fit of weeping, had brought on an incipient headache
that now in the close air of the poorly ventilated
church, threatened to become very violent. It made
her restless to the verge of indevotion, and she was
most thankful when at length Mass was over, and
they were once more on their homeward way.

Immediately that Anne admitted them, she informed Mr. Wilbur that his sister was so ill Miss Liscome had to be sent for, and that lady was now by
Miss Wilbur's bedside; to which information Mr.
Wilbur made no reply, and Anne as she retreated
to the kitchen wondered at his indifference, remembering his anxiety, in a former occasion when Miss
Wilbur had only complained of not feeling well.

"Do you think, Uncle Sydney, I ought to go to
her?" asked Florence, looking heavy-eyed enough
herself to be in bed, though with heroic self-control
she had not said a word of her headache, lest it
should cause any anxiety to Agnes.

"No child;" he replied with an unmistakable decision of tone. Go to your room, both of you, and
rest; you have a full hour until dinner."

They followed his advice. Florence, glad enough

under the pretext of rest to throw herself upon the bed, while Agnes tried to read "Spiritual Perfection." But, somehow, there was no relish in the volume, and she put it down after a struggle to peruse it, and gave herself up to the strange and painful thoughts that had obtained such sudden and complete mastery of her.

When the dinner hour arrived, Florence was hardly able to lift her head from the pillow; but even then, lest it should make Agnes anxious to the verge perhaps of interfering with her appetite, she was silent upon her suffering, and though every exertion made her head throb in a sickening way she kept her lips sealed on that subject. She knew she should not be able to eat a mouthful, but she hoped to conceal that fact by a pretense of doing so.

At table, Sydney said to Anne;

"Go and see how my sister is, and whether Miss Liscome will favor us with her company at dinner."

To which message Anne returned with—

That Miss Wilbur was so very ill, Miss Liscome could not leave her for a moment. Neither Anne nor Mr. Wilbur knew how the heart of the spinster yearned to accept that invitation, and but for the wrathful flash of the black eyes of the little body in the bed, she might have been brave enough to ask her permission to do so.

Poor Florence's hope of being able to conceal her lack of appetite under pretense of eating, was futile. Both Agnes and her uncle speedily discovered it, and the former discovered also, that to which ever since their return from church she had been so selfishly blind, Florence's heavy eyes, and fever-flushed face. She dropped her knife and fork at the sight and exclaimed, her keen self-reproach for not having observed her friend sooner, making her voice sound piteously:

"Oh, Florence! you are dreadfully ill." At the same time Sydney was saying:

"Are you sick, Florence? you do not seem to be eating a mouthful."

She tried to disclaim their charges, and attempted to laugh gayly; but it was a very sorry little effort, and at length she had to admit she had a headache.

"But it is only a headache, and if you will just order a cup of strong tea for me, Uncle Sydney, and not mind if I do not eat, I shall be quite well in an hour, or so."

"But you are positively too ill to continue at table," said Agnes in great distress, and looking as if she would like to leave the table herself, for the purpose of attending Florence.

"Indeed, I am not!" and the young girl roused herself and tried to look very much better, though the effort seemed to send for an instant the table spinning about her, and to make her head throb horribly.

The tea being brought and drunk, she declared she felt better; well enough to join in any proposition for the afternoon.

"Anything—anywhere, that you can suggest, Uncle Sydney," she said, as she poured herself out a second cup of very strong black tea, and drank it without cream or sugar, heroically determined to test to the utmost the virtue of the cure.

"To ask your uncle to propose anything for this afternoon, and Miss Wilbur so ill," said Agnes with a sort of shocked air that might, or might not be real.

"I rather think," she continued, "that your uncle will propose for this afternoon a total and absolute rest for your head."

"Miss Hammond is right," replied Mr. Wilbur; "that is just my proposition for you, Florence."

"For me, it may be, but it need, and should not include anybody else—for instance—"

"For instance," interrupted Agnes, "we are all tired, having been up at an absurdly early hour—" glancing archly at Wilbur—"and we need rest. I at least shall take it, regardless whether anybody else does, or not."

There was no appeal from her decision, but when the girls had retired to their room Agnes showed no desire for the rest of which she had spoken. Instead when she had put Florence comfortably to bed, and bathed the latter's hot brow, she threw herself into the easy chair by the bedside and assumed almost unconsciously, the attitude of painful thought in which recently she seemed so wont to indulge.

The soothing application put Florence into a slumber, and the house seemed to have a death-like stillness. There was not even the rattle of a vehicle over the stony street, and Miss Hammond's thoughts seemed to grow in intensity in proportion to the silence about her.

She looked at Florence; the girl was sleeping like a baby, and with her calm, fair-flushed face almost as much a picture of touching innocence as a slumbering baby could have been. She could not resist kissing lightly the smooth white brow, and then there burst from her in an involuntary whisper:

"Darling Florence! you have envied my seeming piety, but could you see the struggle in my heart you would think far otherwise."

Florence stirred slightly as if she were about to awake, at which in some consternation, Agnes resumed her position in the chair. But, after a little, when the girl's slumber seemed to have grown even heavier, and the silence to have become more grave-like, Miss Hammond's conscience resumed its old struggle, and the struggle was even fiercer, for the temptation to which at first she had not turned a deaf ear, presumptuously feeling that *she* would never yield to such, now clutched her mercilessly.

She felt, she knew, that she must either free herself
by one desperate stroke, or yield to it entirely. She
wrung her hands, and murmured to herself:

"My God! my God! help me! Oh Blessed Mother!
come to my aid."

And then she dropped softly on her knees, and
prayed with such fervor that the tears rolled down
her cheeks; strength seemed to have been given her,
for when she arose, her resolution was taken. She
leaned over Florence, very pale, but very firm-look-
ing, and wishing a little that her friend would
awaken. But Florence slept on for a half hour
longer; then however, she opened her eyes quite refreshed and well, save for a dizziness when she attempted to lift her head.

"Don't try to raise it, dearest," said Agnes.

"But I am so well," replied Florence. "My head
does not ache at all, and I declare if it were not for
that horrid dizziness, I should feel actually frisky."

Her looks seemed to corroborate her words, for the
flush had entirely disappeared from her face, and her
eyes were quite bright.

"Do you think dearest, you are well enough to
have me say something to you?"

And Agnes drew her chair closer, and fondled one
of Florence's plump hands.

"Say something to me—why certainly, I am well
enough—say all that you want to me."

"Well then, dear Florence, after a great deal of
painful thought, I have come to the conclusion that
I must end my stay here, delightful as it is to be with
you, and go to Mrs. Denners, and that I must write
to Mr. Mallaby to that effect, to-morrow."

"*Agnes Hammond!*"

In her amazement, indignation, grief, and dismay,
at such an announcement Florence could say nothing
else, and forgetting her dizziness she sat up in the
bed, and looked half wildly at her friend.

"It does not pain you, dear, a whit more than it does me; the thought of our separation, is almost making me sick," her white face seemed to confirm her assertion,—"but, I could not remain with any regard for your uncle and you, and any respect for myself, in a house where I am so unwillingly tolerated as I am by your aunt."

Her pallor increased a little; perhaps owing to the absolute lie she was telling. The unwillingness of Miss Wilbur's aunt to tolerate her, had nothing to do with her determination to depart.

Florence, implicitly believing every word that Agnes had spoken, was in sad distress.

"I knew," she said, "that burst from Aunt Deb, this morning, would sting you because of her hateful way she said guest, instead of guests; but you seemed to take it so quietly, that I thought you would not mind it any more than I did. Do, Agnes, be sensible enough to think nothing about her. You see, how indifferently Uncle Sydney has taken her illness, to-day, and he is master in this house. And you, yourself must feel how pleased he is to have you here. He seems so attentive to you, that if I didn't know, as I do in your case, how absolutely out of the question is a mixed marriage, I should be suspicious of his engendering some tender feeling on your part."

Agnes bent her head over the little plump hand she was still fondling; but she did not reply; she could not at that instant have trusted herself to do so.

Florence resumed:

"Tell me, dearest, that you will retract this determination of yours."

"I cannot, Florence. I have weighed the matter well and my heart, my conscience and my judgment tell me that I ought to go. Consequently, I must and *shall* go."

When Miss Hammond spoke in that decisive tone, her friend knew there was little use in attempting to combat her, and she threw herself back on the pillow, her head beginning to ache again, and her eyes filling with tears of vexation.

"If you *will* go, Agnes," she said, "then I shall go also. I shall not wait for that friend of my mother's who is to chaperon me to London, and who has arranged not to go for two months yet. I shall get Uncle Sydney to engage a passage for me this very week; he can place me in care of the captain. Then hateful Aunt Deb will be rid of both her disagreeable guests."

But even while she spoke she was secretly, but very confidently hoping that Uncle Sydney would be able to persuade Miss Hammond to recall her determination; the difficulty was to tell him confidentially how matters were, and to tell him before Miss Hammond should write to Mr. Mallaby.

She cast about her for some pretext of getting Agnes out of the way, and she found it at length in a sudden thought of St. John's Park.

"Agnes, dearest," she said, after both had maintained a somewhat lengthy silence, "I think each of us is suffering from the excitement of this resolution of yours. I know my poor head is aching again and your pale face looks as if a breath of air on this close afternoon would do it good. Would you like to take a turn in St. John's,"—the word park was generally omitted—"and would you mind going there alone ? · I fancy Uncle Sydney, not thinking that we would leave the house to-day again, is buried with his books."

The proposition met with favor from Miss Hammond, but she hesitated to leave Florence.

"I shall really be better without you," protested Florence, "for your absence maybe will enable me to forget your cruelty long enough to go to sleep. So, do, dear Agnes, go for an hour at least. You will find the key" (meaning the key of the park) "hanging in the lower hall. I saw Uncle Sydney put it there yesterday morning."

Thus entreated, Agnes donned her bonnet, and went forth. Somehow, though there was a keen sense of suffering in her heart, there was also mingled with it a very exalted consciousness of having nobly done her duty, and instead of being humbly thankful that strength had been given her to do it, she was yielding to some of the emotions that spring from pride and vanity. She was so sure of herself now—so sure that her determination was inflexible.

X.

FLORENCE, heedless alike of her headache that had returned with much of its first violence, and the dizziness that made her hold chairs and table while she dressed, robed herself as rapidly as she could, and groped her way (it seemed like groping the manner in which she was obliged to support herself by baluster and wall) to her uncle's study.

"Come in," he said to her gentle knock, and then seeing how really ill she looked, he jumped up from a reading stand before which he had been idly sitting, and placed a chair for her.

"Why Florence, child, how sick you look," he continued, real alarm in his voice, "and your hands," taking them both in his own, "are very hot. I think I had better send for the Doctor for both you and Deb.

"Never mind me," she replied, "but just help me to do something about Agnes." And then she told him as nearly as she could remember, every word of Miss Hammond's expressed reason for wishing to go, and how she had manœuvred in order to get this opportunity of telling him about it.

He set his teeth together as he listened, and when she finished, there was in his eyes, and about his mouth such a look as upon three occasions in his whole life he had turned upon his sister. Florence felt as she met it, that it were well Aunt Deborah, for her own sake was not present.

"And Miss Hammond is now in St. John's!" he asked.

"I suppose so; she left me to go there."

"Then I shall follow her, and endeavor to reason her out of this foolish determination. She must not be permitted to leave this house on Deborah's account."

"Oh, thank you, Uncle Sydney; I knew you would do something of the kind."

And Florence's little dry, burning hands squeezed his in her gratitude. Their fiery pressure recalled him to some thought for her.

"Florence, I fear you are much worse than you wish to appear, and I think even before I seek Miss Hammond, I had better dispatch Anne for a doctor for you."

"Please, do not: only bring me word that you have dissuaded Agnes from going, and it will be the very best medicine for me."

And she looked up at him laughing quite cheerfully.

He went out, pausing only to take his hat from the stand in the hall; then having heard him close the hall-door softly, Florence dragged herself up the stair, and threw herself dressed as she was upon the bed, feeling happy despite her own physical pain and weakness in the thought that Uncle Sydney might be able to avert the threatened separation.

St. John's Park had beauty and bloom in those days; its neatly-kept walks were bordered with flowering shrubbery, and its patches of grass were smooth and green. Then the fountain played daily, attracting to it the few children whose parents were rich, or aristocratic enough to own a key, and the circular walk about the fountain made a pleasant sort of treadmill for one who wanted to walk without aim, and without regard to apparent progress. The park was guarded rigidly by a gruff old man, who never admitted to it by either accident, or good nature, any one not belonging in some way to the owner of a key; and as he knew well the several owners, and their respective families, it was not easy to deceive him.

On this Sunday afternoon on which Wilbur wended his way thither, but few of the owners had seemed to avail themselves of their privilege; there appeared to be not more than a half dozen people scattered about the little paths, and when having reached the park he waited at one of the iron gates for the old man to admit him, he could see Miss Hammond taking a sort of treadmill walk about the fountain. She went slowly, with her head bent, and as he watched her he became impatient for his own admission: so impatient that he became also displeased with the unintentional delay of the old man, and he returned with undue quickness that person's respectful salute when at length the latter's park duties brought him within hailing distance.

Miss Hammond was so preoccupied that she did not even hear the firm, rapid step on the path behind her, nor was she conscious of the approach of anybody until her name was pronounced just at her ear by Sydney Wilbur.

She started and blushed until her brow and neck, as well as her cheeks, were crimson.

"You are surprised at my appearance. Florence sought me as soon as she had sent you out here, in order to tell me your startling announcement to her, and to tell me from what it proceeded. Now, my dear Miss Hammond," he drew her arm firmly within his own while he spoke, "you must permit me as the uncle of your friend, to have a little authority in this matter."

He spoke kindly, but at the same time with a tone of determination that both pleased and awed Agnes, and then without saying more, he led her unresistingly to one of the vacant benches in a retired part.

When they were both seated, he resumed:

"I regret exceedingly that any word or act of my sister should cause you a moment's unpleasant feeling, but I must say that I think it is carrying your revenge a little too far when you announce that because of it you intend to thrust our hospitality into our teeth, and take your indignant departure."

Hitherto, from the time of her first startled glance, she had not looked at him, but now his queer words and the half stern way in which he uttered them, compelled her to raise her eyes. His seemed to be going through her soul.

"I am not going to depart in any spirit of revenge," she said tremulously, and being so disconcerted by his penetrating look as to know hardly what she answered.

"Then why go?" he persisted. "As Florence told me that she said to you, *I* am master of our house, and what my sister wishes, or does not wish, is of little moment so that I wish and will it. And I wish you to stay, Miss Hammond."

She made a desperate effort to recall her resolution and she succeeded sufficiently to say with a firmness that both enhanced his admiration, and increased *his* determination to have her remain.

"I thank you, Mr. Wilbur, but I *must* go; I must go as soon as I have written to Mr. Mallaby to apprise him of my departure."

And then, determined to avoid the fascination of his eyes, she almost rudely turned away from him, and began to toy nervously with the chain of her watch. Her heart was beating to suffocation, and the blood was surging violently from her cheeks to her brow.

He waited a moment, then caught her hands with a grasp from which she could not free them, and compelled her to turn to him; but she did not, would not look at him.

"I have read your secret, Miss Hammond, you would flee from *me*."

In shame-stricken surprise she lifted her eyes then, only to meet in his a tenderness that thrilled her through.   He relinquished his grasp and stood before her:

"Agnes!"

It was the first time he had called her by her Christian name, and she thrilled again as she had done under his look.

"Become my wife, and thus make my house *always* your home."

He extended his hands to her, and for one wild instant she yearned to place her own in them, and to tell him that as he loved so was he loved in return; but she remembered her recent struggle and her resolution; she remembered these, but she forgot to make even an instant's prayer, and so she had only her own strength upon which to rely.

"I cannot, Mr. Wilbur; you forget that I am a Catholic."

And then she rose also, looking he thought more beautiful in her attempted firmness, than even she had looked to him before.

"But Catholics *do* marry Protestants," he persisted, "and I shall be reasonable, allowing you to practise your religion.   I shall even consent to our marriage by one of your clergymen."

Her temptation was great.   She loved this strong, clever, handsome man with all the virgin fervor of her eighteen years; and she could see no absolute wrong in becoming his wife when he promised to show such a tolerant spirit; then she had forgotten to pray, so that the tempter had fewer forces to fight against, and Wilbur continuing to plead, half laughed within himself, for he felt so certain of victory.

But a sudden thought came to her, and she burst out with it, as if glad that she had it to say:

Do you know that I am quite poor, Mr. Wilbur ? my guardian says that my income is only six hundred a year."

"Do you know that I am quite rich, Miss Hammond?" playfully mimicing her manner, "rich enough to care nothing about your income—rich enough even, to live away from my sharp-voiced sister!

"Oh, Agnes!" his voice taking an exquisite tenderness, "it is you I want, only you, beloved."

He took her hands unresistingly then, and held them, knowing that though she had not spoken, she had accepted him.

And, alas! she yielded to all the fascination of those fatal moments. It was so sweet to be thus loved, thus protected, as again he drew her arm within his own and she felt its supporting pressure—she who had never known a father's, mother's, or even brother's affection—and she walked with him through the flower-bordered paths silent from very happiness. He also was too happy to care to interrupt the silence.

Agnes Hammond, with her beautiful face, her charming modesty, her simple dignity, and even her piety, which—though produced by a religion, that he had been taught to abhor,—he still felt must spring from her own innocence and elevation of soul, won him as never one of the sex had won him before. Occasionally, while abroad a female face had charmed him, but it was only to find on a closer acquaintance that the exquisite features were not accompanied by all the virtues which alone make woman lovely and lovable. In Agnes, brief as was the time he had known her, he fancied he had discovered not alone the virtues already enumerated,—but an admirable truthfulness without which—educated as he had been to adhere to truth in the most minute particulars—he thought no woman worthy of regard.

Miss Hammond had been in the little park before with Mr. Wilbur and Florence, and though she had on that occasion thought it pretty, it had not the beauty that it seemed to possess now. She could have continued for hours that silent walk up one path and down another, imagining that no spot on the whole earth had such strange and exquisite loveliness. The very odor from the flowers seemed to become part of her happiness, linking itself in such a way with her strange and blissful feelings that in the mysterious future when her happiness was but a shadow of the past, it needed only the faintest waft of that same scent to bring before her the scene upon which she now so delightedly looked.

But no suspicion of the clouds that were one day to darken her horizon, entered her mind now—no thought but of her present happiness. Her recent struggles, the Confessor's counsel, her own resolution, were all forgotten, and when, after every path had been twice traversed, and sunset was not far distant Sydney again repaired to a vacant bench, he read in her eyes when they met his, convincing testimony of the return of his affection.

"Before we return to the house," he said, putting his arm on the back of the bench that she might rest her shoulders against it, rather than on the hard wooden support. "I must ask one or two practical questions."

She smiled indifferently, being too happy to care what he asked.

"Being your guardian, do you think Mr. Mallaby will quite approve of your marrying me? Do you think he will interpose the obstacle you mentioned, religion?"

"I am of age; eighteen last month. He has no right to object."

"Well, I shall call upon him to-morrow, declare my intentions, and ask his approval—being *your* guardian, Agnes, he has my warm regard, as any one, or anything must have, that belongs to you, dearest."

She blushed prettily, looked down, and edged away from his hand which from forming a support for her shoulders, had become bold enough to touch her hair. Her action alarmed him lest he had done anything to shock that feminine delicacy which he so admired in her, and he hastened to withdraw his arm from the bench at which action she looked relieved.

"And as you have no home but that Mrs. Denner's, boarding house of which you told me, I think our marriage had better take place as speedily as possible; and in the mean time during our arrangements suppose you and Florence, under good Mr. Mallaby's care, providing he will consent to the double charge, make a sojourn in Mrs. Denner's house. I am afraid it would not be pleasant for either of you to be under one roof with Deborah when I tell her what I intend to do."

"Oh! Mr Wilbur! that will be just delightful. Mrs. Denner is a real motherly woman, and I know she will take Florence right to her heart."

Mr. Wilbur had heard nothing but that formal pronouncing of his name, and determined to correct that instantly, he said with an assumption of sternness·

"*Mr. Wilbur* will listen to nothing except from Miss Hammond. When Agnes desires to be heard, she will please address Sydney."

"Then that arrangement will be delightful— Sydney," making an absurd pause before she pronounced the name, and blushing so shame-facedly, but at the same time so charmingly when she did pronounce it, that it was all her lover could do to avoid snatching her to his heart, and telling her that never had his name sounded so sweetly.

By this time it was sunset, and the old park-keeper was approaching for the purpose of requesting them to depart, as he had already requested everybody else, and they, divining his intention, rose to do so before he had quite reached them.

"Do not write to Mr. Mallaby, until I have seen him," requested Wilbur, as they walked very slowly home.

"But supposing he should be absent—he often is for weeks at a time."

"In that case, I shall see Mrs. Denner; being the good, motherly woman you represent her to be, she will take in the situation at a glance, and become an important ally of mine, until I can reach Mr. Mallaby by letter."

"So you are prepared for any emergency," replied Agnes laughing.

"To be sure! did ever lover woo fair lady without being full of expedients to overcome all obstacles?" he retorted playfully, and then having arrived within the house he said, as she was about to leave him:

"Tell Florence all about it, immediately. I think it will have the effect of making her quite well."

He watched her while she ran lightly up the stair, and she, feeling that he was standing as she had left him peeped archly down at him from over the baluster. Her rosy smiling face set against the dark color of her surroundings, made an exquisite picture; a picture that in the future was to come to him unbidden and unwished.

XI.

FLORENCE was asleep, just as she had thrown herself when she had come up from her uncle's study—so soundly asleep that she did not hear her friend's entrance, nor even her own name when Agnes bending over her repeated it softly two or three times.

"Poor child!" said Miss Hammond, "her head must have ached dreadfully. Her forehead is hot yet, and so are her hands," fondling the latter, and then pressing them to her lips.

"I ought not to disturb her; but I shall have a fever myself if I do not tell her."

And it would seem so from the way her own cheeks and hands were burning.

"Florence," she called with increasing loudness. "Dearest Florence! I am so sorry to disturb you but won't you please awake —I have something very important to tell you."

Becoming desperate, she gave the sleeper a little shake; it had the effect of making the latter stir but nothing more.

"Florence! will nothing arouse you? I am going to be married to your Uncle Sydney."

Whether it was that the words were spoken more into the sleeper's ear, or that their significance because of its very strangeness, had more power to arouse her, Miss Wilbur awoke a second after their utterance, and awoke so suddenly and so entirely, that she opened her eyes very wide, and sat up in the bed.

"You here, Agnes? I must have had the most ridiculous dream—just as I awoke I thought somebody whispered in my ear that you and Uncle Sydney

were to be married. What absurd things dreams
are. And I declare, my headache has quite gone,
and my dizziness too—" putting her hand to her
head, and preparing to get up. "You see, I was
right when I told you to leave me; it *did* give me a
chance to go to sleep. And oh!" as if only then recurring to that which had culminated in Agnes'
leaving her for the park—"did you go to St. John's,
and did Uncle Sydney find you, and did he tell you
what I told him, and did he persuade you to recall
your determination?"

And as if she were glad of an excuse not to listen quietly to what she feared might be an undesirable answer, she was bustling about the room, pre
tending to look for hairpins, ribbons, and other accessories of the feminine toilet.

Though Agnes had been so anxious to pour into
the ear of Florence what had occurred, now that
Florence was ready to listen, she found it absurdly
difficult even to speak, and Miss Wilbur wondering
at length at the protracted silence, paused in her
search for hairpins, and looked at Miss Hammond,
inquiring:

"What is the matter? Is it that Uncle Sydney
was not able to persuade you, and that you are
really going?"

Miss Hammond recovered her voice.

"We are both going—you and I to Mrs. Denner's
—your Uncle thinks it well that we should both be
away from your aunt."

"Dear, darling Uncle Sydney!" ejaculated Florence in her delight that Agnes and she should still
be together. "I knew he would find some way of
averting a separation. Are you not delighted, you
dear, sweet girl?"

And in the exuberance of her own joy, she rushed to Miss Hammond and gave that young lady a
very hearty, not to say violent embrace, her arms

continuing to linger about Miss Hammond's neck, even after her kisses had ceased.

"Yes; I am delighted, but there is something more to be told. That which you fancied you dreamed, was no dream. I whispered into your ear the words that awoke you. I am going to marry your Uncle Sydney. He asked me in the park to become his wife."

The arms twined around her neck dropped away as if that which they held had suddenly become fire or ice, and their owner shrank from Agnes in a sort of speechless horror.

Then, for the first time, owing to the evidently shocked amazement of Florence, there struck through her happiness a chord of keen reproach—in accepting Wilbur, no matter how tolerant he promised to be, she was breaking a precept of the church—she who was supposed to be so pious, so firm in the performance of duty. But she was not going to let Florence see how her conscience accused her, and she strove to say very playfully:

"Are you so unwilling to let me have your uncle. I thought, dearest, your friendship was deeper than that."

"Oh! Agnes! how can you accuse me even in jest of such a thought. It is not that, as you know, but he is a Protestant and you are so good, so fervent a Catholic. How can you be willing to disobey the church? You, whom I thought so good—you to do such a thing and but one week from the Convent, and only this morning at Communion! Oh. dearest Lord! surely our love for Thee is little."

The reproaches were cutting Miss Hammond to the quick; then, her vanity was wounded at having fallen from the pedestal on which her friend formerly had placed her; also, her envy was aroused by a very secret, but a very strong feeling that poor little, plain, common-place Florence, was capable of

greater heroism in spiritual things than she herself
was; and, irritated by these various emotions, she rose
from her seat, and said with unusual sharpness, as she
began to pace the room:

"I do not know why you make such a time, Florence; I am sure very good Catholic women have married Protestants before my day, and many of them
no doubt, have done good service to the Church by
converting their husbands, and bringing up their children strict Catholics. Your uncle has promised to be
most reasonable in matters of Faith, even to the extent
of being married by a priest."

"Oh, has he?" said Florence a little dryly.

And just then, Anne knocked at the door with a
message from Mr. Wilbur to know how Miss Florence was, and whether the young ladies were coming
down to tea, as he had been waiting at table for them
some time.

"Tell him I am much better, Anne, but prefer
taking tea in my room to-night. Miss Hammond
will join him immediately."

"Miss Hammond will remain to keep Miss Florence's company," interposed that young lady, and
Anne in doubt as to which message she should take
still lingered:

"Don't be foolish, Agnes; go down and have your
supper."

"Don't be ridiculous, Florence; come down with
me, and have yours."

But Florence was in no mood to sit at table with
the lovers, and finding that Agnes was firm in her
refusal to go down without her, she bade Anne bring
up tea for both of them.

In a few minutes Anne returned bearing a tray containing alone Miss Florence's tea. "Mr. Wilbur told
me not to bring Miss Hammond's as he wanted her
to come down in order to tell him how Miss Florence
was."

"There! you willful girl; you see what you have brought upon yourself. Now you *must* go," and she absolutely pushed Agnes from the room; then, in a wild burst of grief she threw herself upon her knees. Never had idol been more rudely or ruthlessly shattered than was Florence's. She would have staked her life upon Agnes' firm refusal to do anything that the Catholic Church did not sanction, and now to find herself so absolutely, so cruelly mistaken, was like receiving some painful wound. She blamed herself for having thrown the temptation into her friend's way and altogether she felt very miserable.

"But it is not yet too late, dear Lord," she prayed, raising her clasped hands and streaming eyes. "Only touch her heart with Your grace and she will recall her promise. Oh, Blessed Mother! you to whom she has been hitherto so devoted, do not forsake her now. Oh, my God! do not suffer all her life of piety to go down before this one temptation."

And who knows but the heart-spoken words were heard and answered—that the generous, loving fervor of that unselfish petition won for the sorely tempted girl that which she had not endeavored to win for herself.

XII.

AGNES descended slowly to the dining-room. Despite all her recent happiness she was beginning to feel very wretched. "But a week from the Convent, and at Communion this morning." Those were the reproaches that Florence had flung at her, and the words seemed to be written in the empty air before her. She appeared to herself to be like Judas who after he had partaken went out and betrayed the Master.

"And that is what *I* am doing," she said, as she reached the last step of the stair, and a great gulp came into her throat.

Mr. Wilbur, evidently tired of sitting alone at the table, had gone without tasting of the meal, to one of the windows and stood looking idly out upon the dimly lighted street. He did not hear the light footfall behind him, until his name was called, and then he turned, to behold Agnes, the expression of her face unlike it had ever looked to him before.

In alarm he caught her hands and drew her to the centre of the room where the light might enable him to observe her more fully; then his thought was for Florence, it must be *her* illness that made Agnes look so unlike herself.

"Florence is very sick," he said, "and you are alarmed, my affectionate Agnes."

"No; Florence is better; but I have come to take back the promise that in a moment of forgetfulness of my duty, I gave you. I cannot become your wife, Mr. Wilbur. The Catholic Church forbids mixed marriages, and I must obey her."

She tried to withdraw her hands but he seemed to hold them with a grasp of iron.

"Agnes!" he ejaculated, and in pity because of the very agony in his voice, she looked at him. His face had become as white as her own, and she fancied there were strange, heavy lines about his mouth.

"Have I not promised," he continued hoarsely, "to be reasonable in every matter pertaining to your religion—to be married by one of your clergymen?"

"I know it," she answered, "but all that does not suffice;" and were I not the weak creature I am, I should have told you then what I have just said to you, and what I must repeat; I cannot marry you. Please let me go."

Her hands were aching from his pressure. Not knowing that his grasp pained her, and conscious only that he could not give up, he did not relax his hold.

"You do not love me," he said, his voice tremulous from pain."

Not love him. It needed but a glance at the pale, suffering face which she lifted in reproach, to tell him how false was his accusation. And her simple answer:

"I do love you, but I love my God better," made him think of the sermon of the morning, and the life of the Catholic Saint he had once read and so thoroughly disbelieved; his disbelief in it was not so thorough now. There was even for an instant a thrill of admiration for that religion which could impart such firmness to one so young and so sorely tempted.

Never had she looked so beautiful to him; never had he loved her so passionately. He could not give her up. Yet neither could *he* give up the Faith of his fathers.

"Agnes, beloved! take time to think. Do not be in such haste to recall your promise."

"I must recall it, Mr. Wilbur; and it is unkind of you to press me longer.'

Her determination seemed to increase as if having

taken the first step in right doing, unexpected strength were given her, or perchance it was owing to the passionate fervor of the prayers still ascending for her from the loving heart of gentle, generous Florence.

"Unkind! Oh, Agnes! that ever I had met you, when the meeting meant such a parting as this must be. Do not be in such haste to leave me. I shall let you go after a little, but suffer my presence now, for I shall not inflict it upon you any more. I shall go away, somewhere to-morrow, so that you may remain here with Florence without fear of seeing me again."

At that instant while he still tightly held her hands and looked down with passionate tenderness and sorrow into her face, and while both stood where the light from the chandelier above them, brought them into full and distinct view, the door softly opened and Miss Liscome noiselessly entered. Her entrance was so noiseless that it was neither heard, nor perceived, and after one amazed, horrified, and violently wrathful look at the situation, she went as noiselessly out, and fairly ran all the way back to Deborah's room.

From the moment that Miss Wilbur, in what she termed "holy anger" had betaken herself to bed, she had religiously remained there, complaining of her poor head and heart in a way that taxed even Miss Liscome's accomodating sympathies. Anne also was taxed to prepare the various dainty dishes by which Deborah consoled herself for absence from the table, and which she said to Prudence were necessary to sustain her strength in the trying ordeal. The ordeal was rendered more exasperating by the utter indifference of her brother. He had not once sent to know even how she was, and when evening arrived upon the same neglect, her rage was boundless.

"Just go down to the dining-room, Prudence;" lifting herself on her elbow, and looking like a witch with her little snapping black eyes, puckered face, and thin, wiry, black hair falling about her cheeks, "they're about through with their supper by this time, and see how Sydney is taking my illness."

Miss Liscome, glad of any excuse that would take her into Sydney's presence, instantly obeyed, meeting the scene that made her rush back breathlessly, and as breathlessly give an account of it.

"Your brother was making love to Miss Hammond, Deborah, and she was receiving it. They looked as if they had been kissing each other ever so long the way he held her. Oh! it was the most shocking sight I ever beheld."

Deborah was out of bed, and robing herself in such haste, that she was putting her dress on in backward fashion until Miss Liscome came to her aid.

"Making love to that jade, Prudence, and in *my* house—" Miss Liscome wondered if the house was really Miss Wilbur's indisputable property—"kissing each other! I wonder God's lightning didn't strike them."

And her dress being on, she did not even wait to put back her wildly floating hair, but went with a speed that quite belied her recent illness down to the dining-room, her friend prudently remaining behind, until her curiosity led her to the baluster over which she peeped in hope of seeing or hearing something.

But Deborah was a few seconds too late. That harrowing scene between the lovers had terminated directly after Miss Liscome's noiseless departure; for Agnes, from her own agonizing struggle and the evidence of her companion's pain, seeming to grow faint, Wilbur had become alarmed, and leading her to the door he gave a last pressure to the ice-cold hands

he still held, imprinted a sudden hurried, but burning kiss upon her forehead, and hastened to his
study, while she crept back to Florence.

Thus, Miss Wilbur found no one in the dining-
room, but to test the truth of Miss Liscome's story,
she flew to the study, bursting upon her brother just
as he had thrown himself into a chair in an attitude
of deep dejection.

"What is this I hear about you, Sydney Wilbur?"
she began, her angry tones nowise softened by his expression of suffering, "disgracefully making love to
Miss Hammond in the dining-room."

Astonishment, indignation and disgust made Sydney rouse himself.

"Pray who is your informant?"

Too angry to be warned by even the stern change
in his countenance, she answered in the same shrill,
harsh tone:

"That good soul, Prudence Liscome. She was so
shocked by your attitude with Miss Hammond, that
I shouldn't wonder if her soul's salvation suffered.
As I said, to her, I was surprised God's lightning did-
n't strike you. You, Sydney Wilbur, brought up so
strictly in the Presbyterian Faith, to act so even in
jest with a Romanist, for of course you couldn't have
any serious objects owing to the will."

His indignation was mastering him; and its mastery was becoming so evident in his flashing eyes
that his sister in spite of herself was somewhat
frightened, her fear made her retreat towards the
door.

"Did that good soul, Prudence Liscome," (could
Prudence have heard the witheringly sarcastic manner in which her name was pronounced she would
have regretted her communication to Deborah) "also
inform you that I had proposed to Miss Hammond
and had been rejected, precisely because Miss Hammond is a Romanist?"

Miss Wilbur was speechless from amazement—amazement in the first place that her brother could have been mad enough to so ignore the terms of a certain will as to offer his hand to Miss Hammond, amazement in the second place that Miss Hammond should have refused so eligible an offer, as Sydney Wilbur. But, before she could utter a word either to express her astonishment, at his insane action, or her delight at the rejection he had suffered, her brother took her by the shoulders put her outside of the threshold of the study, closed and locked the door.

Never had Deborah Wilbur been so vexed with herself; now that instead of there being imminent danger that Miss Hammond would entrap Sydney, she had even actually refused him, Aunt Deb wished she had kept her tongue still and had been more civil to her guests, experiencing even a little qualm for having caused the rosary to disappear. She felt that by this last blast she had angered Sydney to desperation, and she did not know what might be the consequence. And in her chagrin as she returned to her room, she blamed Miss Liscome for it all. Indeed, she could hardly wait to be properly within the apartment where she had left that lady, to open upon her the vials of her wrath.

"Prudence Liscome, you're a wicked mischief maker!"

Had a chasm disclosed itself at the feet of Miss Liscome, she could not have been more amazed and horror-stricken; not alone at Miss Wilbur's utterly, unexpected accusation, but at Miss Wilbur's angry tone and manner.

"I repeat it! you are a mischief maker! coming up here and telling me those horrid things about my brother, when actually what you saw was Miss Hammond refusing Sydney's hand. Think of that, you old creature, you; that's more than you'd be noble enough to do if he asked you to marry him. And I

don't know how you can reconcile your conscience
to what you have done—made mischief between a
brother and sister. My brother is so angry with me
for what I said to him, that I don't know what desperate thing he may do."

She talked so fast and furiously that Miss Liscome
could not be heard had she attempted to reply. But
her feelings could be well seen in her face, her
rouge at one moment paling before the natural crimson called up by her anger, and the next, standing
out like daubs in the greenish pallor of the rest of
her countenance. Nothing in the series of reproaches had cut her so much as being called old;
that sting made her bosom heave with emotion, and
at length, her jealousy, grief and rage culminated
in a burst of spiteful tears.

By that time Miss Wilbur's own feelings having
had their vent, were supposed to subside a little, and
even to be less severe with weeping Miss Liscome.
After all, the creature had been devoted to her, and
it would make an unpleasant vacuum in Deborah's
life did she not have Prudence to gossip to. So she
proceeded to mollify her:

"Dry your eyes, Prudence, and don't make a fool
of yourself any longer, crying like a spanked child.
If I spoke a little severely to you, you must acknowledge that you deserved it, rushing up here with such a
ridiculous story as you did. Dry your eyes and
be thankful Sydney is not going to marry that Romish jade. You may be able to win him yet."

She knew in her heart, that for the future, Miss
Liscome would be even beneath Sydney's contempt.

"But you called me an *old* creature," answered
Miss Liscome tearfully, "as if I were an old woman
of forty, when I haven't reached my thirty-fifth
birth-day yet."

"Now, Prudence Liscome you know you're lying.
You look as old as I do, and I was forty, six months

ago. I don't mind you touching up your cheeks a little bit, to make yourself look youthful, but when it comes to lying about age between women of our years I think it is despicable."

"My sister who is ten years older than I am, says I am only thirty-four," again tearfully protested Miss Liscome, her soreness on the point of her age excluding every other thought.

"Then your sister tells lies also," vigorously answered Miss Wilbur, "for, if she's a day, she's fifty, and with that great young man of a son of hers—why Prudence Liscome, he's twenty-five at least. But never mind your age and stop blubbering—" Prudence was gently sniffling—"and help me to contrive something to put Sydney into good humor.

Prudence was not entirely mollified; but she thought it better policy to appear so, and Deborah quite credited the appearance.

XIII.

FLORENCE was still on her knees, when Agnes ascended to her, but she jumped up hastily as the door opened, and turned away her tear-stained face.

"Florence! I have told your uncle that I could not become his wife, and we have parted. I am not to see him any more."

The voice seemed utterly unlike Miss Hammond's voice. Never Florence thought had tones expressed such agony; their appalling accents struck even through the joy which she felt, that Agnes was not going to be false to the principles of their Faith, and when she looked at the white, suffering face turned so earnestly upon her own, her eyes filled again.

"My poor, brave Agnes!"

She forced Miss Hammond into a chair, and knelt beside her, at one moment raining on the latter's face, tears and kisses together, and at another trying to impart to the limp and icy hands some of the heat of her own.

"You are my own heroic Agnes!" she said between her caresses—"I knew you were too fervent, too noble to make a marriage which the Church could not bless."

But her praise caused no throb of vanity this time. Miss Hammond's reaction from the fervor which had led her finally to make the sacrifice, and the bitter thought that she had really parted from Sydney Wilbur, were making her too wretched to yield in the slightest degree to any other feeling.

Florence's attempted comfort changed at length to vehement censures of herself.

"It is *my* fault, Agnes, that you have so much

misery. Why did I bring you here? I might have known that your beauty, and grace, and sweetness would surely captivate Sydney, but I did not think,"—sobbing so that she could not continue.

"You foolish child; to reproach yourself for what you did in such kindness. It is I who am to blame. I should have been stronger. And I *shall* be strong."

She straightened herself in her chair, and held Florence's head up so that she could look into the girl's face while she spoke:

"Don't you remember, Florrie," trying to speak very cheerfully, but failing most miserably to do so, "all that the dear Madames used to say about the crosses that might, and must come to each of us, and how by our crosses we were to be tried and purified? Well, this is my cross and what would you if it did not cut a little. But I shall try to bear it with some of that courage you so generously accredit to me, and you, by your prayers and your cheerfulness, must help me to bear it."

She straightened herself still more, and even smiled a little.

Florence stopped her sobbing and dried her eyes. Miss Hammond resumed:

"Your uncle spoke of going away somewhere. It would be most unseemly that *he* should leave his own house on my account. May we not, Florence, carry out his proposition of going to Mrs. Denner's, both of us? It may not be as agreeable for you, being a boarding-house, as here, but at least there we shall be together until you go to join your mother."

"Certainly, we may," responded Florence, "and as for Mrs. Denner's being a boarding-house, a boarding-house would be a palace with you, Agnes."

"Well, then, go to your uncle now, and tell him our arrangement — also, that I shall write to Mr. Mallaby this evening, so that we may go to-morrow,

or the next day.   If Mr. Mallaby be not at home we
can go to Mrs. Denner in any event. She will accom-
modate us someway."

Florence obeyed, knocking so timidly at the study
door that its despondent and absorbed occupant did
not hear her. When she repeated it, he, thinking
it was his sister who had returned, did not answer;
but when she called softly:

"Uncle Sydney!"

He dragged himself wearily to the door and opened
it. If Agnes had looked changed and suffering, the
change and suffering depicted in Wilbur's face were
appalling. Deep, unusual lines seemed to have come
out in different parts of his countenance, and his
mouth had a painfully set look. Florence started
when she saw him, and wondered with another throb
of keen self-reproach where all the dreadful business
of which she had been the innocent cause, was to end.

"Come in," he said, striving to speak reassuringly
when he saw how she looked.

She gave him Agnes' message.

He listened without looking at her, seeming rather
to watch the motions of a little moth fluttering
about his study lamp; nor did he answer when she
had finished.

"Uncle Sydney," she called, surprised at his extraordinary silence.

They were both standing, he apparently having
forgotten to offer her a chair, or to take one himself,
and when she pronounced his name, moving a step
toward him at the same time, he exclaimed suddenly:

"Oh! Florence! why did you bring her here?'

Why indeed? It needed but that reproach spok-
en impetuously because of the very sharpness of
his disappointment to open anew the flood-gates of
Florence's own grief. She threw herself into a chair
sobbing.

"Oh, that I never *had* brought her; but I did not dream of this, and I felt also so sure that nothing of the kind could happen because she was a Catholic. I did not think you could get to care for her so much."

"You forgot, my poor little niece, that love regards no differences."

And then touched by her sorrow, he said gently, but with so much sadness it was as pathetic as had been his first impetuous burst:

"Miss Hammond has become more to me than any other human being, and the sooner I place miles of distance between us the better for us both. Would it make much difference if *I* took you to your mother instead of this friend for whom you are waiting? I can engage passage for us to-morrow in the first out-bound steamer."

The suddenness of the proposition made her stop crying.

"Agnes," she said, "to leave *her* now, when she is suffering, and looking forward to my companionship to enlighten her trial. How can I do it, Uncle Sydney?"

"Miss Hammond will find consolation in that religion for which she has sacrificed me," he replied a little bitterly, though under the bitterness existed still the admiration which had been engendered by Miss Hammond's very sacrifice.

"And you owe something to me, Florence, for having brought upon me all this wretchedness."

The truth was that he still secretly hoped to move Miss Hammond's determination, fancying that when she found she was to lose so speedily both her lover and her friend, she would, she *must* yield. Manlike, he thought all women were more or less weak, and though Agnes had shown such unusual resolution for her sex, he by no means regarded it as too strong to be eventually broken. Moreover he had never yet an obstacle to his wishes, that his indomitable e will had not found means to conquer.

His gentle, little niece, however, was not without her will, and that will, prompted by her affection for Agnes, made her for some time so stubbornly resist her uncle's persuasions, that he, attributing her firmness, also to the Catholic religion, felt very much tempted to give vent to an anathema upon the same. Indeed, he did smother a violent aspersion upon it, when he found that the utmost to which Florence would at length consent, was to speak to Agnes about it.

"Well speak to her now, and bring me her answer immediately."

He was almost gruff in his command, and Florence as she rose to obey him, both her head and her heart aching, excitement and grief having brought back the former pain, was only restrained by the fear of committing a sin, from the wish that she had never been born.

Miss Hammond, to Florence's intense surprise, approved immediately of the proposition. Perchance, she felt that though her trial would be rendered sharper by separation from Florence, that very sharpness would be better for her, as it would sever her completely from every reminder of Sydney Wilbur.

And she positively coaxed her companion to consent, adding with simulated cheerfulness:

"The excitement of assisting your preparations for departure, Florrie, will be an excellent panacea for me, and if you promise, faithfully promise, to sail inside of a week, I shall brave Aunt Deb for that time, and remain to see you off."

Wilbur smiled grimly, but with secret satisfaction when his niece returned to him with that reply. Miss Hammond would probably yield before the week was out, though with commendable delicacy, he meant to keep out of her sight, until the very last moment.

XIV.

WHEN, the next morning, Miss Deborah Wilbur was acquainted by her brother with his arrangement for Florence, she did not know to which feeling to yield most—astonishment at the sudden and unexpected departure, delight that she should be so speedily relieved of her undesirable guests, regret that Sydney was going abroad, or relief that his disappointment and her recent blast had engendered no worse consequence than a flight to Europe. He would give her no satisfaction on the length of his stay abroad, but that she could bear so long as he had escaped the awful fate of marrying Miss Hammond, and in actual gratitude, she was positively civil to her guest; even more kindly civil than she was to Florence, at which the latter laughed a little, divining whence her extraordinary kindness sprang. Her civility became more marked, when she found that Sydney avoided Miss Hammond's presence even to the extent of taking his meals in his study. Anne, who brought them to him was very much bewildered. That he must be sick to eat in that solitary and secluded fashion, she was sure, but his sister's apparent indifference to the fact made the domestic wonder. That Mr. Wilbur was going away she knew also, by the preparations in which her assistance was required, and altogether, since the young ladies, who came but little over a week ago, and who were now going away before the end of another week, had been in the house, things had seemed strange and quite unlike themselves.

Aunt Deb having concluded the packing of Sydney's trunk, took uninvited a busy hand in Florence's

packing, insisting that as she had done the same in
former years for Sydney, she knew better than any
one else how to pack for European travel.   Florence
was nothing loth to gratify her, as it gave her more
time to be alone with Agnes.   They went out together unattended now, going even in the early
morning to Mass.   On Saturday, Florence and Sydney were to sail, and so the days intervening, were
very few and very precious.   They must not spend a
moment of them apart.

Miss Liscome came every day ostensibly to help
Deborah, but really to obtain a glimpse of Mr. Wilbur, and her heart sank more and more as Saturday
rapidly neared, and she did not once see him.

Whether it was that she was silly enough to hope,
since Miss Hammond had rejected him, he might yet
be won by her faded charms, or that her mature affections had actually twined themselves about him
to the extent of making her unable to resign all hope
of him, even Deborah could not quite determine,
and knowing now how absurdly impossible it
would be for Miss Liscome to inspire in Sydney
anything but a contemptuous regard, she smiled secretly when she saw the daily elaborate array of
Prudence.   But, for ends of her own she pandered
to the attachment of her friend, even expressing regret that she could not invite her to attend the departure, owing to the fact that Sydney, Florence,
Miss Hammond and herself would occupy all availa-
ble room in the family carriage; and her reason was
true, but it was not the only one.   Deborah felt that
her brother would never forgive her for inflicting upon him at such a time, such hateful company, and
that he would be certain to take another mode of
conveyance.

To Miss Liscome, however, who expected the invitation, the disappointment was dreadful; all the
more so because its announcement was not made to

her until the very day before Wilbur was to sail. It was with difficulty she concealed her feelings, and she only consoled herself by secretly determining that she would attend the departure, even though she did not go in the family carriage of the Wilburs. At the same time she also secretly determined upon another action. Since it was evident that she was not to meet Mr. Wilbur, she would send him some token of her remembrance, at which he would be touched by her thoughtfulness, and at least be made somewhat aware of her regard for him. It was awful to think of his going away without knowing of the fond place he held in her heart.

On the pretense of having an errand to perform for Prescilla—Prescilla was her half invalid married sister—she hastened home and looked among her possessions. In an old-fashioned, faded box with a pinless breastpin, and one tarnished earring there was lying a watch-charm in the shape of a gold heart, and having her own name, Prudence, in tiny letters on its face. With that little ornament was connected the nearest approach to matrimony that Miss Liscome had ever been able to make; she herself had presented that charm to her lover in return for his gift to her; but, when he was about to offer his hand, she chilled his ardor by her prudent inquiries about his habits, and her prudent statements as to what she should expect and demand in a husband. So much virtue frightened him, and he prudently withdrew, returning Miss Liscome her golden heart. She put it away in its present resting-place, and only looked at it when she felt low-spirited and inclined to be sentimental over her lost love

She now felt that it would be a most appropriate gift for Mr. Wilbur, and having wrapped it carefully in several folds of tissue paper, she sat down to write an accompanying note. The wording of the note required so much thought and labor that she

had used almost her entire supply of fashionably-
tinted and perfumed paper before she accomplished
anything to her satisfaction. At length, she had to
be contented with:

MY DEAR MR. WILBUR:
  "The accompanying little token is from a heart that holds you in
most affectionate esteem, and that during your various wanderings
abroad will continue to regard you as one of its nearest and dearest friends.

Ever yours,

PRUDENCE LISCOMB."

That language, she thought, while it did not whol-
ly commit her, must convey unmistakably to him
the evidence of her regard.

Then, hastily .donning her bonnet, she ran across
to the Wilburs, seeking admission at the basement
door, in order to have a better opportunity of speaking in confidence to Anne.

Anne had never been favorably impressed by Miss
Liscome, having from the first been disgusted by
the latter's absurd pretensions to youthfulness. She
was always, however, civil, so that Prudence had no
means of knowing to what extent the domestic
might be willing to serve her.

"You dear, good creature," she began, the moment that Anne appeared. Anne opened her eyes a
little at the unusual salutation. Then, having got
fairly within doors, Miss Liscome whispered :

"Is anybody down here ? are we quite alone ?"

"There's nobody down here, ma'am," the tones
in loud contrast to Miss Liscome's cautious accents.

"Well, then, Anne, you good soul, I want you to
do me a little favor. Just slip this little parcel to
Mr. Wilbur without letting anybody else know anything about it. You can do it when you take him
one of his meals. It's just a little remembrance I
want to give him as he's going away, and I don't

care to have anyone in the house know anything about it but just you and him.

"Very well, ma'am," and Anne took the parcel, and returned to the kitchen, while Miss Liscome went up stairs in search of Deborah.

"The old fool!" soliloquized Anne, "giving that young, handsome Mr. Wilbur a remembrance to take away with him, as if he cared for the likes of her. I'll give it to him as she asked me to, when I take up one of his meals, but I'm thinking it's not much thanks she'll get."

Willing, however, as Anne was to oblige Miss Liscome she found no opportunity of doing so that day for Mr. Wilbur went out before even lunch hour, leaving word that he would not return until late in the evening.

Agnes and Florence had been out together the greater part of the day, making little last purchases and finding retired streets down which they could walk and talk. Motion seemed to be necessary to both of them; rest made the anticipated agony of the morrow harder to bear.

Miss Hammond had not written to Mr. Mallaby to apprise him of her going to Mrs. Denner's. She preferred to trust to her chance accommodation there rather than to the certainty of Mr. Mallaby's presence at the parting scene on the morrow, for she knew he would deem it incumbent upon him to give her his personal escort on such an occasion were he not out of the city. Somehow, since he had been at Wilbur's, she had a sort of dread of seeing him in any company, even though he was not her relative and rather than incur the risk of meeting him, she had actually accepted Aunt Deb's offer to drive her. on the departure of the steamer to Mrs. Denner's.

"You know, Agnes," Florence had more than once said, "I may return in a few months, for, if I can't induce my mother to change her mind about making her home in Europe, I may be able to coax her to revisit New York. So we need not be so cast down about this parting after all."

But, despite the hope she strove both to impart, and to feel, and the cheerful tones she assumed, there was a gloom upon her spirits, much more than even the occasion seemed to warrant. It was as if the finger of inexorable fate were pointing to a separation greater than even distance could make between herself and her beloved companion.

At tea, Aunt Deb and Miss Liscome bore them company; Aunt Deb was particularly cheerful, owing to her perpetual gratitude for the awful danger her brother had escaped, and she kept up a light but still, to her three spiritless companions, a sort of exasperating conversation, for it compelled answers constantly from each of them in turn. Miss Liscome wanted to be permitted to observe in silence the face of Miss Hammond who sat directly opposite to her, and to wonder in what special feature was the charm that had won Wilbur. In her opinion Miss Hammond's mouth was too large, and her forehead too low, and just now she was frightfully pale. But she had to acknowledge the charm of the delicate skin and that other more potent charm of youth, Miss Hammond's face bore no lines, nor wrinkles, nor crows' feet.

It never occurred to her to think about Miss Hammond's character, nor to wonder at, or admire, the resolution which could put aside so tempting an offer as Sydney Wilbur's heart and hand—such heroism was beyond even her conception. She was conscious of nothing but a violent jealousy of the girl, and a secret, but none the less deadly desire to crush her if she could. She hated her with all her little vain soul for the love she had won.

All but Aunt Deb were glad when the meal was finished, and hearing her ask, or rather command,

Prudence to accompany her to her room in order to help her finish some sewing upon which both had been engaged during the afternoon, Agnes and Florence repaired to the parlor.

They sat in silence holding each other's hands and looking into each other's eyes with the dreariest attempts at cheerful expressions of countenance, until Florence could bear it no longer. In desperation for something to break the agonizing monotony, she urged:

"Sing for me, Agnes."

Agnes went to the piano; she had little heart to sing, but she could not at such a time, refuse any request from Florence, and thinking it would harrow herself less to sing something from the music belonging to the Wilburs, than the strains with which both she and Florence were familiar, she opened one of the books of melody lying on the piano. They were mostly light airs, but cheerful ones, and when having sung a couple, Florence begged her to continue, she came suddenly upon "Kathleen Mavourneen."

"It may be for years, and it may be for ever,' rang out in her exquisite contralto, and with an expression in the singer's voice that told how her own aching heart was in the quivering strains.

Florence felt her own heart would burst if she waited to hear more, and she stole from the room leaving the singer who now seemed unconscious to everything but that she was giving vent to emotions with which her soul was full.

The hall-door opened, and Wilbur entered, pausing a moment as the strains reached him. Then he stole to the parlor-door; Florence had left it partly open. He looked within, and seeing its sole occupant, went noiselessly in, standing behind the singer and hardly daring to breathe lest he might betray his presence.

But her own feelings were overmastering her; the agony of parting with Sydney, with Florence, the anticipation of an unhomelike boarding house and odd Mr. Mallaby, the craving for the affection of a father, mother, brother, sister to which to flee in order to fill the awful gap that would be made by Florence's departure, seemed to have been rendered more intense by the very words she was singing, and in the middle of the second stanza her song gave way to the great sob that had been gathering in her heart from the first, and she laid her head on the piano, and gave utter way to her grief.

Wilbur could not control himself; he forgot his promise not to appear in her sight; he forgot all his former regard for her extreme delicacy, and rushing forward he caught her in his arms.

"My darling! our separation shall not be—you have consented—you will consent—you will tell me not to leave you."

He held her so tightly that for a moment she could hardly even struggle in his arms; then, with a desperate effort which alarmed him for the result of his impetuous action, she freed herself, and in her horror at having been actually in his embrace, and her fear of yielding at last to him, she shrank from him as though he had been some unsightly thing.

"Agnes," he said, his voice sounding hoarse and unnatural from his own wild emotions, "do you fear me? has it come to this, that you shrink from me?"

He approached her, but she shrank further away, in her desperation praying unconsciously aloud:

'Oh. my God save me! Holy Mother of God help me!"

He stopped short, astonished, grieved and angered at her prayers; astonished and grieved that she should thus fear him, and angered that he was powerless to move her resolution. Could she love him, he argued with himself, and love him as he loved her, and still act in this manner? Other Catholic women equally as good, had married Protestants,

why should Agnes Hammond hold herself so superior? He had not asked her to give up her religion;
he had not even demanded that she should sacrifice
one of its requirements; then, why her refusal to
marry him? Might it not be owing to a sort of natural obstinacy in her character or even a secret
hope that he would prove his love by becoming a
convert to Catholicity for her sake, at which thought
his whole soul rebelled—not even for Agnes Hammond, passionately as he loved her, unless that motive were accompanied by sure and full conviction,
would he renounce the Faith of his fathers.

"Agnes," he said, at length, "you need not fear
me; if in the ardor of my regard for you, a regard
which I now feel you neither understand, appreciate,
nor return, I have forgotten myself, I beg you to
forgive me. It is the last time I shall so offend."

He turned from her, going toward the door, but
before he reached it, something impelled him to look
back. She, stung by his words, knowing how mistaken he was, and feeling that she could not let him
go with that cruel thought of her, had taken a step
toward him, bearing in her face, a wild, agonized
and imploring look. In an instant he was at her
side again, every thought of her gone, but that she
loved him.

"Agnes, my own! your face has recalled me—
your eyes speak the words which your tongue has
so cruelly refused to utter, and remember all that I
have promised with regard to your Faith, all, remember—I demand no sacrifice from you—you will
tell me now that you will marry me."

It was well that the poor, tempted creature lost not
for an instant the thought of prayer. Having learned so sadly the little dependence to be placed on
her own strength, her soul had hardly intermitted
for a second, its silent petition for help; and now she
was enabled to answer with a firmness which even he

felt it were vain to endeavor longer to struggle against.

"If my face seemed to recall you it was because you had wronged me by saying that I neither understood, nor appreciated, nor returned your regard. Perhaps the best evidence of my doing all three is the very sacrifice I am making. I do not love you less, because I love my God more, nor would you in your better and manlier moments even seek to make me do that which was contrary to my principles. Now, in kindness to me, go, or permit me to leave you."

She moved as if to pass him, but he placed himself before her.

"In a moment I shall go, when I have asked once more, is your answer to marry me, irrevocably no ?"

His whole eager passionate soul was in his eyes, and he turned them full upon her, compelling her to meet them.

She answered as firmly as before:

"Irrevocably no !"

He turned away, and went again to the door, and out; she heard his quick step as he strode, rather than walked to his study, and then she went up stairs to Florence who had but just become calm after the burst of grief evoked by "Kathleen Mavourneen."

"Let me cry a little, dear." she said, putting her arms around Florence's neck, "1 think it will do me good."

XV.

IN the bustle of the preparations for departure the next morning, Anne forgot to deliver Miss Liscome's parcel; indeed the domestic was in such bewildering demand by "Aunt Deb," that it was a wonder, as she herself expressed it afterwards, she had any sort of a head left upon her shoulders, and such being the case she did not consider herself to blame for having neglected poor Miss Liscome. But she did not intend to tell that lady that her failure to deliver the message was due to anything save Mr. Wilbur's own absence from home, which was quite true of Friday, but not at all true of Saturday, for though he did not show himself until the moment of departure, he was in his study almost the whole morning.

Aunt Deb wondered a little that Prudence did not come over, but secretly she was just as well pleased; it might be unpleasant to have Sydney meeting her, should he happen to leave his solitude, as he was likely to do on this last day.

Miss Liscome had not made her wonted call on the Wilburs, because she wanted to be early on the pier from which the steamer was to sail; and that she was early, unusually early, was attested by the presence of not another female, and the absence of much of the bustle which attends an out-bound steamer. She had not gone to the house through fear of being unable even there to murmur her farewell to Mr. Wilbur, and she could not with decency announce to Deborah, since the latter had taken it for granted she would not go uninvited, her anxiety to get away in order to be in time for the departure of the vessel. There did not seem to be any impropriety in meeting them all on the pier, and certainly during that meeting there must be an opportunity for her to say something graceful, if not tender, to Mr. Wilbur.

She had arrayed herself, as usual, in some light-colored juvenile costume, as unbecoming as it was unsuitable, and with her rouged cheeks and a great bunch of monthly roses in her bosom, she looked rather an *ontre* sight, on the rough and not overclean dock. What made her appear still more out of keeping with her surroundings, was the morning itself—dark, cloudy, windy, as utterly unlike the summer season to which it belonged, as Miss Liscome herself was unlike the youth and beauty she strove so desperately to counterfeit.

Everybody who chanced to pass looked at her; sometimes even a laborer wheeling his handcart went slower to have a better view of her, and a couple of red-faced, middle-aged, and seemingly jolly tars tried to oggle the "old gal," as they called her, but she indignantly put up her parasol and turned her back to them.

She found patience and consolation in the thought that Sydney by this time had in his possession her little gift; it never occurred to her that he might decline to receive it, or that he might return it to Anne with a message of unmistakable displeasure for the giver. Not dreaming of the utter contempt which her report of his interview with Miss Hammond had inspired, she entertained only her own old pleasant thoughts of him.

At length, the passengers and their friends began to arrive, and as carriage after carriage deposited its load, Miss Liscome felt some anxiety lest *her* friends might come too late for any but the most hurried farewell. To add to her discomfort the day grew more threatening, and the dark, comfortable-looking costume of every lady about her, made her somewhat painfully conscious of her own inappropriate attire.

But her fears were all forgotten the moment the Wilbur conveyance drove into sight, and to the astonishment of its three occupants—Sydney was not there—the first to meet them as they alighted, was startling-looking Miss Liscome. Florence, despite her heavy heart, could not forbear smiling at the creature's ridiculous appearance, and her look of disappointment which she could not conceal, at the absence of Mr. Wilbur.

"What on earth are you doing here, Prudence Liscome?" spoke up Deborah sharply, her sharpness arising from the fact that Miss Liscome might not believe her when she should tell her that she did not know until the last minute Sydney would meet them instead of accompany them, and that had she known it Prudence might have had that vacant seat in the carriage.

Miss Liscome, however, was relieved so long as she felt there was still a chance of seeing Sydney, and she summoned courage to say:

"Do not mind, dear Deborah, about not having invited me; I only felt that in return for all Mr. Wilbur's kind attentions to me, I ought to come to wish him at the last a friendly good-bye."

"Mr Wilbur's kind attentions" to her had consisted of nothing more than common civilty when as his sister's guest he had been obliged to meet her, and even Deborah wondered at the conceit that could thus magnify mere courtesy. Desirous, however, of not offending Prudence, and yet equally anxious to spare her brother a meeting for which he would not thank her, she said:

"We do not know that Sydney has arrived yet, and while we go to inspect the state-rooms, you can get into the carriage, Prudence, and wait for us."

But Miss Liscome was not to be cajoled in that

manner; were Sydney actually on board, Deborah might not tell him, or he might not have the time to come out and see her, so, expressing a vehement desire to behold the interior of an ocean steamer, she followed the party up the gangplank.

Wilbur met them almost immediately, his face having the white, haggard appearance of one who had lost both rest and food, and his mouth set in such a painfully stern way it made Florence shudder to look at him. His sister noted his appearance also, but the anxiety it might at another time have caused, was absorbed in the gratitude she still continued to feel that he was not going to marry Miss Hammond. Agnes, after one furtive, hasty glance, did not trust herself to look again. She guessed well why almost at the last moment he went hurriedly from the house, leaving word that he would meet them instead of accompany them, and she was thankful for the arrangement; it spared them both the agony of that drive together, in which they must be so near, and yet must sternly keep themselves so far apart.

Now, desperately anxious to do anything save look at him, or even think about him if that were possible, she kept close to Florence, giving her little last messages, and for the sake of maintaining an appearance of confidential conversation, saying them over and over.

Florence responded by little nods; did she attempt to reply by so much as a word, she felt she should burst into the wildest grief.

They were in the saloon, pausing a moment before going to inspect the state-rooms, and Wilbur standing beside his sister, saw nothing but Agnes. He had not noticed Miss Liscome by so much as a salutation, and she, a little abashed by such unexpected deportment, kept somewhat in the rear. But, she was devouring both him and Agnes with her eyes, and when they all went forward to the state-rooms she kept still behind the better to watch the conduct of the lovers, and to seize an opportunity for the delivery of her own little speech.

That opportunity seemed to come when, having to pass through a narrow part of the vessel, he waited to let his companions precede him. Miss Liscome was so far in the rear when he paused, that he did not even see her. But, noticing her opportunity, she hurried forward and overtook him just as he had turned to follow his sister.

"A moment, Mr. Wilbur, please; I may not again have the opportunity of wishing you a pleasant voyage, and, hoping that the heart you carry with you will be a *real* charm to you on your journey."

Was the creature crazy? that was his first thought looking at her ridiculous attire. His second thought was that her speech had reference to his attachment to Miss Hammond, and it was with difficulty he restrained himself from giving her a sharper reply than he had ever made to a woman in his life. As it was, he turned from her with an expression of contemptuous indignation which even she, impervious as she was, could not misunderstand. She fell back again to the rear, hating him almost as much as she hated Miss Hammond.

The very last moment had arrived, and Wilbur purposely waited until even Florence had torn herself sobbing from Agnes' arms, and had fled to her state-room there to give unrestrained way to her grief, before he extended his hand in good-bye to Agnes. He had already kissed his sister, and he had waited even until she had begun her retreat to the gangway near the head of which Miss Liscome had taken her place.

Then he extended both his hands to Agnes, and since it seemed likely to be the last time, she placed her own within them.

"Is your answer still the same?" his voice was fairly quivering.

"Still the same."

He had to stoop to catch the words as tremulously uttered as his own had been.

"You are willing to make this a final farewell and to crush my heart as you are doing—oh Agnes! you are cruel, you are merciless."

She felt his hot breath on her face as he spoke, and but too surely she read in the working of his countenance the evidence of what he said; but her own pain was no less.

"It is *you* who are cruel to thus harrow me. You know that I cannot consent to that which you ask. Good-bye."

He released her hands while she was speaking, and in order to maintain her self-control she had turned away with the last word, to which he did not respond, upon her lips; owing to the great dumb agony in her heart, she was going blindly forward, not well knowing whither her steps were leading until some one set her right, and she found herself descending the gangplank almost the very last of the loitering visitors. Neither caring nor thinking of the direction Deborah had taken, she stood on the pier among others who waited to see the departure of the steamer.

The cloudy, gloomy, though still rainless day, seemed to be in accord with her miserable feelings, and every strain of the cordage, every creak of the timbers as the vessel prepared to depart, was like a heavy blow upon her heart. Slowly, majestically the steamer detached itself and headed for the broad water, while an awed silence seemed to fall upon the spectators. On board the decks were crowded with the passengers ready to wave their adieus.

In the front line stood Wilbur, his hat off as were the hats of most of the gentlemen about him, and his head bowed. Agnes saw no one else. He looked up when the waving of adieus began, and so that he might see her she forced her way to the very edge of the pier and waved her handkerchief. He waved his in return, and then her blinding tears that could be restrained no longer, prevented her from seeing him again.

"Miss Hammond! a pretty chase you've led me looking for you, everywhere: why in the world did'nt you follow me when I left the steamer, and not make me lose you in this manner."

It was Miss Wilbur's sharp, shrill voice; Miss Wilbur accompanied by Miss Liscome. Together they had been searching for her and the search had not made either of them amiable judging from the scowling looks darted at her by both.

"I beg pardon," she said, drying her eyes and turning to accompany them, "I had forgotten that I was keeping the carriage waiting."

"I never believed," continued Miss Wilbur as they treaded their way to the family vehicle, "in the sickly sentimentality of waiting to see a steamer off. You have said good-bye on board, and what more is there to do?

"When Sydney went away before and when I knew he was going to be gone a whole two years, or more, I went home immediately that I said good-bye to him on the vessel, and plunged right into my work. That's what *I* did, Prudence Liscome," as if it were Prudence who had been guilty of the sentimentality she deplored.

"I have no doubt of it in the least, dear Deborah," mildly answered Miss Liscome, and by that time they had reached the carriage.

Agnes shrank into a corner, thankful that a drive of little more than a half hour would free her from the presence of her companions.

The exterior of Mrs. Denner's house was more pre-

tensious, than either Miss Wilbur's, or Miss Liscome's, but as Prudence said afterwards to Deborah,
it was utterly without style, and in a very unaristo-
cratic neighborhood.

These facts, however, did not trouble Miss Hammond, as she hurried out of the carriage. She stood
a moment at the carriage door to thank Miss Wilbur for her hospitality, and to say a brief adieu to
each lady, without however, offering to accompany
it with her hand. Then she went quickly up the
stoop of the house, and the carriage drove away.

XVI.

MRS. DENNER was absorbed—hands and mind in dessert making when one of the little wide-eyed, tow-headed Denners rushed down to the kitchen and announced "Miss Hammond's in the parlor and she wants to see my ma."

"Merciful sakes! Miss Hammond!" and Mrs. Denner's eyes in a sort of dismayed astonishment, opened as wide as those of her offspring.

"Whatever shall I do? I am not in trim to see such an elegant young lady as she is," and she looked down ruefully at her soiled calico dress, and then leaving the batter she had been vigorously mixing, she went to survey herself in the piece of looking glass that hung near the dresser.

"She said she wanted to see you right away, Ma," urged the little Denner.

"Merciful sakes! then, I'll have to go up just as I am." And smoothing her dress as if that were to give it a more cleanly look, she ascended to the parlor.

It was two years since she had seen Miss Hammond, the latter preferring to spend all the holidays of her last school year in the Convent with Florence, and Mrs. Denner could hardly help mingling with her kindly welcome, expressions of delighted astonishment at the way the young lady had grown.

"Mr Mallaby kept telling me that you were getting tall and handsome, but you beat everything that he said. Excuse me for saying so Miss Agnes, but you're an out and out beauty."

Agnes smiled a little, but it was in a dreary sort of way. She felt as if her recent trial had crushed

beyond chance of resurrection, every emotion of
vanity.

"I have come to stay with you, Mrs. Denner; unexpected circumstances causing me to terminate my
visit sooner than I thought to do.   But I suppose it
makes little difference—you can find some accommodation for me, can you not? I shall be easily satisfied."

She looked so tired and sorrowful as she spoke,
that Mrs. Denner's motherly heart was touched; she
could not refrain from calling the young lady "dear
child," instead of the formal "Miss Agnes."

"My dear child! *you* should be accommodated
though the whole house had to be turned upside
down.   Mr. Mallaby told me as you would come in
about two months, and knowing that, as the house
was slim in boarders—it always is at this season—I
just set apart a room for you, and though it isn't as
freshly furnished as I want to have it, perhaps you
won't mind it for the present."

So far from not minding it for the present, Agnes
thought, when she was ushered into the large comfortable apartment, that it would do very well for
all the time.   Its neatness certainly belied Mrs.
Denner's own appearance, from which Agnes had instinctively, but secretly shrank; but Miss Hammond was speedily to learn that Mrs. Denner's own
appearance was the only slovenly thing about Miss
Denner's boarding-house.   Whether it was that
combined cares of matrimony and boarders
made her insensible to the effect of soiled, and un-
tidily hung skirts, collarless waists, and torn aprons,
or that, did she bestow care upon her person it
might seem like the evidence of an unworthy vanity,
not even the boarders, finding such strange contrast between the appearance of the mistress and
the appearance of the house, could determine, and
every day, save for an hour or two on Sunday,

Mrs. Denner was to be found in that condition which necessitated when anybody called to see her, the ejaculation:

"Merciful sakes ! whatever shall I do, to go up to the parlor in this trim."

Her heart, however, was in its proper condition— large, sympathetic, and kindly, and perhaps no one of her boarders who rarely left her save to return, experienced that fact in shorter time, than did poor heart-sick, home-sick, lonely Agnes Hammond.

She felt it in the delicate and tempting little repast which was brought to her by Mrs. Denner's own hands, and by the tender, motherly manner in which that good woman insisted that Miss Hammond after partaking of the repast should lie down and have a quiet little slumber; and she waited in order to place the "dear child" comfortably in bed, and to draw the blinds so as to exclude the light. Then she went out softly, and back to her dessert making, wondering a little what could have been the "unexpected circumstances" which had terminatd so surprisingly soon Miss Hammond's visit. Neither could she quite control her desire for Mr. Mallaby's return from business—fortunately he was not away on one of his suburban trips—in order to see how he would take his ward's unexpected coming.

She heard him on the stoop at length, the sound of his voice mingled with the voices of the children by whom he was surrounded, coming into the kitchen through the area window, and she hurried to meet him, receiving him just as he had let himself in with the whole boisterous crowd hanging about him.

"Go away, every one of you ! you're a disgrace to any house, piling in, in this manner, and how Mr. Mallaby can stand it, I don't know."

Mr. Mallaby was as much surprised as were the children who had become instantly and simulta-

neously silent; never had Mrs. Denner before objected
to anything they did when they were in company
with Mr. Mallaby.

He hastened now to apologize for them.

"They mean no harm, ma'am, and its my own
fault."

"But I want to speak to you, Mr. Mallaby, so just
go away every one of you," and she turned them
all out, unceremoniously, even slamming the door
upon them, and then she drew Mr. Mallaby into the
parlor, the door of which room she also shut.

"Miss Agnes has come—she's here now."

"Miss Agnes has come," he repeated, looking bewildered, and as if he quite doubted the fact.

"Yes ; she said that 'unexpected circumstances,'
them's her very words, made her end her visit so
soon. She looked awfully sad and tired but I didn't
ask her any questions as I didn't think it was
my place to do so. I just got her as a bit to eat and
made her lie down as soon as possible."

"Unexpected circumstances made her end her visit," awfully sad and tired-looking," "made her lie
down as soon as possible," these were the statements
that worked themselves into Mr. Mallaby's brain,
and as they did so, the expression of his face changed to one of positive pain and anxiety. His brown
eyes were full of that sad wistfulness which had ap-
pealed so to Florence Wilbur's heart, and which now
almost brought the tears to Mrs. Denner's eyes.

"Do you think she is sick?" Even his voice seemed tremulous from anxiety.

"No, I don't think as she's sick, but I think she's
unhappy some way. Just stay here, and I'll see if
she's rested enough to come down to you."

Miss Hammond, unable to sleep, had remained in
bed but a very short time, so that she was quite prepared to descend to Mr. Mallaby, and she rose at
once from her pensive position by the window and ac-

companied Mrs. Denner to the parlor. That good-hearted, but somewhat curious woman would like to have entered with the young lady, and it was with more than one sigh of regret she kept on her reluctant way to the kitchen.

Mr. Mallaby was standing just as Mrs. Denner had left him, the same anxious expression on his face, the same wistful look in his eyes. Never, perhaps had even his ward observed that look so plainly before.

"Welcome, Miss Hammond," he said, his look changing to one of genuine relief and pleasure, as her appearance, she had forced a smile to her lips, seemed to deny the probability, at least of illness.

"And how have you come to us so unexpectedly?" shaking the hand she extended, and speaking playfully, as if to hide the evidence of much deeper feeling.

She told him in a few words of Florence's unexpected departure, and in order to account for any dejection she might in the future be unable to conceal, she told how acutely she felt that departure, Florence and she having loved each other as if they had been twin sisters. And, of course, Mr. Mallaby dreamed of no other pang, that his ward could have suffered when she bade farewell to her friends; and while he sympathized with her sorrow, he felt that, arising as it did only from a friendship formed at school, it could have neither the strength, nor the constancy to cause him much anxiety. In that manner he expressed himself when he told Mrs. Denner why Miss Hammond had left her friends so soon, and Mrs. Denner quite agreed with him. She said that, in her opinion school-girl friendships were like pills, "Sticky while you're swallowing, but forgotten when they're down."

XVII.

MRS. DENNER's boarders were few—owing as she said to the season of the year—comprising but four very staid gentlemen, and a couple of exceedingly deaf, old ladies. The gentlemen breakfasted early, did not return to lunch, and at the evening dinner seemed to pay an entire, and very solemn attention to their plates. The deaf old ladies made but few attempts at conversation, but they atoned for their silence by attending religiously to their appetites and demanding from every one in their vicinity constant attention in the way of passing to them articles that were often within their own convenient reach.

Thus, Miss Hammond, when she went to breakfast the next morning, found not such a public table as she had dreaded to meet. Mr. Mallaby sat next to her having the old ladies on the other side of him. The four staid gentlemen had breakfasted an hour before. He introduced his ward to the old ladies, and Agnes heavy-hearted as she was, found it difficult to refrain from laughing as one of the bewigged dames stiffly responded:

"How do you do Miss Apple?"and the other said, with a piping voice like that of a chicken.

"I am happy to meet you, Miss Hatter."

"Hammond!" shouted Mr. Mallaby, his florid face growing more florid in his exertion to make the deaf old creatures hear.

"Oh, Hartache," exclaimed the first, and "Hastate," chimed in the second, and then they both begged pardon together for having in the first instant so dreadfully misunderstood the name, and instantly fell to demanding of Mr. Mallaby, the attentions that it was evident they were accustomed to receive from him, thus preventing him from making any further effort to correct them in the matter of his ward's cognomen. But that fact did not make him less thoughtful and kindly in his attentions, and while he was delicately watchful to see that Miss Hammond had everything for which she cared, neither did he neglect the gluttonous old ladies in any particular. His ward noticed that the very waitress attended him with an alacrity and manifest pleasure not bestowed upon anybody else, and she suddenly, and involuntarily felt an increased esteem for her guardian.

"What will you do with yourself to-day, my dear?" he asked after the meal.

"Occupy the time with my books and music. As my trunk has arrived, I shall have reading matter, and as there is a piano in the parlor, I shall not be at a loss for practice."

She spoke cheerfully enough, and he not knowing that the cheerfulness was assumed, went to his daily avocation quite satisfied that with such pleasant occupation she would be neither lonesome, nor homesick; but, he kept thinking as he went down the street, what he should bring her when he returned. Books and music; those were the things to which her tastes inclined. He remembered the time when his tastes were similarly inclined, and then he seemed to feel a sudden chill—a chill that made the perspiration which the heat of the morning had brought out upon his forehead to become as cold as if it were a death dew. He had to cross to the sunny side of the street, and to put down his umbrella in order to get out of the grave-like-shiver. And he walked on briskly, in order to crush the awful remembrance that had caused the chill, and he set his face into the expression that reluctant debtors dreaded, and he caused his eyes to assume the hard, keen, persistent stare which few cared to encounter a second time.

On Nassau street where his office was situated, he was so well known that his sad appearance had long since ceased to excite comment, and as his reputation for integrity had also become well established, he was held, despite his eccentric ways in no little regard by business men.

On this morning, at the very door of his office he was met by as odd-looking a figure as he was himself—a tall, lank, long-haired young man.

He was evidently young from the absence of all down upon his face, and a certain infantile expression that denotes the spooney age; but he was so tall, and at the same time so slight, that the high, carefully brushed beaver on his head, and the bright blue of his broadcloth pantaloons, and swallow-tailed coat, made a very gaudy and absurdly attractive sight. His feet were exceedingly small and encased in brilliantly polished boots, and it was evident from the admiring looks he frequently cast upon them, that he regarded them as the most important portion of his very slim person. Certainly, from the shape of his head, and the expression of his short-chinned narrow face, the quantity of his brains must have been limited. His pale blue eyes were small, placed close together, and had the white rim about the pupil, which physiognomists say denotes "a bad eye."

Mr. Mallaby, odd as was his own appearance, gazed with a sort of amused wonder at this apparition—the young man's attenuated person might almost pass for such.

His wonder increased when the apparition, said in a very high, shrieking sort of voice—the kind of voice one hears from hoydenish girls trying to be masculine.

"Say, boss, are you Mr. Matthias Mallaby?"

"That's my name," answered Mallaby in his gruff, business tone.

"Well, then, boss; just let me preface my remarks by assuring you it is with no idle curiosity that I've approached you this morning for the purpose of saying that, which, while it may cause in you some emotions of displeasure, will on my part only come from a respect that is tempered by—"

He was cut short by Mallaby fairly roaring at him: "What the devil are you trying to say?"

The apparition retreated a little, but immediately resumed in the same shrieky voice:

"A moment, boss; just let me explain. I was going to tell you, that as I said before, it is with no idle curiosity I approached you this morning; but I'll preface my remarks by saying that in view of the mistake which has occurred, I would only say, so that you may be quite clear in the matter—"

"And I would only say that you are a consummate jackass!" came again from Mallaby, indignant that both his time and his temper should be thus tried.

"Either say what you want to say, you fool, without so many prefaces, or begone."

"Oh, now boss, listen a minute while I preface my remarks by telling you that a letter came to you for me—I mean came to me for you—I mean came to both of us for each other—" and at that stage of his explanation he became so uncertain himself of what he did mean, that he stopped short, turned very red in the face, looked down at his exquisite feet as if they might help him, and began to fumble in his breast-pocket.

"You're a born ass!" ejaculated Mallaby, unable to contain himself, and not to be detained longer he turned shortly on his heel to go within the office.

By that time however, the strange-looking youth had produced a letter, the broken seal of which showed that it had been opened, and he pulled Mr. Mallaby back and placed it in his hand.

Mallaby turned to the superscription, reading with new wonder his own name, Mr. Mallaby, only that the b carelessly made, and not of sufficient height, might be taken at a cursory glance for another letter. Then, he turned again to the broken seal and from that to the youth with a most indignant glare : the glare had the effect of enabling the latter to say without prefacing his remarks:

"I thought the letter was for me, boss—my name's Mallary—and I read it; then I thought it must be for you."

The florid hue in Mallaby's face died away to ghastliness, and his hand shook violently as he opened the letter: it had been folded so as to make its own inclosure. Still, while he tremulously unfolded it, he endeavored to reassure himself by the fact that the penmanship was utterly unfamiliar; but the foreign postmarks upon it—those made his heart quake.

It bore no formula of date or place, at the head, as letters do, nor was there any form of address; it began at once:

"Your last was not satisfactory. The spectre of the past is only to be laid by prompt and full compliance. I, *Jared*, tell you this so that you may know what to expect.

> Yours,
>
> JARED.

Mallaby breathed more freely. There was nothing in the letter to reveal his secret; and if there had been he doubted its comprehension by the dolt who had read it: but he did not know that the dolt had already shown it to some one of more intelligent, and more evil comprehension than he himself possessed, his aunt, Prudence Liscome.

Malliflower Mallary had become recently attached

to an office almost next door to that of Mallaby, and hence the mistake that put into his hands on the previous day an epistle that so bewildered him, he took it home for some members of his family to explain it. The only one who seemed able to do so was his aunt, and she, sagely concluding that it must be meant for somebody else, asked her nephew if there was anyone in the vicinity of his office who bore a similar name, or a name even somewhat like his own. After a little thought he remembered Mr. Mallaby, of whom, brief as was the time of his own connection with a firm on Nassau Street, he had heard, and whom on one occasion he had even seen, Mr. Mallaby being pointed out to him by a companion.

"Then he is the man," said his aunt, and having obtained from her nephew as full a description as the latter could give of Mr. Mallaby, her soul was secretly gladdened by the thought that he must be the very Mallaby to whom she had been introduced, the guardian of that hated Miss Hammond. Should such be the case, and if that mysterious letter were really for him, what satisfactory consequences for herself might not follow. Perhaps even the inclining to her favor matrimonially of Mr. Mallaby himself through that very letter which had fallen so strangely into her hands. Her nephew, in his idiotic fear at having actually read a letter not intended for him, wanted to destroy it, and never breathe a word about it to anybody; but his aunt, in well-feigned, virtuous horror, exclaimed violently at such a proposition, and protested that in such an event it should become her religious duty to acquaint Mr. Mallaby herself. That threat frightened Malliflower's very soul, and he hastened to promise compliance with whatever Aunt Prudence should advise. She advised that her nephew should go early the next morning to Mr. Mallaby's office, tell him the mistake that

had occurred, and deliver to him the letter, not neg-
lecting at the same time to watch carefully the effect
of his communication upon Mr. Mallaby. She even
prepared a speech to accompany the delivery of the
letter, but her nephew in his semi-idiocy, had forgotten one part of it, and had ludicrously distorted
the other part. His stupidity, however, did not prevent him taking in more of Matthias Mallaby than
the latter dreamed the dolt was capable of doing,
and when with a deep-drawn sigh of relief he put
the letter into his pocket bidding at the same time
a curt "good morning," to Mallary, and turned into
the office, he had not the slightest suspicion of how
faithful a description of his agitation was to be given
a few hours later to Prudence Liscome.

On that same morning, hardly an hour after the
departure of young Mallary, Anne, out on a domestic errand, made time to call upon Miss Liscome,
delivering to that lady the parcel and note which
were to have been given to Sydney Wilbur.

"I couldn't manage to give them, ma'am, Mr. Wilbur wasn't home at all on Friday, as you know yourself, and he was out on Saturday," secretly assuring
herself that she was telling no lie, so long as Mr.
Wilbur had left the house on Saturday to take the
steamer.

"And you couldn't get any chance? oh, Anne!"
said Miss Liscome in a sort of dismayed disappointment, as she took back her gift.

"But you haven't mentioned it to Miss Wilbur,
nor anybody," her dismay changing a little to fear.

"No, ma'am; I never yet made a fool of myself,
by meddling in things that didn't belong to me, or
putting myself forward, and I hope I never shall.
Good morning, ma'am."

And Anne faced immediately about and departed,
thinking to herself as she went.

"I wonder if the old creature took what I said,"

But Miss Liscome took it no further than to think that Anne was rather impertinent, and to feel that only she was somewhat in the power of that domestic, she would like to have given her a good setting down; and then she went back to all the feelings engendered by the return of her charm.

Wilbur's look on the steamer when she had made that remark to him, had caused her to doubt a little his acceptance of the gift; still, as Anne had not returned it on the preceding day, she had felt he must have taken it, and that fact consoled her not a little; now, however, to find it had not even been offered to him, she knew not whether to yield to disappointment because it had happened so, or to be glad that he had not the opportunity of rejecting it.

The incident, however, in connection with her recollection of his indignant and contemptuous look, awoke within her the desire to crush him as mercilessly as she would crush Agnes Hammond.

It made her also wish with a sort of fierceness to win Mallaby. Why should she not, remembering the attention he had paid her on that only time of their meeting, and, as the wife of Miss Hammond's guardian, what might she not be able to do in the way of revenging herself upon Miss Hammond? Then also matters in her sister's household were becoming rather uncomfortable; unpleasantly frequent demands being made upon her for loans from her own little private annuity, so that a combination of undesirable circumstances seemed to point to Mr. Mallaby as a very happy settlement. She put her little charm into its old resting-place with the single tarnished earring and the pinless breastpin, and she felt as she closed the box that it might not be very long until the golden heart would be again brought forth and presented to Mr. Mallaby as a token of of her maidenly regard.

XVIII.

MISS HAMMOND tried to occupy herself with her books and music, taking from her trunk its little store of volumes—they were all either histories, philosophies, or religious works—and arranging them for convenient use, and then removing from the same receptacle, a neatly-bound volume of music with which she repaired to the parlor. Mrs. Denner was there, having just finished her daily careful dusting of the apartment, and she assured the young lady she would not be disturbed by the entrance of anyone, the gentlemen all being out, and the old ladies engaged in knitting in their own room.

So Miss Hammond played unrestrainedly, bravely determined not to yield to her sad feelings and trying to fortify herself by remembering instances of heroism in the lives of the saints. But for all her efforts it was melancholy work. Florence's tearful face seemed to mingle with the notes as she played, and more than once instead of the music, she heard Wilbur's last words.

"You are merciless, Agnes!"

And in spite of herself her thoughts would wander to the life of the two on ship-board, to the foreign shore to which they were going, to conjectures about Wilbur's future movements—whether he would remain with Florence and her mother, or go still further abroad; and then she longed with a sort of wild, fierce longing, for the letter that Florence had promised to write on the steamer, and to post the first opportunity. But so many days must elapse before she could receive it, that her heart sank, and it was only by beginning a wild, loud, brilliant passage of music, she managed to suppress a passionate burst of tears. When Mr. Mallaby returned to lunch, which it was only occasionally convenient for him to do, and which he did to-day, with a good deal of inconvenience, he bore with him a package of books and music for his ward. The selection gave evidence of so much taste and culture, in such matters, that the young lady was further puzzled to understand her odd-looking guardian, while she was also not a little touched by his kind thoughtfulness. And when she would have thanked him with more feeling than she usually manifested, he turned away hastily, as if he were either offended, or that he could not bear the exhibition of her gratitude.

Every day she experienced in numberless ways evidences of his watchful regard, and yet he seemed positively bashful in her presence, speaking but little, and always acting as if he feared he were guilty of some intrusion.

Sometimes, she could not help being amused by it all, but oftener she was touched; touched to sudden tears by his rare, and woman-like gentleness. Nor was she long in ascertaining the devotional regard with which he seemed to have inspired everybody in the house; the deaf old ladies had a positive affection for him, the staid gentlemen often in turn consulted him, and in return seemel less staid and more cheerful after the consultation, while the affection of Mrs. Denner and the little ones was visibly and audibly demonstrated many times a day. He was so modest and gentle in all his requirements, and so grateful for the smallest service, that to wait upon him was a pleasure of which every servant in the house gave convincing testimony.

Thus, despite her former half-contemptuous regard for Mr. Mallaby, and her intense satisfaction that he was no relative, Agnes was daily experiencing an esteem for him that did not seem unlikely to

grow into positive affection. She even found herself when Florence's first letter came, announcing its
arrival to him, with a freedom and abandon that she
might have used with Florence herself, and only that
she was too eager to go to her room in order to read
its contents in solitude, she might have noticed the
singular look that came into his face at her manner.

The letter written on the steamer though lengthy,
contained little more than expressions of the writer's
affection for Agnes, and the pain that absence caused.

Of Wilbur it said no more than:

"Sydney does not mention you, dear Agnes, and when I do, he
remains sternly silent; but, oh, dearest, how nobly you have done
your duty, and I feel that our Blessed Lady to whom you have been
so devoted, will find means of compensating you even in this world.

But the little attempt at consolation was ineffectual, for Agnes, woman-like, was thinking only of
the cold, cruel fact that Sydney never mentioned
her. She seemed to forget for the time that she had
given him up irrevocably, and that ever since, while
she prayed for him fervently, she had been trying
desperately to put every other regard for him out of
her heart and mind. As she read the letter a
third time she became indignant, saying to herself:

"*I* should not have been so sternly silent about
him."

Then her old pride that had seemed to be quite
crushed, but which had only slumbered, biding its
time, flashed up, drying the tears, before they did
more than moisten her eyelashes, and flushing her
pale cheeks.

She put the letter into her trunk, and immediately
made a very fierce renewal of her resolution to compel *her heart* to be sternly silent about Sydney Wilbur; and, to strengthen her resolution, she determined to devote part of her time to some charitable
work. She had already begun to go to Mass in the

mornings, concealing her pious practice under the
pretense of a morning walk in Washington Square
which was almost in the immediate vicinity of Mrs.
Denner's, and, she had even conquered her pride
sufficiently to accompany Mr. Mallaby to the High-
Mass on Sundays. The latter victory cost her no
slight struggle, for Mr. Mallaby's dress on the Sab-
bath, even to the item of the green umbrella, did
not differ from that which he wore on weekdays; to
be sure he was always spotlessly clean and neat,
never a speck appearing even in his nails that were
suffered to grow a full eighth of an inch beyond his
white, freckled fingers; but all that did not detract
from his exceedingly odd appearance. In her strong
desire now for spiritual distraction she thought of
offering her services in the Sunday School, and the
thought became more ardent as she pictured a Sunday School class of poor children to whose homes she
might make charitable visits. It was true her be-
nevolent intentions would probably cause serious in-
roads upon her slender annual allowance, but in
her present zealous mood she felt equal to any personal sacrifice.

In the fulfilment of this determination, on the very
next Sunday, instead of accompanying Mr. Mallaby
to the High-Mass, she asked to go with Mrs.
Denner's four tow-headed youngsters to Sunday
School, at which Mrs. Denner ascertaining the young
lady's intention, was much surprised, honored, and
edified; but, Mr. Mallaby, when apprised of his
ward's design, only smiled, it might be in approval,
or it might be in doubt. of her perseverance in the
good work.

Miss Hammond introducing herself, but at the
same time keeping the little Denners about her as a
sort of testimonial of her character was received with
no slight welcome by the Sunday School Superintendent, and she was assigned immediately to the

veritable class in which were the four little wide-
eyed, restive Denners. The latter were delighted,
whispering to their companions that the young lady
was their "Ma's boarder," that she "played the pian-
ner," had "a heap nicer dresses that the one she had
on," and so contrived to interest the other members
of the class in Miss Hammond's apparel, that when
she applied to the teacher of the class adjoining for
information relative to the mode of instruction, she
was obliged to turn back in short order, the skirt of
her dress being most violently plucked—it was in
the admiring hands of the whole motley dozen.

She speedily convinced, even the Denners, priv-
ileged as they felt themselves to be, that she was not
there for ornament, nor amusement, and when the
hour for dismissal arrived, she felt that the session
had indeed been a time of distraction. Owing to the
buzz about her, and the ceaseless vigilance required
by her own restless and mischievous charges, she had
not been able to yield for an instant to her wonted
thoughts. She wondered a little, as tired and spiritless she wended her way home, whether she had not
been premature in committing herself to such an
uncongenial spiritual work, as this, her first experience of Sunday School teaching seemed to be.
How much more pleasant would her books have
been; but, with that thought her stronger, and better
nature aroused itself; she felt her cheeks growing
hot at the realization of her spiritual sloth and cow-
ardice, and she began to walk very fast as if to atone
by exertion for her secret weakness.

There were pattering steps behind her, and she
turned to behold her whole Sunday School class
headed by the redoutable Denners—to whom she had
not even hinted the slightest desire of their company
home—close in her rear. They had maintained a
very respectable distance until Miss Hammond's ac-
celerated gait put them off their guard, when in a

sort of unconscious boldness they had increased their own pace until it suddenly brought them almost up to her. Their look of dismay at being detected was comical, and the way the more bashful ones endeavored to hide themselves behind their companions caused a scrambling that was ludicrous; even the dignified young lady had to laugh a little, and then her amusement gave place to wonder, as the whole pack encouraged by the Denners, rushed past her in pursuit of another object. That object was Mr. Mallaby who, on *his* way home from church, was just turning a corner a whole block in advance of the party.

Miss Hammond slackened her gait, thankful that she was so near home, for she felt that Mr. Mallaby being speedily informed of her proximity, would wait to give her not alone his own escort for the rest of the distance, but the attendance of the whole twelve children. He did not, however, linger a moment, when they reached him, and if the little ones told him he did not even look back to ascertain the proximity of his ward, but devoted himself at once as he always seemed to do, to the childish interests about him. It was evident that the Denners had introduced their companions, and that Mr. Mallaby was delighted with the introduction, by the exceedingly friendly terms which immediately appeared to ensue, between all parties. They walked on each side of him trying to arrange themselves so that each one could get as near to him as possible, and whatever charm he used, even the boisterousness of the Denners became subdued, and they, as well as their companions were listening to him with a silent, but evidently delighted attention.

Miss Hammond felt increased esteem for her guardian; an esteem so much increased that she forgot to take the slightest note of his odd appearance; and, mingled with her admiration of his unselfish qualities was a sort of shame of herself; her

secret consciousness whispered that it was very selfishness which had moved her to the charitable work
of that morning—her selfish desire to escape the pain
of her own fruitless longings and that same consciousness whispered that her work had been done in a
sort of half-hearted and ungraceful way, utterly unlike the manner in which it would have been done by
truly good and zealous people.   Her feelings were a
little intensified when Mr. Mallaby, having arrived
at his own stoop bade good-bye to the little strangers,
—the Denners, sniffing the odor of the dinner, dived
into the area, and waited smilingly until his ward
joined him.

"I fear you have tired yourself, my dear," he said
gently, but even while he spoke he seemed to avoid
looking at her, and when he had opened the door
with his latchkey, and held it back for her to pass,
he looked beyond, rather than at her.

Distasteful as was Sunday· School teaching, and
visiting the parents of Sunday-Schoolchildren, when
the latter were delinquent in the matter of attendance, or lessons, Miss Hammond faithfully persever-
ed in each; and owing to her acute consciousness of
selfishness in it all, her acts were not corroded by
the vanity that might at another time have destroyed
their merit.   She hated herself for being so selfish, and she hated herself fiercely for not being able
to forget Sydney Wilbur.   She never mentioned his
name in her answer to Florence's letter, and she was
constantly summoning her pride to aid her in repelling every thought of him.

Her very prayers were made in a sort of desperation
that had more of rebellion than submission in them,
and her soul, despite its endeavor, would sometimes
question why had such a blight come upon her early
years, when the long lives of others seemed so
happy.

The very heat of the crucible in which she was

being tried, made her powerless to know how much
of the canker of imperfection was destroyed, and her
keen self-distrust rendered her as unaware of the
merits that her perseverance entailed, as it caused her
to be utterly unconscious of the strength she was
achieving for the time when her soul should be more
cruelly tried.

XIX.

In the little town of Annecy whose fame is more from its connection with a saint than even from its historical value, as being in the centre of Savoy, the cradle-land of Italy, Sydney Wilbur found himself, hardly two months after he had parted in London with Florence and her mother. Why or how he had come there was somewhat of a mystery even to himself. He had left London solely because he wanted to get away from even accidental mention of Agnes Hammond's name—Florence had secretly irritated him by her frequent use of it—and he had wandered to France without purpose, and without desire. He seemed to himself like a man in a sort of nightmare unable to control, or to protest against the feeling that was urging him on. From one country-place to another—he shunned the cities—he went stopping only long enough to recover from his fatigue, and thus, his circuitous journey brought him one day to Aix les Bains ten miles distant from Annecy.

There he overheard a rather noisy and emphatic dispute between a couple of tourists, one wishing to remain and continue the baths, the other to go immediately to Annecy and present some letter of introduction that was to enable him at once to see the relics of St. Francis de Sales.

"Relics of St. Francis de Sales." Curiously enough that phrase brought back to Wilbur all the thoughts about Catholic saints to which his brief acquaintance with Miss Hammond had given rise and he found himself again recalling that which he had read once accidentally of one Catholic Saint, and wondering whether Agnes had not just such heroism of character; and then, more curiously still he felt that *he* would like to go to Annecy, "not to see the dust or bones of any dead man, be he saint or not," he said to himself, but yet he could not have assigned a defi- nite reason for wishing to go.

In those days the little trip from Aix les Bains to Annecy was made by diligence, and when Wilbur descended from his high seat on the top of the vehicle he found himself in a quiet, quaint little town, the houses of which had that peculiar light color common to buildings in France and Italy.

Wilbur, looking about him in his slow walk through the street at the end of which, according to information obtained in Aix les Bains, he was to find a place of refreshment, smiled a little as he won- dered how long would be his stay in Annecy, and whither he should next set his face.

The day was somewhat chill and dark, but the people he met looked cheerful and friendly, and many of them, noticing that he was a stranger, saluted him with a courtesy common to European countries. As he neared his destination, he saw approaching him a tall, thin, stooping gray-haired man. The figure of the man, remarkable because of its height and at- tenuation was rendered more so by the strange fashion of its garb; the latter was in color sombre to such an extreme, that not even the white of a collar showed about the neck, nor was there the suspicion of any- thing upon the wrists beyond the loose, hanging sleeves that barely covered them. His coat from its limited length was more like a jacket, and his pan- taloons went quite over his shoes. A low-crowned clerical-looking hat was pressed tightly on his short, thick, curly gray hair, and the face beneath the hat was smoothly shaven, and very pale. Looked at in connection with the gray hair one would have said at the first glance, that the man must be sixty;

looking longer, and looking at the face alone, one would be inclined to think that even fifty years would be too many to assign.

His eyes were small, but very bright, his whole countenance refined and intellectual, but his mouth and chin indicated weakness; not the weakness that comes from a bad moral nature, but a lack of ability to resist the influence of a stronger and more evil will.

Wilbur, at the sight of him seemed to be transfixed, coming to a halt so suddenly, that the attention of the strange figure was attracted. Their eyes met even lingering upon each other, but without any apparent result, for Wilbur feeling that he had been mistaken, recovered himself, and with a slight bow was about to pass on. The stranger also, had seemingly failed to make any recognition, and returning the bow he too appeared to be about to resume his way. But some other thought impelled him to turn and accost Wilbur, speaking in English.

"Your pardon sir, for detaining you, but you looked at me so earnestly, it has excited my curiosity; that you are English, or American, I judge by your dress and general appearance, and if you be either, you may have met me before."

His voice had a clear, pleasant ring, and his face while he spoke broke into a kindly, genial expression.

The sound of the tones recalled to Wilbur's countenance the look which had come into it on the appearance of the stranger.

"I am from America," he answered, "and the sight of you recalled in an indistinct manner, some one I have not seen since my boyhood; one of my professors in college—his name was Hale."

"I am the man, and you—I recall you now—my old pet pupil, Sydney Wilbur."

He had caught Wilbur's disengaged hand with both

of his own and was wringing it, his loose flapping sleeves disclosing with every motion his own bare, bony wrists.

"And what a man you have become, my dear fellow," he continued, seeming to forget how many years there had been in which to make the man, "and how in the world have you hit upon this little place, and where are you stopping ?"

Wilbur laughed at the slight reason he had to assign for having hit upon that particular spot, but he parried the question by asking in his turn:

"How in the world do *you* come to be in France? the last I remember of you was, after a vacation spent in Boston with a wealthy uncle you gave up your seat in college to go abroad somewhere—was not that it ?"

"Yes; that was it."

The words were spoken in such a changed voice and accompanied by such an altered expression of face that they hardly seemed to belong to the same speaker, and Wilbur felt himself becoming curiously and mysteriously interested.

"That was it," he repeated in the changed voice. " I went to spend my vacation with that uncle and there was subjected to an influence—but about that no matter—" recovering his former pleasant tones, and straightening himself as much as his curved shoulders would permit him to do, "my interest is with you now, my dear fellow, to know how and why you came here, and where, and how long you are going to stay."

"As to how I came here," laughed Wilbur, "that is easily enough told. I came by diligence from Aix les Bains; but the why I don't know myself, further than I have been aimlessly wandering through Europe for the past two months, and happened to bring up here. I am going to put up at the—, recommended to me by some party in Aix les Bains, and

I am going to stay a couple of days. Now you have
the story of my coming to Annecy."

"Then, Wilbur, you must accept my hospitality,
for those couple of days. I have a complete bachelor's establishment and shall be delighted to show
you the interesting mysteries of its management."

Not waiting for his friend either to decline or protest, he turned quickly about and led the way into
another street, Wilbur following, and rather hailing the incident as a distraction from his yearning,
restless self.

The *menage* into which he was introduced, was as
complete as its owner had declared it to be, and so
luxuriously and artistically comfortable that it was
difficult to believe no woman's hand had assisted in
the arrangement. Hale as he bustled about, endeavoring to make his guest feel quite at home, said:

"You see, if you can remember so far back, that I
have forgotten none of my old habits of comfort, and
when you have spent a day with me you will say
my life is as pleasant and comfortable as you have
already done me the honor to say that my house is. "

Sydney did say so even before the day had passed,
and he repeated it that evening at their early supper
adding, as the male attendant having served them,
retired to an adjoining room.

"Is that solemn-looking man your maid of all
work also? I have noticed no female about the
house."

"Female," repeated Hale in a tone of ludicrous
wonder, "female about *my* house. What would become of my life of quiet them? I should be miserable, for a woman must either love, vex, or grieve you.
It is her nature; she can no more mind her own business and leave you alone than she can eat straw in a
mistake for pudding. No, my dear fellow, when my
uncle died and left me that money as I told you, I
made up my mind to have a quiet, easy life, and no

life was ever very quiet that had a woman connected with it."

Wilbur colored slightly knowing the uneasiness of his own life since a woman had come into it, and lest his host might observe the blush, he hastened to say:

"But you have not yet told me how you came to select Annecy as your permanant abiding-place."

"True, I have not; but I fear the account will have little interest for you. You were in religious principles, if I remember correctly, Wilbur, a staunch Presbyterian."

"And I am yet," answered Wilbur quickly, and with sudden force.

"I did not for a moment doubt it," was the reply, "and it is for that very reason I fear, the story I am going to tell will have little interest for you. When you saw me last, I had just become a High ·Church Episcopalian, and youth of sixteen though you were then, you did not hesitate to show your abhorrence of a religion so much like the Catholic Faith."

"Yes; I remember quite well," replied Wilbur, who, despite the little interest predicted for him by his host, seemed to be listening with the closest attention.

"After a brief residence with my uncle I was induced by a cousin who was also a nephew of my uncle, and who lived in the house with us, to accompany him to the West. On our way we fell in with a young Englishman who had come to America to try his luck. We induced him to accompany us, and we went to California, where eventually we three drifted to the gold mines; it was in the very beginning of the gold fever. There, while we were at work in the mines something happened,—but, that is not necessary to my story—" pausing abruptly for a moment, and passing his hand over his forehead as if he were brushing away some unpleasant memory.

"Our luck in the mines," he resumed, "not being what we had expected, my cousin and I left California, and after some time, during which we had made another stay in Boston, we went to Sydney, Australia. When we were there a number of years, my uncle died, leaving me sufficient means to live comfortably, and being tired of life in Australia, and very tired of life with my cousin, I determined to separate from him. As he had not been remembered in my uncle's will beside a trifle to buy a souvenir, and as he thought he would benefit by keeping me near him, he vigorously protested against my intention, his vigor considerably increased when he found that I had become attached to an acquaintance we both had formed in Sydney, and that I had induced this acquaintance to accompany me in my departure. By a gift of money I appeased him, and Mr. Wylie— whom you shall see in a day or two; he has only taken a run to Paris for some books—and I, set our faces to Italy. There, having leisure and means for observation and thought, I became attracted to the Catholic Church; in this attraction, when I began to speak of it, I was assisted by my companion, he having been born and educated in the Catholic Faith, but having fallen away from its practices through the influence of companions.

Fearing, despite my cousin's promise not to annoy me since I parted with him on such liberal terms, that he would constantly harass me for money, I turned to account a singular coincidence and actually sent to him by my companion, Wylie, news of my death. Awaiting his return—, he was to rejoin me in Paris—, I changed my name from Hale to Todlebein, the name by which I am known here, and spent my time in studying the Catholic religion. When Wylie joined me I was ready to become a member of that Church, and Wylie penitently resumed his abandoned religious practices.

"We selected Annecy as a quiet, and retired spot, one of the least likely to attract the attention of my cousin who seemed to have no doubt of my death, and one where we could pursue the literary studies to which we were both attached, and here we have been living for some time."

Wilbur was silent from surprise, and perhaps a little displeasure. He was annoyed to find that this old friend, and ex-college professor of whom he had been very fond in his boyhood, had gone over to Miss Hammond's religion; but he said after a little:

"You spoke of a third party, a young Englishman,—what became of him?"

Hale, or Todlebein, as he preferred to be called, looked surprised:

"Ah, Wilbur! with that young Englishman is connected something of which I prefer not to speak. I purposely refrained from saying much of him. I did not think I had said sufficient to cause your present inquiry.

"You ask me what became of him. I do not know; but lest, some day the world may hear of him, and my testimony may be necessary, I subscribe for all the most prominent daily papers published in the United States; a fact that will account to you for the number and kind of American papers you saw in my study two hours ago."

"That you may hear of him through the papers?" questioned Wilbur profoundly interested.

"That I may," repeated Todlebein, "but we will change the subject to something of yourself," he continued, "to what you have been doing since you left college which is, how many years ago?" leaning slightly across the table as if to look more closely at his guest.

"About twenty, but they have not been twenty very productive years. I have studied law because I liked it, and not with any very definite plan of ever

being admitted to the bar. I have had a course of
travel in Europe less aimless than my present wanderings, and for the rest, I have done nothing."

"So there has been no woman in your case
either," said Todlebein, but as he did not look at
Wilbur when he made the remark, he did not see an
expression on his guest's face that might have revealed to him how greatly he was mistaken.

Todlebein's secret mingled with Wilbur's dreams
that night, and he found himself thinking of it the
first thing the next morning, and thinking of all that
Todlebein had said about his conversion. While
waiting the summons to breakfast he repaired to the
little study expecting to meet his host ; finding the
apartment empty, he went about looking at the
books. Most of them were religious works, contro-
versial, or lives of saints, and with mingled feelings
of impatience, disgust and curiosity, he took down
one of the former. The first page awakened his
interest, the second riveted it, and by the time he
had finished the chapter he was oblivious even of the
signal for breakfast; his host was obliged to come in
search of him.

Angry and annoyed with himself he closed the
volume with a snap, and at the breakfast-table he
turned the conversation with a sort of desperate earnestness on topics utterly foreign to religion. But,
for all his efforts his thoughts would recur to what
he had read, and when later in the day, he yielded
to the desire to read further, he did so, protesting
to himself that he was only doing it in order to learn
in all its fullness what sort of a religion was that
to which Miss Hammond belonged. Under the same
secret protestation he came at length to asking questions of his host, relative to the Catholic Faith, and
his interest increased with his enlightenment, Wylie
returned from Paris, and Wilbur found him a simple,
genial gentleman, somewhat older than the ex-pro-

fessor, and not unlike him in appearance being equally tall, spare, and gray-haired; but his features
bore less evidence of refinement and cultivation. In
such cordial society he was induced to protract his
stay several weeks, and when at length he parted
with his friends the latter felt though they did not
betray their thoughts, that the Presbyterian principles of their guest had been sorely shaken; neither
of them dreamed that it was the heroism of a woman
which had awakened in Wilbur's breast the first
gleam of admiration for the Catholic Faith.

XX.

FLORENCE wrote with conscientious regularity to
Miss Hammond, and her letters were like oases in
the existence of the home-sick, heart-sick girl; for
though after the one that told of Wilbur's departure
from London, he was not even named, Agnes opened each succeeding letter with the secret hope that
something would be said of him.   And in addition
to that hidden hope there was a charm about the
cheerful, affectionate, and lengthy missives that always lifted for a time the pall which hung over her
spirits.

One day, when six months of her aimless life had
passed, there came to her a letter from Florence containing a most unexpected invitation.

"As I told you in my last letter, dear Agnes; it
ran, "mamma and I have fully decided to go to Italy.
In her state of health the English climate is too trying, and we shall start to-morrow for France, and
thence by easy stages to Florence where we shall remain a whole year. Having imbibed from me an affection for you, she desires me to ask you to join us.
Knowing your independent spirit, dear one, I can
assure you that your income will be ample for all
expenses, and as we must, because of mamma's
health, live very quietly, your wardrobe need not be
extensive.   There will be no danger of meeting Uncle Sydney, for yesterday brought one of his brief
and most infrequent letters in which he said that he
had been wandering through France, but was about
to start for Germany, and thence home, after which he
would go probably to the western part of the United
States to remain permanently in order to comply with

the terms of some queer will of which I believe my mother knows, but neither he nor she, has ever taken the trouble to inform me. So, dearest, if that dear Mr. Mallaby, having had the felicity of your presence. for all these months, can bring himself to relinquish that felicity for a time, come to us; and write immediately so that I may send you all the necessary directions without further delay. I am so happy at the prospect of seeing you again, that I can hardly contain myself, so come, come, come.

"Your own Florence."

The information that Sydney on his return home would go probably to the West to remain permanently, brought a dash of pain to Miss Hammond's heart. She could no longer persuade herself that she did not love him as ardently as ever, and she had to acknowledge to her own hidden consciousness that she was as keenly wounded by this evidently total forgetfulness of her, as if she had not voluntarily resigned him. She knew now how way down in her secret heart had been the thought of his return when she could at least have the comfort—slight though it might be—of feeling that they were both in the same city; now, however, even that must be given up since it was evidently his intention to continue to keep a long distance between them.

How in her pride, she hated herself for her weakness, and in a desperate endeavor to conquer her bitter and painful feelings, she turned again to the letter, to consider the invitation. Her aching heart hailed it; its acceptance promised change of scene, distraction from her yearning, restless, unhappy self, and more than all, renewal for a time of the companionship of Florence which she so sorely missed. Never, it seemed to her, had she so longed for a mother, she whose earliest memory could not recall one, and in her wild, strange, bitter yearning, she bowed her head upon the letter and wept on it scalding tears.

When she became calmer she quite decided to accept the invitation, and she only waited Mr. Mallaby's return in the evening, to acquaint him. But while she made her decision, she could not help feeling a sort of regret for him: she knew that he was attached to her; his quiet, gentle, generous care of her told her that, and the very unostentatiousness of his tender watchfulness touched her, though at the same time his timidity, and even sometimes, embarrassment in her presence, puzzled her. Remembering all these things she felt that he would miss her, perhaps even object to her departure; but at the thought of that she straightened herself involuntarily, feeling how sternly she should meet his objection knowing the little right he had to urge any, being no relative. And then, her reflections seeking the more practical part, she almost regretted having made certain expenditures in the cause of charity that drew largely out of the income of the present year; she remembered with a sort of dismay how painfully hesitating was her guardian's manner when she requested her semi-annual allowance before the usual date of its payment.

However, she met him the moment of his return, before even he had ascended to his room, and she drew him into the parlor, feeling that if she waited until after dinner, they would have the eyes of some of the boarders upon them.

Being a December evening, daylight had vanished early, but before the last beams departed, the parlor was well lighted, Mrs. Denner taking especial pride in the lavishness of her parlor illumination.

"What is it, my dear?" asked Mr. Mallaby, wondering that his ward should meet him at the very threshold of the hall-door, and wondering still more at the summary manner in which she drew him into the room. She seemed unusually excited, a crimson spot glowing on each cheek, and until she answered him it seemed as if his own breath stopped because of a sudden and horrible foreboding.

"I received a letter from Florence to-day; she and her mother are going to Italy, and they have invited me to join them. I should like to do so for a few months."

Mr. Mallaby's breath came back to him; her announcement was not that which he had feared, but though it was not, it contained sufficient to produce in him anxiety, dismay and pain. Despite his efforts to conceal the feelings they showed themselves for an instant so plainly upon his countenance, that his ward saw them. She was annoyed almost to anger, and her annoyance made her eager to have him understand as quickly as possible that she had quite decided to accept the invitation, and that he must be prepared to meet any exigencies her decision might entail.

"Florence says the expense of living abroad will come quite within my limited income, but as I have already overdrawn my allowance for the present half year, and have disposed of it, I must ask you to let me have at once the amount that will be due on the next date of payment. I can make it all up by future economy."

Mr. Mallaby did not reply; instead, he retreated a little, as if to prop his back against the wall, and then he continued to look at her—an anxious, grave, sad look that, though it did not curb entirely her impatience for his answer, made much of it vanish.

"I suppose," she resumed, speaking very rapidly, "you, with your strict business habits are inclined to censure my extravagant mode of overdrawing my allowance: but 1 assure you this shall be the last time. I shall live entirely within my means in the future, and should I find on my visit abroad that I cannot do so, I shall return immediately."

"It is not that, my dear," replied Mallaby at length

with strange hesitation, "that I was considering. I was thinking—that is, I fear I may not be able to let you have the money you desire. Unexpected liabilities in my business have crippled me financially just now, and—"

He could not finish the sentence, for his ward was saying with sudden indignation.

"Liabilities in your business? pray sir, does *my income* go to defray liabilities in *your* business?"

He started from his position by the wall as if he had been stung, and he approached her with a sort of deprecatory motion of his large, freckled hands.

"Yes;no;" he said in a sort of breathless, frightened way, "that is I mean Miss Hammond—" and then he stopped short, the perspiration breaking into his face, and his hands dropping helplessly to his side.

"What did he mean?" The question whirled through Miss Hammond's brain bringing in the horrified amazement of the moment but one cruel answer; that he had been false to his trust, using for his own purposes, her money, and that all his kindness to her was but a sort of atonement for this breach of duty; how did she know even but that her income ought to be much more than its present paltry sum. Hatred of him mingled with her indignation, and gave to her voice an emphasis that smote him to the soul.

"It is time, Mr. Mallaby, that you rendered to me some distinct account of how *my* financial matters stand. I was of age five months ago, but trusting you so entirely I did not then demand any further knowledge than you had chosen to impart to me that last Sunday afternoon in the convent, when you told me that my income would be six hundred a year. I recall now the hesitation with which you made that statement and connecting it with your present manner I can come to but one conclusion, that you have not fulfilled the trust reposed in you by my father;

or if I wrong you by such an accusation, give me the proofs of your honesty. From what investment do I derive my income? Who were the witnesses of this trust reposed in you?"

He lifted his hands again as if there might be something in the action to counteract the painful force of her impetuous accusation, or to bring some assurance to his own dismayed, cowering self.

"There were no witnesses when that trust was given to me, and the little that was left to you, was swept away by false securities some years ago. I did not tell you this before, because, as I had promised to be your guardian I thought it better that you should remain in ignorance of any dependence upon me. You might have considered yourself bound to me by some claim of gratitude, when I was but fulfilling a promise made to the dead, I who had neither wife, nor child."

A sudden huskiness affected his voice for a moment.

"I have tried to be true to my trust, and I should not have made this revelation, but, that in justice to myself it was necessary to make it. I could not let you continue to think me guilty of the dishonesty with which you have charged me."

He retreated a second time to the wall, wedging himself against it, and appearing as if he would like to break through it for the purpose of getting away from Miss Hammond's presence; and though he glanced nervously about him, he studiously avoided looking at her.

She stood as if frozen to the floor; the crimson spots had gone suddenly out of her cheeks, and but for her eyes, her face, from the pallid rigidity of every muscle, might have been taken for the countenance of one already dead. Her eyes opened to their widest extent and fixed on Mallaby showed the struggles of her soul. Could she believe him? and were

his story of such a noble fulfillment of trust entirely
true, what debt of gratitude did she not owe him,
and with what indifference, and on some occasion,
almost contempt, had she not repaid it? Were his
statement *not* true how villanous must be his character. But what means had she of proving either, and
at that stage of her wild thoughts her heart seemed
ready to burst. In any case, her visit to Florence
must be given up, and she must find some way of
being no longer dependent upon Mr. Mallaby.

"If you had only told me all this before," she said
at length in a sort of tired, dreary way that pierced
him to the heart, and made him raise his eyes instantly to hers.

"I should have acted so differently. I should have
been neither the incumbrance nor the care that I
must have been to you."

"You have never been an incumbrance," he said
quickly, but with so much trembling earnestness that
she was fain to believe him, and in a grateful impulse she tried to smile in order to assure him while
she replied:

"It is very good of you to say so, but in spite of
your assertions I feel that I must have been. I shall
endeavor not to be so much longer, however; for I
feel that I can turn to some account the education
you have so generously given me."

She had striven to speak kindly, but despite her
effort her words sounded cold to him who listened
to them with an anguish of which she did not dream.
He felt that his statement had carried to her mind
but half conviction, and again making that deprecatory motion with his hands, he said with trembling
earnestness:

"There is no necessity for any endeavor to turn
your education to account. My finances are not so
embarrassed but that they will continue to suffice
for your usual support, and in a few weeks, if not

further unexpectedly embarrassed, I can get or borrow enough to let you make this visit abroad."

Somehow, his very readiness to get, or borrow for her, instead of touching her by the kindness it implied, made her incline more to the thought that he had violated his trust; but when she looked at his face, sad and softened as it was by emotions of which she had not a suspicion, and when she met his tender, wistful eyes, she could not let him see how she still doubted him.

Forcing into her own manner and tones a warmth that it was impossible for her to feel, she went up to him and took his hand.

"If, Mr. Mallaby, I have been wanting in the gratitude and kindness you seem to have so well deserved, I beg your forgiveness; perhaps in the future I may have opportunities of atonement; but my present duty of doing something for my own support is so clear that I cannot slight it; nor will you, good Mr. Mallaby, in the generosity and regard for my feelings that you have always shown, object to the fulfillment of my duty now. Again, I give you my poor thanks for all your goodness to a friendless orphan."

She had retained his hand while she spoke, pressing it in her burning clasp, and she did not once turn her eyes from his face. But with the last word she dropped it and turned away so suddenly that she had reached the door before he found voice to recall her. Then, as he was about to speak, she looked back at him saying:

"Please tell Mrs. Denner to send a cup of tea to my room; I cannot go to table to-night," and smiling, she vanished.

XXI.

THE letter declining Florence's invitation was written, but written so carefully that its affectionate recipient would not be able to glean from its contents
anything of the revelation that had come so unexpectedly and so bitterly to her friend.   Somehow,
Agnes could not bring herself to write that, her
pride revolted from acknowledging even to Florence, her great indebtedness to this man who was no
relation, if indeed his story were true; and she shrank
equally from a confession of her own doubts and
fears about him.   So she put her refusal on the
score of an economy which was absolutely necessary
for her to practice during the coming year, and she
added that a residence abroad with Florence would
make a subsequent parting, much harder than their
first had been.   But these statements were mingled
with so many warm, and earnest expressions of affection, that Miss Wilbur though she might be
bitterly disappointed, could hardly feel hurt.

That letter promptly sent, Miss Hammond began
immediately to devise some plan for earning her living.

Her music seemed to be the part of her education
she could turn most readily to account, and on the
very next morning after her startling conversation
with her guardian, and without again speaking to
him on the subject, she went out, taking her way to
to the home of the Superintendent of the Sunday
School.

He was always gracious to her, and he was said to
be rich. On one occasion when he had invited the ladies of the Sunday School to meet at his house for the

purpose of devising some entertainment for the children, she had been particularly pleased with the gentle, cultured air of his whole family. That he *was* rich the appurtenances of his home had seemed at that time to give ample evidence.

His graciousness did not diminish when he learned the object of Miss Hammond's call, and he was too polite to express his very great astonishment. He was glad to say that he thought he could help her in the matter of obtaining pupils; he had no doubt that within a week she should have at least a half dozen; he did not tell her that four of the half dozen would be his own children; it seemed prudent to withhold that statement until he had conferred with his wife.

Agnes thanked him, and kindly declining his invitation to protract her visit, hastened home.

The promise of six pupils within a week seemed to make unnecessary, any further effort on that day even did she know in what way to make a further effort, for her circle of acquaintances was so limited.

The Superintendent kept his word. The very last day of the week brought a polite note from his wife requesting Miss Hammond to call upon the ensuing Monday in order to make arrangements for the musical instructions of her own four children, and also for two pupils of a neighboring family.

When Agnes read the note, smiling with a sort of dreary satisfaction at its contents, it did not occur to her to show it to her guardian; but, when at the dinner table, that evening she raised her eyes occasionally to his face and saw as she could not help seeing, its preoccupied, troubled look, she felt that she must show it; it would seem too indifferent to enter opon this new course of life without even his knowledge, and if he were all that he represented himself to be how much more was it her duty at least to acquaint him with her plans.

So, directly after dinner, she whispered to him to come into the parlor, and drawing him into a retired corner, she told him what she had done and she put the note into his hand.

The room was sufficiently lighted for him to read it in the remote corner where both were seated, and he did so in a sort of mechanical way, as if he were still too preoccupied with his own thoughts to be enabled quite to understand her. And he held it a long time open before him; long enough to have perused it a half dozen times it seemed to Miss Hammond who was somewhat anxiously watching him.

At length he said, still holding it before him, and without looking away from it:

"You are really going to give music lessons?"

"Yes; I am really going to give music lessons."

"You were afraid to depend upon me, " he said softly, almost as if he had intended the words only for his own ear .

"Not afraid to depend upon you,"she answered quickly, "but ashamed to do so longer. I thought it was my duty to tell you about this note; having done all that you have done for me it would be unkind to enter on another course of life without at least acquainting you."

"Duty," he repeated, as if that one word had been all that he caught of what she said, or as if it were part of his own mysterious thoughts. And then he folded the note, handed it back to her and stood up.

"Duty," he again repeated, "you owe me no duty further than the kindness of your own heart prompts you to render. What I have done was but in the fulfillment of a promise to the dead. Since you are of age I have no right to protest against this thing you intend doing, but there is no more need of your doing it now than there has been heretofore. When you find the labor too much, or too irksome, give it

up immediately. Is there anything else you wish to
see me about?"

"Nothing" she answered a little stiffly, half angry
with herself for having told him of the note; he had
seemed so preoccupied she was sure it made little
difference to him; and then her doubts of him
all returned, and when that night she laid her head
upon her pillow it was with a heart sick from
doubt, longing, and pain.

What Mr. Mallaby's real thoughts were about his
ward's new course of action not even Mrs. Denner,
who speedily ascertained the cause of Miss Hammond's daily departure, could learn. She had sought
deftly enough to obtain his opinion, making apparently incidental but nevertheless, shrewd remarks
of her own upon the subject; beyond a smile however, or an indifferent answer, Mr. Mallaby did not
commit himself. Nor did he even show in his manner
that he was either pleased, or hurt by Miss Hammond's steady plying of an avocation which took
her out in all sorts of weather, and sometimes left
no small trace of its fatigue upon her countenance.

For himself, his habits remained unchanged; he
came and went, accompanied by the children as he
had always been; and within the house he was
the same quiet, gentle, kindly man who won boarders and servants alike. Agnes was unable to settle
to any permanent conviction about him. She liked
and disliked, doubted and trusted him alternately,
and hardly a day passed that something about him
did not produce one or all of these emotions. If she
could but be sure that all he had told her were true;
how her heart would go out to him and how anxious
she would be for opportunities to convince him of
her gratitude.

One morning that they both left the house together, Miss Hammond having obtained another pupil whose time of instruction was so early it came

shortly after her own breakfast hour they were met
at the foot of the stoop by the postman.

"Any letter for Mallaby?" asked that gentleman
quickly, and shifting his umbrella from one arm to
the other, as is by that action he would cover the
nervousness accompanying his question. There was
one; one bearing a penmanship similar to that of the
mysterious letter which Mrs. Denner so deplored,
and as Mallaby took it his hand trembled violently.

"I must return to the house, my dear, and read
this letter." he said.

Miss Hammond wondered a little that he should
have to return to the house in order to read a letter,
but she wondered still more when she looked up at
him and saw his face covered with perspiration; the
day was cold enough to make her shiver under her
heavy cloak.

He vouchsafed no further explanation but with a
gentle "good morning," turned back into the house
mechanically noticing two of the little Denners who,
issuing from the area on their way to school saw him,
and immediately began to take their usual possession
of him. He shook himself from them and hurried
to his room. For over an hour he remained there
locked in, and with that mysterious letter—it was
of unusual length compared with former ones—open
before him. The January day might have been one
in mid summer from the fever in which he seemed to
be as he read again and again the clear handsomely
written pages. At length, in the desperation of his
thoughts, he crushed it in his hand; then, after a
moment, he smoothed it out, replaced it in its envel-
ope and put it into the secret drawer where the former ones were kept.

He walked to the open window, to let the cold air
blow upon his throbbing temples; then he paced the
room until his agony wrung from him:

"Oh, God! that it should come at last! and now,

now when she is what she is. How shall I face it?"
But I *must*, for it is coming. There can be no escape."

He seemed to brace himself with the last words,
even giving himself a sort of shake as if that action
must do something toward freeing him from the en-
tanglement of the cruel circumstances, and having
bathed his face to cool the fever that yet fired his
veins, he went once more on his down-town course.

"There is a lady waiting to see you, Mr. Mallaby,
she has been waiting with extraordinary patience
over an hour."

The peculiar smile accompanying the announcement told both of amused wonder caused by the fact
that a lady should want to see Mr. Mallaby, and
that any lady should be able to exercise such extraordinary patience.

The announcement caused actual amazement to
Mr. Mallaby. His avocation never by any possible
chance brought him into contact with females, and
what one of the sex could possibly require of him
that made it necessary for her to wait over an hour
in his business office, he could not imagine. To solve
the mystery he went at once to the inner room to
which his visitor had been shown. Before he had
well-crossed the threshold, and before he had even
time to discern the elaborately-dressed form in an
armchair by a dingy window, he was saluted by:

"Dear, *dear* Mr. Mallaby; I am almost overcome
by the delight of meeting you again."

As she had not moved from her chair, and further
than the smile which displayed all the crows' feet
in her countenance, she did not seem to be overcome,
Mr. Mallaby was not very much impressed by the
veracity of her salutation,

Transferring his umbrella to his left arm, he made
his way to her;

"Dear, dear Mr. Mallaby," this time she arose,

shaking out gracefully her crinolined skirts, and extending from her muff a hand covered with a kid glove of the very lightest cream color.

"You have forgotten me, I suppose; but I, dear Mr. Mallaby have never forgotten you, nor the delightful evening I spent in your company—the duet, we sang, do you not remember," as Mr. Mallaby continued to wear a look of ludicrous bewilderment, "at Mr. Wilbur's house on Hubert Street? I am Miss Liscome whom you met there."

"Oh yes, yes!" replied Mr. Mallaby, remembering at length the event she recalled, and then, knowing nothing more of Miss Liscome, than the fact that she was the friend of Miss Hammond, he deemed it his duty to be very courteous to her; so he bade her resume her seat, and depositing his umbrella in a corner he drew a chair forward for himself. But all the time he felt a sort of bewildered wonder as to what could be the purpose of her visit.

Miss Liscome delighted with her gracious reception desired to show her gratitude by being very genial and communicative.

She took both of her cream-colored hands from her muff, and clasped them together as a sort of testimony of her earnestness, while she said:

"You were so kind and attentive on that delightful evening, Mr. Mallaby, that somehow, ever since, almost unconsciously, I have considered you a friend. Then, my friends, the Wilburs, knowing you as Miss Hammond's guardian, have spoken so nicely about you; (Prudence did not mind an occasional lie of that kind in her own interest) and added to all this report gives you such a reputation for integrity, I could not refrain from coming to you for some advice pertaining to my own business."

To show her extreme confidence in him, she placed one of her hands upon his knee. He shrank involuntarily but that did not deter his fair visitor: she even went so far as to place both of her hands upon his knee while she continued.

"I have some money to invest, my dear Mr. Mallaby; and to you I come as the person best fitted, and possibly best disposed to advise me how to invest it."

Mallaby shrank so unmistakably from her this time that she was obliged to remove her hands.

"My dear Madam," he replied, "I really am unable to advise you on that matter; that is out of my line of business.

"Surely not so far out of the line of your business but that you may give me some advice.

But Mallaby still shrinking from her persisted:

"I do not know how to advise you, Madame, further than to refer you to the firm of Kent & Co., up the street here. They are reliable parties, and possessed of the means to give you all the information you need." And then he nervously edged his chair away.

But Prudence was neither daunted nor discouraged, she had not reached the determination to make this visit without preparing and fortifying herself for every emergency, and feeling that she was in possession of something that might bring Mr. Mallaby to her own terms she became more assured and with her assurance, more smilingly importunate.

"Dear Mr. Mallaby," moving herself to the extreme edge of her chair as if to recover some of the distance he had put between them, "you do not know what a bashful and timid creature I am; the very fact of going to entire strangers, as the gentlemen of the firm you mention, are to me, would produce such a palpitation of my poor heart as might be extremely dangerous. Indeed, never could I have summoned courage to come to you had not your attention to me on that delightful evening caused me to regard you as a friend: and I have only summoned

this courage after a long time, being eight months
since I saw you, and only summoned it now when
my business affairs demanded very urgent attention."

She paused, trying to look very trustingly and
very appealingly into the brown eyes opposite. But
the owner of the brown eyes was neither flattered,
nor touched; indeed, his face showed more distrust
than any other emotion, and Miss Liscome reading
that, resolved to defer no longer her last shot at him.
She rose, giving a little graceful shake to the ample
skirt of her light silk dress, and letting her hand rest
on the outside of her ermine muff as if to display its
slender shapeliness.

Mallaby thinking she was about to depart, rose
also, thankful that the unusual interview was so near
its close.

Instead, however, of the adieu which he expected,
there broke upon his ear, accompanied by a very
fixed look:

"I have another reason for my confidence in you,
Mr. Mallaby; I did not mention it before, because I
thought I still could rely upon the kindness with
which you first met me. That reason is Jared."

She pronounced the name in a lower tone and with
a marked emphasis, but neither the subdued voice
nor the emphasis carried such dismay to the listener
as the absolute fall of her voice when she uttered it.
That significant inflexion, more than anything,
seemed to convey to him her entire knowledge of
his secret with which that name was connected.

He stared at her like one who had suddenly lost
his reason, his eyes opened wider than one would
think him capable of doing, and the florid color of
his face deepening to a purple.

Miss Liscome was satisfied. Her shot had told
well, and it only remained for her to exercise her
skill in keeping the wound open.

"Dear Mr. Mallaby."

The cream-colored gloved hand was taken from the white muff and placed on his arm.

"Do not permit what I have said to disturb you. I thought it better to be frank, but I assure you everything is safe with me. Indeed, I *could* not betray a confidence so sacredly given, and again I assure you that I have only said what I did in order to enable us to understand each other—to help *us* to be friends."

She smiled sweetly, and still retained her hand upon his arm.

A vise appeared to bind him; he did not have the power even to shrink from her touch, and he could only glare at her, his wide, wild, fixed stare was little less—while his thoughts went whirling through his brain. Was his fate approaching him from all sides? Had his secret gone forth not alone from the source he dreaded, but from another also? or was the one in whom he was compelled to trust, false alike to promise and principle? How did this woman get her information? Did she possess it when she met him on Hubert St., or had it been imparted to her since? Was she in communication with Jared? Had Jared always known her? Was Jared in the city?"

With that thought volition seemed to return to him. He took a step backward, causing Miss Liscome's hand to fall suddenly from his arm, and he opened his lips to speak. But they closed again without the issue of a word. Did he question to ascertain the extent of her knowledge, his very questions might betray to her more than she knew, and reveal to her the fear in which he lived. Better he deemed, in the hurried agony of the moment to get away from the subject as best he could, and try to cover by an assumed calmness the agitation that he felt he must already have betrayed.

"As I said before, Madam," he began hurriedly, thinking to cover by his haste the tremor of his

voice, but his very haste gave to his visitor a more
cunning assurance of the effect of her shot.

"I do not know how I can help you further, than
to recommend you to the firm I mentioned, or if you
like I could accompany you there."

It was in a sort of desperation, hardly kowing
what he said, that he made the offer, but Miss Liscome seized it immediately; to her it was a very
palpable sign of the power which she wielded to
compel his attention, and her acceptance of it might
promote a more desirable acquaintance with him,
so she answered in her gushing manner:

" Oh, if you would, dear Mr. Mallaby. Your presence would give me an assurance, a courage I could
not otherwise have."

Mallaby put on his hat, took his umbrella from
the corner, and without another word went forth
with her, creating no little amusement and wonder
among the clerks in the outer office through which
they passed, and also on the street where Mallaby
was such a well-known figure. Many stopped to
look after the odd-looking pair and comments, such
as:

"What woman is that with Mallaby ?"

"What is that odd fish, Mallaby, up to now, that
he's got a woman with him!" were frequent and many.

The subject of the comments was in too anxious
and bewildered a frame of mind to have heeded
much had he heard them, and Miss Liscome trip-
ping by his side was too well satisfied with the result
of her morning's work to have been very much concerned.

XXII.

That Miss Liscome was satisfied and pleased with the result of her visit to the office of. Kent & Co., the smile on her face, and the gushing manner in which she parted with Mr. Mallaby on the corner of Nassau Street, fully attested. She insisted on shaking hands with him twice, and on saying not only loud enough to drown the noise of the numerous vehicles, but so loud her voice could be heard by everybody in the vicinity.

"I do not know how to thank you, my dear Mr. Mallaby. You have been so kind. But I treasure it in my heart. I assure you, in my heart, Mr. Mallaby."

And then at length she swept away from him, and he returned to his office, to give such attention as he might to the business that awaited him. But all that day a spectre seemed to be behind him; a spectre that only awaited its opportunity to clutch him, and when in the discharge of his duties his voice became sharper than was its wont, and his manner more aggressive, it was only because the cruel hand of the phantom seemed to approach so near.

Even the children, who, according to their custom met him that evening on his return, seemed mystified by his preoccupied and gloomy manner. He hardly seemed to know that they were about him and instead of lingering upon the stoop with them, he went in immediately, leaving them all in the doorway too much abashed to follow him, and yet in too much uncertainty to make their own retreat until he disappeared in an angle of the stairway on the way to his room.

When he had locked the door he looked about
him in a quick, wild way as if he half expected to be
confronted by further evidence of the presence of the
grim, and ghastly spectre that had seemed to accompany him all day. Then the went to the secret
drawer, opened it, and took forth a large bundle of
letters. They were mostly written in the same clear,
bold hand, and as Mallaby seemed to seek for one
in particular, his own hands shook like one stricken
with palsy. He came to it at length, the letter that
had gone to Malliflower Mallary, instead of Matthias
Mallaby, and as he read it again and again, it
never occurred to him to think that the mistake in
the delivery of that letter might have led to Miss
Liscome's extraordinary and mysterious knowledge.
Not knowing that she was related to Mallary, and
not dreaming that Mallary had given it to anyone
to read before he discovered to whom it belonged,
Mallaby had not a suspicion of the true source of
Miss Liscome's dangerous information. He could
only believe all that it seemed to imply, and arrive
at but one conclusion, when he had read it for the
fourth time.

The conclusion that " Jared" was in some treach-
erous way responsible for Miss Liscome's use of his
name.   Then with his hands still violently shaking
he sought to arrange the letters according to their
dates.   How many of them there were, and over how
many years they extended, the date of the first was
nearly ten years before— nearly ten years since the
spectre which was alluded to in the mysterious
note, had assumed its present huge, and terrifying
proportions; and as the miserable man lived over
again in retrospection, the horror and anguish recalled by those letters, he leaned his head forward
on the little table near him and groaned aloud.

But for that oath to the beloved dead he could
fling off the burden at once. He could take the let-

ter to Agnes, and let her know the wretched story. Her horror and contempt could be borne better than the ghastly load he carried now.

But his oath forbade, and the white face of the shrouded dead seemed to be before him, and to look at him with the same expression it had worn when its living owner had alternately shrieked and begged for the taking of that awful pledge.

There was a knock at the door but he with his face still bowed forward on the table, did not hear it; another, and a violently loud one sounded; he lifted his head, looking strange and wild enough to have been taken for some one else than Matthias Mallaby.

"Mr. Mallaby, if you don't open the door, I must have it forced, for I am sure you are sick or dead not to answer all my knocking. And Miss Hammond also is dreadfully worried because you don't come down to dinner."

It was Mrs. Denner's voice full of a sort of shrieking entreaty and dismay.

Mallaby roused himself.

"I am not sick, Mrs. Denner, thank you; and tell Miss Hammond I'll be down presently."

His voice was so husky and utterly unlike itself, that Mrs. Denner shook her head in a very doubting way, and instead of returning at once to her domain paused as if for some further sound from Mr. Mallaby's room. She heard nothing but a rustle of papers—he was gathering up his letters and about returning them to the secret drawer when another thought made him pause. Why did he keep those reminders of his agony; what purpose did they serve save to renew his fears, and now more than ever he needed strength if he would keep his pledge until the end. He took them to the grate and in bundles of twos and threes shoved them between the burning coals, waiting with a sort of sullen satisfaction until the very last was reduced to ashes.

Mrs. Denner, returning at length to the kitchen wondered whether he had received another of those mysterious letters; not knowing that Mr. Mallaby had met the postman, she was inclined to be sure that he had not received any, unless it had gone to his office, which she did not think was likely as the letters came at such regular intervals to the house.

It was a full half hour before Mr. Mallaby appeared at the dinner-table. Miss Hammond, in no little wonder at his unusual want of promptitude, was waiting for him. He had delayed his coming in order that no trace of his recent agitation might be perceptible, and though his tardiness had restored something of his wonted composure to his manner, it had failed utterly to give back to his face its usual look. Instead, it had left a haggardness, and an expression of such dejection and anxiety, that his ward said with involuntary concern:

"You are certainly sick, Mr. Mallaby."

"No my dear;" he replied with a little cough between the words; the cough was a pretence to hide the huskiness of his voice. And then he smiled; the very saddest smile Miss Hammond thought she had ever seen.

Gentle as he always was he seemed to be more so on this evening; as if it were a gentleness born of some pathetic sorrow, and Agnes found her eyes reverting more frequently to his face than to the plate, and she felt at the same time more touched by his manner, and more strangely drawn toward him than she had been in her whole life before. Every doubt of him seemed to vanish, and her eyes filled with tears as she thought that his present dejection might be owing to business embarrassments, with which he doubtless imagined that she not only did not sympathize, but by which she was actually imbittered.

In the ardor of her unwonted impulse she could not refrain from whispering to him:

"You look worried and sad, are business cares the cause?"

He lifted his eyes to hers; the first time he had done so during the meal, and for an instant flashed upon her a look so grateful and kindly that it caused within her a keen reproach for all her indifference to him. Then he dropped them to his plate, and answered in his gentle way.

"My business cares have been a little trying to-day; but the day is over now, and things will go on as usual."

As he spoke however, he was thinking within himself.

"For how long will things go on as usual?"

XXIII.

PRUDENCE LISCOME was still Deborah Wilbur's friend and confidant; perhaps, even more intimately such the longer that Sydney protracted his stay a-broad. Deborah, in her ever-increasing delight that her brother had escaped both the awful fate, and the pecuniary loss which a marriage with Miss Hammond would entail, felt that she must have some one to whom to impart that delight, and Prudence, with her servile attention and flattery seemed to be a most desirable selection. In this way Prudence came to live as much in the home of the Wilburs as she did in that of the Mallarys; but for all the hospitality which was thus extended to her, and for all the intimacy which she so servilely maintained, she was extremely reticent upon her own affairs. No syllable, relative to her transaction with Mr. Mallaby, or to the mysterious letter which she had used with such startling effect, dropped unguardedly from her lips; not a word, even pertaining to her investment with Kent & Co., escaped her, and while Deborah, with a sharp and self-satisfied frankness gossiped of everything pertaining to herself and Sydney, Prudence, with the quality for which she was named, was silent on everything relating to her own affairs.

Nor did she make much comment on the contents of Sydney's brief and irregular letters to his sister; but Deborah usually kept up such a running fire of angry remarks on her own account, because of their brevity, that Miss Liscome had little opportunity to speak. One letter however, had given Miss Wilbur supreme satisfaction. It was that in which he announced his return, and his further intention of making his home in the West, for the purpose of complying with the terms of a certain will.

"I knew he would come to his senses at last," said Deborah, when she had read the letter for her friend, her sallow, puckered face reddening a little from actual pleasure. "Just think of it, Prudence Liscome, a half million of money going begging for want of an heir who has been ridiculous enough not to claim it. He could have been in possession of it these six months. But it is better late than never, and I can not be sufficiently thankful to Providence for saving him from that Miss Hammond. In that case he *never* could claim this mony: *never*," giving a sort of spiteful emphasis to the last word.

Prudence was stirred to a painful curiosity. What could be this mysterious will which in addition to prohibiting Sydney Wilbur's marriage to Miss Hammond required him to make his home in the West; but as usual, not daring to ask for an explanation, she looked at Deborah in a very wistful and inquiring manner. That lady, however, delighted to mystify her friend upon that one subject; not that it was necessary to affect such mystery, but to do so, ministered to her love of importance. She always felt vastly the superior of Miss Liscome, when she alluded to that will.

"I wonder how I shall like living in California," Deborah continued, half in soliloquy and seeming not to take the slightest notice of Miss Liscome's wistful look of curiosity. "In order to comply with the terms of that will as I have told you we shall have to live there, Prudence; just think of it, actually live there."

But Prudence made no answer; she only continued to look, and Deborah having paused for a second, resumed.

"I suppose I ought to begin right away to think what disposition we shall make of this house."

Then, Miss Liscome ventured to remark:

"Does Mr. Wilbur mention in his letter the precise time of his return?"

"Oh, dear no! but that is not to be expected from
him. He does everything on impulse, and I would
not be surprised if he had started homeward right
after sending this letter."

Despite however, her emphatic statement about
impulsiveness, she was not to be gratified by any
instance of it in this case, for three months elapsed
bringing only a line from him, saying that he was
going to Italy, and not making the slightest reference to his return. Deborah was thoroughly incensed, and she answered Miss Liscome's inquiries for
him with a savageness which made that lady hesitate to repeat them.

Prudence had, however, so much to console her
in the thought of Mr. Mallaby, that the Wilburs
were a sort of minor consideration. She visited the
business office of that gentleman at such regular intervals that she had become a subject of no infrequent, and amusing remark. No one knew the object of her interviews; even Mallaby, if interrogated
upon them could not have clearly told. That she
had some pretext in wanting to be informed of the
fluctuations of the money market, he could have
answered, but had he said that, his business acquaintances would have laughed; it was so droll
that she should apply to a man in Mallaby's position
for such information.

And he, himself, had protested his unfitness
to supply such knowledge, and he had stated his
readiness to introduce her to other and responsible
parties, but without avail either to avert her visits, or
to reduce their number. Every week she presented
herself in some ridiculously juvenile attire, and if Mr.
Mallaby were not in, she waited for him with extraordinary and unruffled patience. Feeling and fearing
the mysterious power she wielded, he dared not be

rude to her, but he bore the inflictions of her visits with an agony of spirit that was rapidly turning his grizzled red hair to an entire gray, and putting a curve in his shoulders that had not been there before. He hailed the opportunities that took him from the city, but if his absence were protracted beyond a week, it was only to be met immediately on his return by the rejuvenated spinster. Sometimes his desperate fears urged him to ask his ward about her; her former acquaintance with the lady might help him to understand Miss Liscome's mysterious knowledge of "Jared". But, often as the words were upon his lips, they were unuttered, for he feared to betray his own agitation, his own awful, and heavy secret. Nor did Prudence ever mention Miss Hammond's name. With the intuition of her sex she felt that Mr. Mallaby was purposely silent about his ward, and she was not sorry, for with equal feminine astuteness she divined that her cause with Mr. Mallaby would hardly gain, did Miss Hammond know of the present acquaintance.

At length, Deborah received a letter that stated the precise time of her brother's return; in other respects it was most unsatisfactory, and even alarming, for it spoke in a sort of mysterious way of the writer's delight to get back to New York, and his hope that his wanderings were now over. Not a word in the letter (more lengthy though it was than any former one) bore reference to complying with the terms of the will, and Deborah tried to solace herself by thinking that as he had already mentioned his intention to go to the West he did not deem it necessary to do so again. And now that he had escaped marrying Miss Hammond, surely he would not be mad enough to let a half million of dollars slip from him.

But, when she read the letter for Prudence, and in a moment of unwariness gave expression to the doubt

and anxiety engendered by her brother's silence on
the subject of their removal to California, Prudence
though she did not say so, fully concurred in the
doubt. She was shrewd enough to detect a vein of
buoyancy in the letter, very unlike his former epis-
tles, and from that she divined that Sydney Wilbur
was unusually happy. Perhaps he had married
while abroad, or was about to marry, and that he
did not care to inform his sister until his return; that
thought made Miss Liscome wish wildly for her own
marriage; her own marriage to anybody so that she
might be introduced to Sydney Wilbur on his return
as the wife of some one. That fact would show him
how little he had affected her heart, and how unim-
paired was her ability to enter the matrimonial
state.

Mallaby was her only hope, though thought of
matrimonially, he was a most forlorn hope. Not the
slightest approach to a tender regard could be dis-
cerned in his manner, and all Miss Liscome's little insinuations, and affectation of gushing ingenuousness
fell as blank as though they were showered upon a
stone wall. He was always deferential, but at the
same time he seemed always utterly oblivious of her
little arts. But she never lost confidence. The fact
that his deference did not lessen, owing though she
knew it to be to the secret which he thought she possessed, made her constantly take fresh courage in
the matter, and she continued to pursue her aim.

Wilbur's letter announcing his speedy return, increased her matrimonial eagerness. But how to get
Mr. Mallaby quickly to the desired point was difficult. She reflected upon it long and deeply, and at
length decided that she herself must bring matters
to an issue. Her partially-invalided sister, Mrs.
Mallary, had been ordered by her physician to spend
the approaching month of June in some country-
place in the interior of the state. Miss Liscome pre-

ferring housekeeping cares to those of nurse, had rejected the proposition to accompany her, and it was decided to hire an attendant. Now, as Prudence cogitated about Mr. Mallaby, she determined to change her mind with regard to bearing her sister company.

The announcement to Mallaby of her approaching departure from the city could be made the occasion of something more pointed than had been any of her former gushing expressions, and that she might be enabled to try her plan as soon as possible she informed her sister immediately of her changed determination and that very afternoon she was taking her way to Mr. Mallaby's office.

That gentleman was in, having arrived such a short time before his visitor, that though he had removed his hat, he had not yet taken his umbrella from under his arm. As it was barely two days since her former call, he was startled and dismayed by her presence now.

Had she come because of further developments of *his* secret which she knew? Was she sent by *him* who had so basely betrayed every principle of honor?

These were the thoughts more than any of annoyance or displeasure, that leaped instantly to his mind, and kept him looking at his visitor, as she stood for a moment in the doorway. with a sort of daze and horror.

But Prudence was nothing daunted; she smiled her very broadest, and having carefully closed the door behind her, she tripped forward until she was directly in front of him.

"Dear Mr. Mallaby," prolonging the first word and throwing into it a ridiculously affected tenderness, "I know you are surprised at seeing me so soon again, but I shall state at once the object of my visit."

"The object of her visit." It put him into a cold perspiration and he transferred his umbrella to the other arm, and began to wipe his face.

"I have something," opening a fancy purse which was suspended by a slender chain to her wrist, and beginning to fumble in it.

Mallaby edged away from her, wiping his face violently, and then he shifted his umbrella from arm to arm as if he did not quite know what he was doing. Was she going to confront him with the proof of her secret knowledge? was she going to show him that his doom was upon him?

But she only brought forth from several folds of tissue paper a little golden heart.

"I am going away Mr. Mallaby, she said, holding the trinket up before his bewildered gaze. "and I wanted to present you with a little souvenir of my gratitude. You have been so kind to me, that I thought this little golden emblem would be the most fitting token I could give you. It is the symbol of all my earnest feelings for you, and I assure you that it is with sincerity I present to you, dear Mr. Mallaby, this little heart."

She had tried to find her way to one of his hands in order to place her gift within it, but either in his astonishment, or from an instinctive feeling of self-defence, he had shifted his umbrella to his breast, and folded both of his arms tightly across it. Nor did he make the slightest effort to remove them.

Prudence, despite her hardihood, winced just a little at this rebuff, but she was not going to desist until she had exhausted all her tactics, and she affected the pathetic, saying with an overdone tremor in her voice :

"You know, Mr. Mallaby, how rare are true friends in this world, and you have been such a true friend to me—you have taken such a brotherly interest in my affairs—you have so kindly advised my youthful inexperience—"(His interest and advice had consisted in tolerating her visits) "In a word, you have been *so* kind that I could not think of going away without leaving with you something that would remind you of my feelings for you. So, do, dear Mr. Mallaby, accept my heart."

"She attempted to lay it on the sleeve of his coat, seeing that his arms were so tightly folded, but Mallaby actually sprang from her, saying, with a sort of fright in his tones:

"I don't want your heart, ma'am."

But Prudence pursued him.

"It is your delicacy, Mr. Mallaby, that prevents your acceptance; you would fain not be thanked for what you have done. But my gratitude will have vent, and you must accept this little souvenir of my regard—you must positively, my dear Mr. Mallaby, accept my heart."

He had kept retreating until he had actually wedged himself into a corner of the room, and she had followed, standing before him in a way that seemed to afford him no escape.

"I have no use for your heart, ma'am," he said, in desperation, not thinking that her proffer had a deeper significance than his mere acceptance of a souvenir, but, feeling with the instinct of his manhood an aversion to the taking of any gift from a woman, and from one who was in reality so little indebted to him.

Miss Liscome was beginning to consider herself insulted and aggrieved. That this man would not come to terms under her present course she was at length convinced, and drawing herself away from him with the look and manner of one deeply injured, she determined to make some allusion to "Jared." But, while she sought the words best to say, and while Mallaby releasing himself from the wall to which he had seemed to be pinned, took his hands from their folded position and placed his umbrella under one of his arms, the door suddenly opened, and a clerk from the outer office announced:

"A gentleman to see you, Mr. Mallaby."

The gentleman was close upon the heels of the clerk, and immediately that the latter had turned about, walked quickly and confidently into the room.

He was a tall, finely formed man, about Mallaby's age, but flashily dressed, and with a countenance that indicated great penetration of character and shrewdness. But his eye was bad, with a white rim about the pupil, and when he was not on his guard an unpleasant sinister expression.

"Well, Mallaby, old boy, here I am at last."

His voice corresponded to his appearance, producing a prepossessing effect at first, but leaving, when it had ceased to sound, a doubtful impression.

His effect upon Mallaby startled even Miss Liscome. He looked like a man who had come face to face with some sudden horror, his eyes distended, and the florid hue of his countenance almost entirely displaced by a greenish pallor.

"No welcome, old fellow, when I have come so many thousands of miles to see you. I can forgive you, however, as you are dazed by surprise. But, rouse yourself, old man, and give me at least a 'how-do-you-do.' "

He accompanied the last words by a slap on Mallaby's shoulder, and then he took one of Mallaby's hands and began to shake it violently. But there was no return of cordiality in the forced grasp nor the slightest evidence of a welcome in the ghastly face.

"And this friend of yours, this lady," the stranger resumed looking towards Miss Liscome, and endeavoring by his own garrulity to restore Mallaby's speech, "is wondering who I am to cause you so much astonishment. Introduce us. Is she *Mrs. Mallaby?* You know you kept so precious shady about yourself that you may have married a half dozen times without my knowledge."

Miss Liscome could not refrain from simpering: "I am not Mrs. Mallaby. But, dear Mr. Mallaby has been so kind to me that I feel under many obligations to him."

"Of course," answered the stranger, with a short and sort of doubtful laugh. "Mallaby's always kind. That used to be his character among the boys. Remember the old times, eh?"

And again his hand descended with no light blow on Mallaby's shoulder; then, without pausing to see whether Mallaby had yet regained his voice, he turned once more to Miss Liscome.

"Since your friend defers introducing us, I shall introduce myself. I am Nathan Kellar all the way from across the seas to see this old time companion of mine; and now Madame, may I have the honor of knowing your name?"

Prudence pursed her mouth into its very sweetest look, and gently simpered again:

"I am Miss Prudence Liscome."

"A fine name, Miss; one every way worthy of your handsome presence."

Miss Liscome's rouged cheeks grew slightly redder from pleasure at the unusual compliment. She was too deficient in delicacy to notice its coarseness, and too full of vanity, and too ignorant of the art of reading physiognomies to know that the stranger had shrewdly divined her weakness, and was pandering to it. In her paramount vanity and desire to make an impression on some masculine heart, she was conscious of nothing but delight at Mr. Kellar's flattery, and a sort of relief and satisfaction that he was not the mysterious "Jared". From his effect upon Mallaby, she had feared at first he might

be, but even in that case it would not have been
difficult for her to invent an excuse for *her* use of
the name. And thus satisfied and delighted she
was prepared to enhance the impression she fondly
believed she had made upon the stranger.

Mallaby had recovered from his apparent daze
and horror, though the pallor was slow in leaving
his face, and his voice at first had a husky, uncertain sound.

Your sudden appearance startled me" he said to
Kellar; then he turned to Prudence; "You will excuse me, ma'am, for giving you any more time to-
day. I want to see this gentleman on private matters."

Prudence felt indignant and insulted. His remark to her, more like a command, and uttered in
a tone so cold, and expressive of his desire for her
departure, together with her disappointment at
being compelled to forego a further acquaintance,
with Mr. Kellar stung her vain, little shallow soul.
Her rouged cheeks blazed with the crimson of
her own anger, and rendered reckless by her very
situation, and burning to give some revengeful thrust
to the horrible Mallaby, she said, as she went toward
the door.

"Mr. Mallaby must remember that I never should
have presumed so much upon his kindness, but that
I was assured I might do so by *Jared.*"

There was the same peculiar falling inflection
which she had given to the name on a former occasion, and which had so startled Mallaby; it startled him now but not to the degree it had done then,
but the name itself acted like an electric shock upon
the stranger. He fairly jumped forward as if to
make some violent demand for an explanation, and
then as if checked in his progress by some
doubt, he turned and looked at Mallaby. Mallaby
was glaring at him.

"Good-day, gentlemen," said Miss Liscome hurrying out. She had seen enough to know that she had mystified the two, and she hastened her departure lest one or both should demand an explanation. She was even in some trepidation as she went up the street, lest one or the other should pursue her, and she only drew a composed breath when she was seated in an up-town car.

So far, however, from thinking of pursuit, the two men continued to glare at each other for several seconds after she had left the office.

Then Kellar spoke.

"Who is she? How does she know Jared?"

"She knows Jared through you or he, having broken faith with me," answered Mallaby fiercely.

"By G——d you wrong me," replied the stranger. "As you witnessed yourself, I never saw her before. I never even heard her name."

"But can you say as much for Jared?" asked Mallaby somewhat mollified by the earnest manner of his visitor, and continuing:

"Tell me why Jared, who never wrote before, should write to me a few months ago, and send the letter here to this office?"

"Did he?" said the stranger manifesting considerable surprise.

"Don't you know that he did?" asked Mallaby, becoming fierce again, "and if he did that without your knowledge, how are you able to assure me of his silence?"

"Don't be so quick, Mallaby, to scent danger where there is none. I tell you Jared has broken faith no more than I have. Whatever knowledge this mysterious woman possesses does not come from him, no more than it has came from me. You ought to know Jared better than that. Let me see his letter."

"I burned it," answered Mallaby, his fierceness relapsing into dejection.

"I burned it with every one I ever received from you, in order to get rid of such reminders."

For an instant the white rim about Kellar's eyes seemed to dilate, and a covert smile appeared to play about his lips, but he said in an earnest, hearty way:

" I shall set myself to find out what this woman knows. I am sharper than you are, Mallaby, in such matters. Just tell me the extent of your acquaintance with her."

Mallaby briefly detailed his first acquaintance with Miss Liscome, and her resumption of the acquaintance within the past few months.

Kellar could glean nothing from the account that would help him to an explanation of Miss Liscome's mysterious knowledge; on the contrary, it puzzled and frightened him, but he did not betray his feelings to his companion. He pretended to be confident that she was on an entirely different track, and that it needed but a little clever pandering to the lady's vanity to discover her secret. Mallaby was somewhat reassured, but his very reassurance upon the point made his thoughts revert with renewed agitation to the object of Kellar's sudden and unexpected arrival.

"You said nothing in your last letter about coming, though you must have started almost immediately after writing."

"I did not decide to come until the day after that letter was mailed; and I am here just now solely in my own interest; the interest of others is involved in my coming, and your interest as well—an interest that is to make money for you—so don't look so cowed old boy. You are not going to be hurt this time."

Mallaby breathed a little sigh of relief, but it was not accompanied by any other sign of satisfaction.

"Where is Jared?" he asked as he dropped wearily into a chair. " Has he returned to New York, also?" Kellar also took a seat, and then he answered carelessy:

"No; he did'nt care to make the journey to New York, this time, and as I was coming only upon business interests in which you are to help me, Mallaby, old boy, I did not press him to accompany me."

Mallaby looked at him, but the expression of Kellar's face told no more than did his carelessly-spoken words; he would wait a little before making a full disclosure of his errand to Mallaby.

XXIV.

FLORENCE WILBUR and her mother were sojourning in Italy; in Florence "the beautiful," and there was only wanting to complete Miss Wilbur's happiness, the company of her friend, Agnes Hammond.

A dozen times a day she spoke of her, and not an object of art, nor a place of interest she visited, but called forth such enthusiastic accounts of the enjoyment it would have afforded Miss Hammond, that her mother said with some impatience on one occasion:

"I do wish, Florence, you would enjoy things a little, on your own account, and not constantly drag Miss Hammond's name into every place we visit. I am sure you did all you could to get her here, and so long as she chose to decline your invitation, I don't see why you must be forever thinking about her."

"You dear, fond little jealous mamma," answered Florence laughingly, "if we were not here in this public place," (they were in the Laurentian Library) "and in the presence of so many people, I should hug you until you cried for mercy. Don't you know that Miss Hammond's rejection of my invitation is only another instance of her highly spirited, noble character. She has probably been devoting her purse to charity, and would not come to us lest in some way her sense of independence might be wounded. She is one of the rarest girls, and I love her just next to you, my tender little mamma." The tender little mamma could not help being conciliated, her daughter turned upon her such a look of eloquent affection, while at the same time as a further endorsement, she squeezed her mother's prettily-gloved hand.

Short as was Florence in stature, her mother was still shorter, but with a slender shapeliness utterly unlike the stout and rather heavy figure of her daughter. Then, her complexion always very fair had imparted to it from her partially impaired health, a delicacy and spirituality which enhanced its attractiveness and made her seem but little the senior of Florence. Indeed, people more frequently supposed them to be sisters, than mother and daughter, and fragile-looking Mrs. Wilbur, with her spiritual face, and exquisitely tasteful dress, rarely failed to excite even both attention and remark, while plain common-place Florence was never the object of more than a passing look. But it did not trouble the simple unselfish girl, instead, she derived no small amusement from the fact that her mother was occasionally thought to be her younger sister, and she seemed to delight in the admiration that same little, youthful-looking matron enlisted. And so far from seeking to enhance her personal charms it was rather a penance to don the adornments upon which her mother insisted; if left to her own choice she never would have worn any but the plainest costume, and she would hardly have taken the trouble to see that it was quite properly adjusted. But her toilet had always to be subjected to her mother's critical examination, and that examination was the little plague of poor Florence's daily life.

Notwithstanding that, however, and her constant desire for Miss Hammond's company, she was deriving each day a vast amount of enjoyment from her Italian sojourn. Despite her disparagement of her own appreciative faculties as compared with those of Agnes, she keenly enjoyed her sight-seeing, and her sense of the humorous found so much to attract it, that her emotions were almost always equally divided between the sublime and the ridiculous.

They had been there three months, Mrs. Wilbur's health seeming to be much benefited by the genial climate. They made few acquaintances, and beyond an afternoon drive in the Cascine saw little of the gay world of Florence. That drive they both enjoyed, perhaps enjoyed more the road leading to the Cascine than the latter itself. Generally they took the road near the Arno, and bordered as it was with hedges of laurel and myrtle, it seemed to suggest to both of them pleasant memories of a far distant land.

One afternoon that they had arrived at the Cascine a little before the fashionable hour, they descended from the carriage in order to wander through the woodland solitude adjacent. Its shade and lonely beauty often before had tempted them to do the same, for though planted by the hand of man the forest trees breathed the spirit of nature as fully as did the oaks of the Appenines.

As they walked slowly along leaving the carriage to await their return, both were attracted by the sound of quick steps just behind them, as if in pursuit. They turned simultaneously, and beheld Sydney Wilbur.

Amazement kept them for a moment from doing more than ejaculating in a breath, "Sydney," but directly after that, both mother and daughter, showered upon him greetings, questions and expressions of delight, until he playfully cried for mercy. They had given him no chance to put in a word.

"If you only give me an opportunity," he said laughingly, "I shall tell you all about it. I arrived this morning, and was on my way to your quarters when some lucky chance made me perceive you both. I have come direct from Baden-Baden, and if you are willing to sacrifice your afternoon in the Cascine, and will accord me the honor to accompany you home I should like to do so, for I have something to tell you."

"Sacrifice our afternoon in the Cascine, when you are the compensation," said Mrs. Wilbur laughing. "I think we would be willing to sacrifice our whole stay in Italy for the sake of having you, Sydney."

Sydney bowed almost to the ground in a sort of mock deference and gratitude, while Florence laughed heartily, but said as soon as she had recovered from her mirth:

"Uncle Sydney knows we would sacrifice a good deal to have him with us, and as a proof we shall return to the carriage immediately, and drive home."

"In order to gratify your curiosity regarding what I have to tell you, eh?" he said playfully.

"No sir;" replied Florence with assumed indignation. "I disclaim any curiosity in the matter, and own only to a pure, unmitigated desire for your company."

"Oh, wonderful among your sex," rejoined Wilbur, as he offered an arm to each lady. "But, nevertheless my little disinterested niece," he continued, as they retraced their way to the carriage, "my news nearly concerns you."

"I do not care," rejoined Florence, determined to be consistent and abide by her assertion of disinterestedness. "I am only desirous of your company and nothing more."

"But it may have something to do with Miss Hammond," he persisted:

"Oh, will it? what is it? Do tell me," and she stopped short in her walk, bringing her companions also to a sudden stop.

Wilbert laughed heartily:

"I knew you had the curiosity of your sex, and now I have proved it; but you will have to mortify it until we get home. I shall not tell you another word."

"Miss Hammond is the one vulnerable point on

which you may wound, rouse, or fire Florence," put
in Mrs. Wilbur playfully. "She does nothing but
quote her, think of her, and I verily believe, dream
of her."

"She is not the only person who thinks and dreams
of Miss Hammond," said Wilbur softly.

His sister-in-law gave a gentle pinch to his arm on
which she was leaning and then she said very softly:

"Heart-sore still on that subject, Sydney? Have not
your travels banished her image?"

They had arrived at the carriage and he seemed to
make the matter of assisting the ladies to enter the
vehicle a pretex for not answering.   Nor did he refer to the subject during the homeward drive; instead, he seemed endeavoring to divert the thoughts
of his companions from it by making constant remarks
about the narrow streets of Florence, its unfinished
churches, and its gloomy, massive and frowning architecture.

But once within the medieval-looking apartment
to which they repaired on leaving the carriage, he
burst out as if unable to defer his communication
for a single instant longer:

"I have determined to become a Catholic, and I
have come here to you two for assistance in my final
preparation."

Amazement seemed to have transfixed both mother
and daughter; they stood and looked at him as if the
power of volition and speech had gone from both.
Florence was the first to recover, and she sprang to
him throwing her arms about his neck, and fairly
crying upon his bosom:

"The sacrifice that Agnes made has won this,"
through her happy tears, and then she continued:

"Have you told her? does she know?"

"Not a syllable of it," he answered, "nor do I wish
her to know until I bear it to her in person."

By this time Mrs. Wilbur had recovered herself.

"You have indeed brought us news, Sydney, and I congratulate you." ·

Her eyes were misty, and Sydney touched by this unexpected evidence of feeling in her his sister-in-law, disengaged himself from his niece, and crossing to Mrs. Wilbur folded her in a very warm embrace.

While he bent with inimitable tenderness over the fragile little lady, an unpleasant doubt seemed to come to the mind of Florence. It was so strong and so painful, she burst out with it immediately:

"Are you going to embrace our Faith because so doing, will bring you Agnes?"

"No, my orthodox, and careful little niece," he replied, lifting his head, and releasing himself from his sister-in-law. "I am not going to do so base a thing as that. My change of creed is produced by an absolute and entire conviction of the errors in my own belief, and the truth of yours. Doubts of my own religion began in Annecy where I met an old-time friend who had become a convert to your Faith. I struggled against them, and for the purpose of crushing them I fled to Germany, to Worms, to catch as it were, something of the spirit of that archreformer, Luther.

"While there, I tried to make up my mind to end my wanderings, return home and actually gladden Deborah's heart by consenting to go out West and claim what was left to me by Uncle Derwent's will. I even wrote to Deborah to that effect, but I did not mention the time of my return. I could not yet make up my mind as to the precise date. The very day on which I dispatched that letter, I drove upon my fate, for going to visit one of the suburbs of Worms, the vehicle in which I had engaged a seat met with an accident upon the road. The accident caused an hour's detention and one of my fellow-travelers, to pass the time, began to converse with me. Finding that I was a more fluent speaker in

French than in the German, he used that language.
He was a most interesting and instructive talker, and
when we resumed our journey, it was, on my part,
to be more delighted with him, than with any point
of interest on the way. The acquaintance continued, and before long I discovered that he was one
of your Catholic priests in disguise—the disguise
was owing to the severe attitude of the government to
Catholic ecclesiastics. When I learned that fact, I
could not resist the desire to confide to him my
doubts on religious matters.

"Unlike what I expected, he was not eager for my
conversion. He seemed more anxious that I should
wait, examine, and reflect. I remained in his vicinity
several weeks reading the books he recommended, and
having many lengthy conversations with him. Then
as a last effort to get away from myself I went to Baden-
Baden that I might be diverted by the gay life there.
It was useless. The very gayety only seemed to
bring more forcibly to my mind all that I had learned of nobler things from my German friend, and
the life, the warmth, the soul of the Catholic Church
in contrast with the coldness of my own faith.
Conviction overpowered me. I could no longer resist
it and I determined to become a Catholic. Then,
my dear friends, it occurred to me to come to you;
to give you the pleasure of supertending my final preparation, as a sort of reward for having neglected you
in the matter of correspondence. I wrote irregularly,
and was silent upon all that I have told you because I
could not bring myself to mention the subject
more than seemed to be absolutely necessary. Am
I forgiven by you both, and are you, my scrupulous
Florence, reassured about the *motive* for my conversion?"

Mother and daughter clasped each one of his hands
and answered in a breath:

"Quite forgiven;" and Florence continued: "And

quite reassured as to the motive, dear Sydney."

"And Agnes," she resumed, when the three were seated, and Mrs. Wilbur was declaring for the fourth time that it was so very wonderful she could not realize it, "happy Agnes. Heaven has at length rewarded her."

"Rewarded me, you mean," replied Sydney, "in not alone enriching me with the gift of the true Faith, but enabling me again to woo Miss Hammond."

"And that will cut you off forever from Derwent's will," said Mrs. Wilbur.

"To be sure," replied her brother-in-law, "but I shall not need it. I have my profession to turn to should it become necessary, and I am so rich in what I gain by resigning my title to this will that I think I am rather to be congratulated on my loss."

"Do please enlighten my curiosity," pleaded Florence. "I have heard occasionally about some queer will in which you, Uncle Sydney, are greatly concerned, but never, to feel the desire to know about it that I do now. Please explain it to me."

"On condition that you do not enlighten Miss Hammond; that you promise never, by word, hint, pen, or pencil, to drop a syllable to her that shall make her think, guess, or know there has ever been in existence such a thing as Uncle Derwent's will."

He spoke playfully, but his niece could not help feeling that he was quite in earnest, and she hastened to assure him that she would be as secret as the grave.

"Since then you make so grave a promise," he resumed with a ludicrous affectation of great solemnity, "I shall not hesitate to give you the particulars.

"Uncle Derwent was my mother's brother, and so rigid in his particular form of Protestant belief, that when my elder brother married your respected mother," bowing to his sister-in-law, "being baptized in the

Catholic Faith ou the day of his marriage, it was feared that the old gentleman in his frenzy would lay violent hands upon himself, or somebody else.

"My brother had been his favorite, and as Uncle Derwent had never married, it was well known that my brother was almost his sole heir. On my brother's marriage, however, he straightway had the will altered, substituting my name for that of my brother, and putting in a proviso which had not been there before. The proviso was that in the event of my marrying a Catholic, every cent of the fortune was to pass to public institutions. Sometime after the making of the latter will he went, for his health, to California. Liking the country and the climate he remained there, and with the whimsicalness of an odd, old man, he actually had another proviso added to the will. One which said that in order to claim the bequest I must reside in California, and take his name, and not receive my inheritance until I had passed my thirty-sixth year."

"But, with all his provisos he was strangely short-sighted. He bound me not to marry a Catholic but he said not one word of the possibility of I myself becoming a Catholic.

"Whether he stupidly thought that the fact of my not having a Catholic wife would avert all danger of conversion from myself, or that it was actually an oversight on his part, I know not. Certain it is that he died, leaving the terms of the will as I tell you."

"And so it is really for Agnes that you renounce this fortune. How the dear girl would feel did she know it,"mused Florence.

"That is the precise reason I do not wish her to know it,"answered Sydney . "There is no telling to what further depths of sacrifice her high spirit might impel her."

And though Florence did not answer it, she silently concurred in the opinion.

"But how will Deborah receive all this?"asked
Mrs. Wilbur." Have you written to inform her?"
"Not I,"laughed Sydney shrugging his shoulders.
"I prefer to face the storm in person and have it
over at once. Did I tell her by letter, the tempest
would only gain violence because of the length of
time which she would have to excite herself before
my arrival. I wrote to her just as I left Baden-Baden,
that I was coming here to Italy, but I did not even
say that I expected to meet you. By to-morrow
however, I shall decide on the date of my return,
and I shall then write and apprise her of that."

Happy Florence! never was her sunny, unselfish
heart so gladdened before, and never before did she
say such fervent prayers of gratitude.

"It was Agnes' daily rosary that brought about
this,"she said to Sydney the next day as she was
accompanying him to see one of the priests attached
to the church of San Lorenzo.

"She never omitted saying her rosary, " she continued, " and how distressed she was, when, during
our stay in your house she happened to lose a little
pearl rosary given to her by one of the Madames on
the morning of her departure from the convent. She
could hardly be consoled for it."

Wilbur did not reply, but he was nothing loth to
hear his niece talk of Miss Hammond; indeed, contrary to his feelings when he was in England, it
was the subject he liked best to hear about, and when
occasionally,Florence was silent for a time about her
friend, he found pretexts for introducing her. Once,
he hinted his fear lest she might have found another
suitor.

Florence turned upon him indignantly:

"That shows you do not know Agnes Hammond.
She does not wear her heart upon her sleeve for
every daw to peck at, and having loved you once,
she will continue to love only you. You wrong her
by the supposition of another suitor."

"Granted, my little, fiery niece, but what has Miss Hammond been doing all these months? Denying myself all news of her, I am actually hungry for some now."

"Why, have I not already told you all I know about her?" replied Florence in a sort of dismayed astonishment that was ludicrous. "Did I not tell you that she was living a very monotonous life with her guardian, diversified alone by her works of charity which I only suspect, because she is almost absolutely silent upon them?"

"Yes," returned Wilbur, "and that she had refused your invitation to visit you here— if she only had" he added in a tone of doleful regret."

"Yes; if she only had for just your satisfaction, I suppose," mimicked Florence with pretended indignation, "as if nobody else felt keenly her rejection of that invitation. But, as I told you before, it is only another instance of her real nobility of character. And now, Uncle Sydney," changing her voice to a tone of playful gravity, "I shall doubt the sincerity of the motive you allege for your conversion, if you continue to talk and think so much of Agnes Hammond."

"As if all my thinking and talking of Miss Hammond were not atoned for by the visits you compel me to make to numerous shrines. And when your tyranny extended as it did yesterday to making me say in the Medicean Chapel a thousand Hail Marys, I think I may be permitted a little latitude in the matter of Miss Hammond."

And he made a most wry face.

"But I intend to repay you, Florence," he continued, "for our wedding-tour shall include Italy, and Agnes and I shall make a stay of some months with you."

"You are a good, charming uncle," she replied, "and to reward you, I shall be more lenient with you.

I shall insist on no more preparation for your baptism than that you shall hear Mass every morning, make every afternoon a visit to some chapel, recite daily the rosary, and the Litany of the Saints, beside Spiritual reading for an hour, saying a few Hail Marys and pious ejaculations, and—"

The burst of laughter from her uncle in which she was compelled to join, stopped her.

"You want me to out-Herod Herod, in my Catholic prayers," he said as soon as he had recovered his composure.

Despite Florence's pretended fear of the motive which actuated her uncle's conversion, his demeanor on the day of his baptism in the chapel attached to the Church of San Lorenzo indicated the seriousness, and in some measure the sublimity of his thoughts. It was in the early morning, and there were no witnesses but Florence and her mother; the latter, and the priest who performed the ceremony were his sponsors, and as Florence heard his firm responses to the demands which form part of the rite, her eyes filled with happy tears.

A little after, and the three received Holy Communion. Even in the ardor of her own thanksgiving Florence could not refrain from looking at her uncle who knelt beside her: but his face was buried in his hands, and his motionless attitude indicated how deep and absorbed were his devotions.

XXV.

DEBORAH WILBUR was in a glow of happiness, a letter having arrived from Sydney naming the very day
on which he intended to begin his journey homeward.
The one thing needed to fill the measure of her delight, was the presence of Miss Liscome. That lady
had accompanied her invalid sister to a quiet country-
resort, and from the tone of her lengthy letter to
Miss Wilbur written not an hour after her arrival at
her destination, she was hardly likely to return for
a month or more, at which prospect Deborah chafed.
She wanted Prudence to talk to, and even to assist
her preparations for a final departure from New York,
for, though her brother had not said a word of going
to California she felt assured that he was coming
home for no other purpose.

When the excitement consequent upon her satisfaction seemed beyond control, she found some relief
in talking to Anne, thereby astonishing not a little
that practical and undemonstrative domestic, while
her bustling preparations went to the extent of dis-
arranging the whole house, in order, as she said, to
have everything ready for immediate sale, or trans-
portation, on Sydney's return.

Anne stared agape at the litter and confusion,
thinking it a funny welcome to give the master, and
wondering at such hasty preparations for a journey
the date of which had not been even hinted.

The only apartment Miss Wilbur spared, was that
which her niece and Miss Hammond had occupied.
Having denuded Sydney's own room of its furniture
in order to show him how certain she was of their
speedy removal to the West, it was necessary to have

some chamber prepared for him, and Anne was set to work dusting and polishing, but with orders not to disturb the texts that still ludicrously enough stared down from the walls. Thus, Anne's sturdy arms belaboring the bricks that formed the back of the hearth of the wide, open fire-place, caused some of them already loosened by time, to project still more from their cavities; in this way she even disturbed the little case containing the pearl rosary which so long had lain hidden from sight. It came slightly to view, but at that moment an authoritative ring of the hall-door bell made Anne in such haste to obey the summons, that she finished her work at the hearth without perceiving anything more than the scoured surface of the bricks.

The visitor was a flashily-dressed, but fine-looking man, whom Anne had never seen before, and he asked for Miss Wilbur with such a self-confident and partronizing air, that she went immediately to find her mistress.

Miss Wilbur saw him at once, her fringe of corkscrew curls pushed ludicrously up from her forehead and her puckered face expressive of intense curiosity.

"Miss Wilbur, I presume."

The stranger bowed very low, Deborah nodded, and puckered her face still more in her desire to know the business of the visitor.

"I have come to learn the address of Miss Liscome. She is an esteemed friend of mine but not having seen her for some time I am in ignorance of her whereabouts. I ascertained by accident, her acquaintance with you, and learning your address, I have taken the liberty of calling for the information."

Deborah's curiosity began to be mingled with indignation at Prudence for never having mentioned this gentleman who claimed her as such an esteemed friend, and her indignation made her for the moment impervious to the stranger's suavity. She eyed him all over with unpleasant sharpness as she answered:

"I don't know that it's my place to give people's addresses to every stranger who inquires for them. And may I ask who referred you to me for imformation about Miss Liscome?"

The gentleman, instead of being daunted by her rebuff, only smiled the broader, and seemed to put himself more at his ease, while he said very suavely;

"Your prudence is to be commended, my dear Madame;I dare say it is upon that quality my friend, Miss Liscome, has based her excellent friendship for you.   But in this case you may safely waive the virtue; my object in desiring to see Miss Liscome is purely to benefit her."

Deborah in spite of herself was slightly mollified by the suave, confident air of the visitor, and feeling that she would serve little purpose by continuing to withold Miss Liscome's whereabouts, she not only gave that lady's number on Hubert Street, but actually produced Miss Liscome's letter, and permitted the stranger to copy the address which headed it.

"And what is your name?" she asked with a little snap, when the visitor seemed about to depart without giving any information on that point.

"Kellar, Madam; Nathan Kellar, entirely at your service for your graciousness of this morning," and he bowed again very low.

Deborah would have put a few more questions, but he gave her no opportunity, for with a hurried adieu that was in marked contrast to his former easy manner, he seemed to dart from her presence and out of the house.

She relieved her feelings by writing immediately to Miss Liscome; adding to her graphic description of the visitor an account of her own displeasure at being treated with such reserve byPrudence, as not to know something about this old-time friend of the latter; then she concluded by hinting that unless Miss Liscome speedily returned she would find the Wilbur homestead quite deserted and even possibly sold to strangers.

Mr. Kellar also wrote to Miss Liscome a flattering epistle, but so coarse in its flattery that to any other woman it must have caused a sort of indignation and disgust; in Prudence it raised emotions of the keenest vanity and lulled even her fear of discovery as to her true knowledge of "Jared." Mr. Kellar had devoted a page of large letter paper to the impression made upon him by Miss Liscome—his inability to forget the charm of her manner, his longing to behold her again and how that longing had impelled him to seek her address from Miss Wilbur to whom he had been referred by their mutual friend, Mr. Mallaby, as the person most likely to know where Miss Liscome lived; that in accordance with an impulse of prudence, not knowing what degree of friendship existed between Miss Liscome and Miss Wilbur, he had witheld from the latter all mention of Mr. Mallaby. Then was added an artful description of the unfavorable contrast Miss Wilbur presented, in the eyes of the writer, to Miss Liscome.

Prudence read it repeatedly, each time becoming more delightfully agitated, and more anxious to return to the vicinity of her new and ardent admirer.

To the dire consternation of her sister she announced her intention of starting for the city the very next day, and she was unusually indifferent to entreaties, protestations, and reproaches. Mrs. Mallary having come to the country at the mercy of Miss Liscome, was obliged to return home at the will of the same lady, before the expiration of half the time allotted for her sojourn.

Her first visit was to Deborah, and full of the flattering contents of Kellar's letter she felt that she was very much the superior of Miss Wilbur. Indeed,

there was a sort of inward chiding of herself for
not having before impressed her superiority upon
that lady, but she intended to atone for her remiss-
ness by beginning to do so at once. She felt quite
bold and exultant as she tripped along the sidewalk,
not even ruffled in thought by the indignation and
tears of Mrs. Mallary whom she had just left—that
lady being both aggrieved and insulted by her hurried and untimely return.

Miss Liscome's resolution to assert her superiority
weakened at the first sight of Miss Wilbur, and it
gave way entirely before the extravagant welcome of
Deborah, who, answering the bell herself, could
hardly get Prudence into the house quickly enough
to impart some delightful information.

It was to the effect that Sydney had arrived from
abroad that morning and had gone out not ten minutes
before Miss Liscome came. She was so full of her
own communications that she even forgot to allude
to the gentleman who had called for Miss Liscome's
address, and she also forgot to reproach Prudence
for never having told her that she had such an acquaintance.

"Sydney has grown handsomer than ever," she
rattled on, not giving her visitor the slightest chance
to put in a word, "and he is in the best of spirits, a
clear proof that he has completely forgotten that forward chit, Miss Hammond. He was just delighted that
I had the house so torn up, and things in readiness
to depart, for he said he guessed it wouldn't be long
until we should leave here. So, you see the dear fellow has actually preserved his common sense, and in
a little while we shall be in California in full possession of that fortune."

She was obliged to pause to take breath, and Miss
Liscome seized the opportunity to remark mildly:

"I am very glad Mr. Wilbur has returned so
well, and I'm sure I shall be quite lonesome when

you go to California;" and then Deborah's breathing.
spell being further protracted by a cough the speaker
ventured to continue:

"Since your preparations are all made, I suppose
you will start for California before the month is out."
It was then the early part of June.

"Dear me! I hope we shall," answered Deborah
with increased vivacity as if to make up for her enforced silence of the moment before. "I don't know
what we'd be doing staying here with the house all
upset as it is. There isn't a room fit for Sydney to
sleep in, except that one I fixed up for the girls.
You remember, Prudence, the one where I hung all
the texts—" Prudence nodded; "well, that room I
didn't touch just because it had those blessed texts in
it: I do think it was owing to them, somehow, that
Sydney was kept from marrying that forward
piece."

"No doubt," simpered Miss Liscome, at the same
time venturing to look around at the disordered condition of the parlor.

"You can guess how busy I have been," continued
Deborah observing her visitor's look, "and how
much I needed your help, but you can do a good
deal for me yet before we go. And oh, Prudence
Liscome," suddenly recollecting the person who had
called to know Miss Liscome's address, "who is that
Mr. Kellar who came here looking for you?"

Remembering her former indignation at not having been told anything about him, her voice had
taken a sharper accent.

Prudence colored, but it did not show very much
owing to the partially darkened state of the apartment, and the quantity of rouge on her cheeks.

Expecting the question from Deborah's fierce letter to her just before she had left the country, she
had prepared her answer, and she gave it with assumed carelessness:

"He is a friend whom I have not met for some time."

"Singular you never spoke about him. You've told me at one time or another, about your friends, but you've never mentioned *his* name."

And Deborah went to one of the windows, and threw back the venetian blind as if to let in more light on Miss Liscome's face. But that lady retained her self-possession.

"You couldn't expect me to mention everybody I ever knew, Deborah; and it was some time since I had seen Mr. Kellar."

"But where did he get directions to find *me?*" persisted the questioner, remembering with some vexation how she had omitted to insist upon that information from Mr. Kellar himself.

"I don't know; I have not seen him yet," replied Prudence.

"But he wrote to you, didn't he?" asked Deborah again in half indignant astonishment, "he copied your country address from one of your letters to me, and that meant, if it meant anything, that he was going to write to you."

"Oh yes; he wrote to me; I got his letter about the same time I got yours."

"And do you mean to say, Prudence Liscome, that you don't know where that man got my address? You're keeping something back, Prudence, or you're lying, and your lying will be found out, and the wrath of God will strike you."

And Deborah who had remained standing after her return from the window, drew her little form up and looked with severely virtuous indignation at her visitor.

Prudence, however, endured the ordeal, emphatically reaffirming what she had said.

Baffled on that point, Deborah probed to find another.

"When and where are you to see this friend?" there was a slight and rather unpleasant emphasis on the last two words.

"I shall write to his office on Nassau Street, and invite him to call on me."

That sounded plausible enough, but Deborah could not yet withdraw the probe:

"Is he married, or a widower?" she asked.

"Neither," hazarded Miss Liscome. "He is a "single man."

"Ah! "ejaculated Deborah, and then feeling that her visitor had evidently fortified herself by the quality which her name represented, and that no more definite information could be elicited from her just then, she abruptly changed the subject by desiring Prudence to take off her bonnet, and accompany her up stairs; she needed her advice regarding the sale of certain articles.

But, though Prudence advised according to her economical judgment, and though she endeavored to appear as if she were interested alone in the articles submitted to her inspection, her thoughts were in an excited whirl, because of her untruthful answers to Deborah's questions about Mr. Kellar. What, if by some means the Wilburs should learn of her acquaintance with Mr. Mallaby, and through that, the real extent of her acquaintance with Mr. Kellar? she was not even sure that Mr. Kellar was not in the category of married men, or widowers, though to Deborah she had asserted the contrary; to do her justice, she did not dream for a moment that he could have a wife living and write her such a letter, but her confidence was founded on blind trust, however. She knew that nothing disgusted Deborah so much as a lie; a downright, cold-blooded lie even in a trifling matter would be sufficient to alienate Miss Wilbur's friendship. As the Wilburs were so soon to leave New York, there seemed really little to fear in that respect, but despite such an assurance Miss Liscome was secretly ill at ease. Not that she need care for Deborah's friendship now, she argued to herself, when they were to be separated speedily, but it was the fear of ignominiously losing that friendship which made her so uncomfortable. Regarding Sydney, her old feelings for him were considerably blunted by her delight at Kellar's sudden and seemingly violent esteem for herself.

XXVI.

KELLAR was a daily visitor at Mallaby's office coming early and staying late, or, if when his call was short repeating it after as brief an interval of absence.
If he had definite business it was not apparent, but that his visits were not particularly cheering to Mr. Mallaby, was very apparent. Even the clerks of adjacent offices noticed the frequent dejected appearance of Mallaby since the advent of this fine-looking, flashily-dressed gentleman. But, no one on the street knew more of him than that he was an old, and long absent friend, and not a few wondered that odd Mr. Mallaby should ever make such a companion of one so unlike himself.

But, that Kellar *had* definite business in those leisurely and seemingly aimless visits, Mallaby felt more and more each day; felt it with a terror akin to the old terror produced by Kellar's letters which he had burned, Kellar himself, in his random conversation dropped hints, and made allusions that caused Mallaby's soul to quake. But he did it in his careless way, and with a guffaw at the conclusion of hint and allusion, as if he had been telling some very funny story.

Frequent as were his visits to the office, he was never invited to visit Mr. Mallaby at Mrs. Denner's.

Mallaby steadily, and even sternly ignored every hint on the part of his friend to win from him such an invitation: nor, did Kellar ask one directly, until he had been a month visiting the office. Then, one morning at the conclusion of one of his mysterious allusions instead of his wonted burst of laughter, he said, suddenly:

"By the way, Mallaby, you have not yet asked me to spend an evening with you. It is well enough to see you here in the office, but dang it man I want to pay you a more social visit , and I want to see that ward of yours, whose letter to her "dear guardian," I saw when she was a child. Ask me up there for to-morrow evening."

There was no opportunity for Mallaby to answer, for at that moment the office-boy brought him a card, bearing the name, "Sydney Wilbur."

"He's waiting outside, and he wants to see you right away," said the boy:

"Tell him to come in," said Mallaby in a half-dazed manner, not having recovered from the shock given by Kellar's unexpected and emphatic request.

And then standing up, the card fluttered from his agitated grasp to the floor. Kellar lifted it and retained it long enough to read the name.

"Ah!" he said to himself, as he placed it upon the desk, but he had no time to give audible expression to his thoughts, for Wilbur was ushered in."

Mallaby remembered the young man distinctly, and having somewhat recovered his self-possession, he advanced to meet him.

"I have just returned from abroad, "said Wilbur shaking cordially the hand extended to him, "and I have come immediately to you in order to settle some important business. May I see you alone?" glancing at the other occupant of the office.

"Ye-es; certainly," said Mallaby, but the hesitation with which he pronounced the words belied their significance, and he also glanced at Kellar, but it was in an appealing way that Wilbur could not help noticing.

"Oh, I shall leave you, gentlemen, to your confidential business," said Kellar, feigning an agreeableness that he did not quite feel, and moving to the door; "but Mallaby and I are old friends," he continued ad-

dressing himself to Wilbur, "Mallaby will tell you so
—*very* old friends;" and then he went out quietly
closing the door behind him, and whistling as he
continued his way.

"Sit down, Mr. Wilbur," said Mallaby, attempting to cover by a show of cordiality his own very apparent embarrassment; he knew that whatever might
be Wilbur's business with him he could not hope to
withold it from Kellar. And, though Wilbur did
wonder a little, and was secretly not favorably impressed by the company in which he found Mallaby,
no trace of his feelings was suffered to appear. He
seated himself with a quiet dignity, and began to
state his business in a simple, straight-forward manner. Surmising that Miss Hammond had not
told her guardian of his proposal to her when she
was his guest, and that her rejection was the cause
of his going abroad, he began with that part of the
story, and he continued without a pause until all of
the events in his own life during the time he had spent
in Europe had been told.

"I have been thus explicit," he added, "that you
may be assured, my conversion to the Catholic Faith
is the result of conviction, and not due to my regard
for Miss Hammond. But now, that the obstacle has
been removed, which prevented her acceptance of
my suit, I have come back to renew it. Before doing
so, however, I desired to acquaint you, to receive your
approval, and to ask you to break to her the news
of my return, and its object. Whatever information you may desire of me, or of my circumstances
in order to know thoroughly the person who asks for
the hand of your ward, I think can be easily and fully obtained." •

He ceased, throwing himself slightly back into his
chair, but continuing to look into Mallaby's face.
During the whole recital Mallaby had not once withdrawn his eyes from the young man's countenance;

his look had been so fixed that it seemed to be held there by a power outside of his own will, and save for the great beads of perspiration which toward the close of the account broke upon his forehead, it was not easy to tell the effect upon him. But when after a few seconds of strange and impressive silence he attempted to give Wilbur some reply, the effect was then only too apparent, for his voice was husky and tremulous, and the hand that he slowly raised to his head shook violently. Feeling that it was necessary to make some excuse for this emotion, he said:

"All this has come so suddenly upon me, Mr. Wilbur, that you must pardon me if I do not seem to be myself. Miss Hammond has never intimated to me a word of that which you say happened while she was a guest in your house, and having had the charge of her from babyhood, it can hardly surprise you to hear that I have acquired something of a father's affection for her.

"At the same time, however," regaining his composure, "I not only yield approval to your proposal, but, for the sake of my ward, I am delighted with it. Regarding the information which you say I may require of your circumstances, your father was too well known as one of the substantial business men of the city, for me to doubt the character and easy circumstances of his son. And since you have become a Catholic, and my ward is of age, there can be no reason for the slightest objection on my part. Having been courteous enough to ask my sanction and approval, be assured Mr. Wilbur, that you have them both. When shall I tell Miss Hammond to expect you?"

He had quite recovered his self-possession, and he stood up smiling, and with something of the expression in his brown eyes which had won Florence.

"Would this evening be too soon?" asked with an eagerness that made Mallaby smile the more.

"No; I shall tell her immediately that I get home."

"Thank you," and in the glow of his gratitude, the young man wrung both of Mr. Mallaby' hands, then Mallaby having written Mrs. Denner's address on one of his own business cards, and handed it to Wilbur, the latter with a brief, but very warmly-spoken adieu, took his departure. On the street he encountered Kellar who had evidently been waiting for the termination of the interview.

"Finished your business with my friend, Mallaby?" he said, speaking as confidently as though an introduction to Wilbur had given him the right to thus accost him.

The young man was somewhat annoyed at the stranger's unwarrantable familiarity, and instead of replying, he flashed upon him a surprised and indignant look and passed on. But while he did so, he was conscious of a very strange sensation: as if an inner voice had told him that man was again to cross his path, and in a far more unpleasant manner. He smiled a little at the oddity of such a feeling, mentally classed it with the ridiculous fancies some old women are supposed to have, and by dwelling on the anticipations of his meeting with Miss Hammond, he succeeded at length in banishing it.

Kellar had returned to Mallaby; returned with a self-confident smile, the significance of which Mallaby knew too well how to interpret. He was standing as Wilbur had left him, save that one hand was pressed tightly to his forehead, and the fingers of the other were working convulsively by his side.

Kellar threw himself into a chair, elevated his feet to the desk, and having otherwise made himself very comfortable, said with an affected yawn:

"Well, old man! what has the talk been about?"

"My ward," answered Mallaby, slowly removing his hand from his head, and looking steadily at his questioner. "Mr. Wilbur desires to marry her. He wanted to do so at the time, when, as I told you, she' was a guest at his house, but the difference in their' religion prevented. While abroad he became a Catholic, and now there is no obstacle to their union."

In the first moment of his unguarded surprise at such information Kellar jerked his feet from the desk, and sat erect; then suddenly remembering himself and desiring to cover his momentary betrayal by an assumption of very great indifference, he resumed his first position, and said nothing more than: "Ah!"

"I am glad to sanction his suit," continued Mallaby, and speaking very rapidly as if the courage to which he had nerved himself might fail him if he lingered in his delivery, "it will place Miss Hammond in better circumstances than she is at present; *and it will relieve me of considerable anxiety.*"

His emphasis on the last words, made Kellar smile broad enough to show almost the whole of his two rows of even, well-kept teeth, raise his eyebrows, and ejaculate once more that careless sounding: "Ah!"

"I am to tell her when I go home that he has returned," still pursued Mallaby with the air of one who is anxious to communicate all the circumstances once, and finally, " and he will call upon her some time this evening."

"Rather fortunate that I did not assign this evening for the time of my visit, eh?" said Kellar with the same apparently careless air, and he took a huge jackknife from his pocket, and began to open one of its numerous blades.

"I named to-morrow evening; do you remember, Mallaby?" beginning to trim his already wel-ltrimmed nails," to-morrow evening, "he continued, speaking as slowly as Mallaby had spoken rapidly, "when I should like to see Miss Hammond. She must be handsome to have won the heart of such an elegant fellow as this Sydney Wilbur appears to be, and she must be admirable in morals and manners having been the ward of so conscientious a man as my friend Matthias Mallaby."

He looked up for an instant from the nail he was cutting and laughed as he always laughed when there was a hidden meaning to his words. Then he continued:

"Will you apprise Miss Hammond of *my* visit to-morrow evening?"

Mallaby's hands hanging by his side clinched for an instant, and a fierce expression came into his face; he even advanced a step as if in obedience to the ferocious impulse well-nigh overmastering him; but Kellar looked up and laughed again.

"It won't do, Mallaby," he said, "the *past* remains, and can neither be forgotten, nor erased; we both as well as Jared, remember it too well. But you are safe, and everything is safe that you have been promised, so long as you yourself fulfill the conditions. It is a harmless whim of mine to see Miss Hammond: one that need cause you no anxiety. I shall not seek to win her from that handsome Wilbur. So, rest assured old man, and give me a cordial invitation for to-morrow evening. Should Wilbur be there also it will be so much the better."

He had jumped up while he spoke, put his knife back into his pocket, and slapped Mallaby vigorously upon the shoulder.

"You may come to-morrow evening," returned Mallaby, but with none of the cordiality in his manner required by Kellar, and a moment after, he threw himself into a chair and groaned heavily.

Kellar whistling went out again to the street.

Miss Hammond was surprised that evening when on leaving the dinner-table her guardian requested her to come into the parlor as he had something to tell her.

There were so few private conversations between them, that the request even startled her, and she looked quickly into his face to learn if its expression boded anything unpleasant. But he returned her looked with a smile which somewhat reassured her.

"A friend of yours called at the office to-day to see me," he said quietly, when they were seated in a corner of the parlor.

"A friend of mine?" her eyebrows were arched, and her lips apart in astonishment at his information. She had no friends outside of her little circle of music scholars and none of them would be likely to call at Mr. Mallaby's office.

"Yes; a very warm friend of yours; Sydney Wilbur."

He had given this additional information thus abrutly to test more assuredly its effect upon his ward; and possibly to learn by means of that effect how deep was *her* regard for this returned suitor.

"Sydney Wilbur!" The very tone in which she uttered the name, betrayed her regard, and the fiery wave of color that mantled her neck and cheeks, and ascended to her brow told unmistakably her delight at the news. But in a moment she had recovered herself, her color disappearing as suddenly as it had come, and her whole glow of delight fading in the thought of what happiness his return could bring to her since the obstacle which had parted them still existed. He had probably some business interest with her guardian, and perhaps through a necessary politeness had asked for her. These were the thoughts which flitted through her mind in the brief interval from her utterance of the name until her guardian spoke again "

"Mr. Wilbur told me all that occurred during your visit to his house."

Miss Hammond with a little of the inconsistency of her sex began to be slightly indignant. What right had Mr. Wilbur to tell that story to her guardian; had he done it in the wantoness of gossip? and her anger at what seemed to be such uncourtly conduct tempered the delight she would otherwise have felt at his return, and the manner in which she replied:

"Has he,"made her guardian doubt a little his previous conviction of the depths of her regard for Wilbur. He resumed:

"He has returned from abroad to renew his suit, the obstacle which existed two years ago, being removed. He became a Catholic while he was away, and he came to me to-day for my approval. It is hardly necessary to say that I cordially gave it."

"All the evidence which her guardian wanted of her regard for Wilbur, appeared then. Her whole face was aglow with a pleasure that could hardly be contained; in her delight she could not even remain seated, and rising she caught both of his hands.

"You are so good to bring me such news," she said;"you have made me very happy."

The glad tears filling her eyes prevented her from seeing how his face had changed color and how persistently he avoided looking at her, and when she released his hands he moved away from her, saying quietly, but with his face partially averted:

"Mr. Wilbur is coming here this evening. I shall leave you now, in order that you may prepare to meet him."

He was gone before she could recall him, but she was too happy to think of any thing just then save her own approaching pleasure.

Mallaby went to his room thinking as he heavily ascended the stair that he understood now the cause of Miss Hammond's dejection when she returned from that visit to Hubert street.

XXVII.

NEVER had Agnes Hammond been so happy, and her happiness was so great, so sudden, so strange and so utterly unexpected, that she feared to find it but a dream; in her uncertainty she actually rubbed her eyes and pinched herself in order to be convinced that she was quite awake; then she fled to her room and immediately sank on her knees before an image of the Blessed Virgin. To that dear patroness she felt her happiness was due, and too full to give voice to the gratitude which filled her heart, she could only lift her clasped hands and look all of the exquisite feelings of her soul.

How thankful she was now, for having made that sacrifice nearly two years ago, and how her heart went out in love and gratitude to Florence, but, for whom, the sacrifice would not have been.

As she rose from her knees she heard the tinkle of the door bell, and without waiting to take even a hasty glance in the mirror, she bounded down the stair, becoming instantly impatient when she found the bell had not been answered. It seemed to her that there never had been such a tardy response to the summons, and unable to contain herself, she stood just within the parlor, with the door only partially closed.

In another moment the girl answered the bell, and Miss Hammond heard the loudly-spoken "yes sir," to the inaudible question of the person she had admitted.

Agnes could wait no longer; she flung back the parlor-door, and rushed forth with:

"Oh Sydney!"

But instead of Sydney there confronted her, a tall, fine-looking, flashily-dressed man whom she had never seen.

"Oh," she said in terrified dismay, and retreating hastily.

But the stranger laughed.

"Thought I was somebody else, eh? I feel obliged to the mistake, since it has given me the pleasure of an earlier introduction than I should otherwise have had. You're Miss Hammond, I presume. I am Nathan Kellar your guardian's old friend. He told you, I suppose, that he invited me to spend to-morrow evening with you both but unexpected business makes it necessary for me to see him to-night. Just show me to Mr. Mallaby's room," turning to the amazed girl, who had admitted him, "I would rather see him there than anywhere else; and you, Miss Hammond, I shall probably have the pleasure of meeting again, a little later."

The servant felt constrained to obey him, and Agnes turned into the parlor with a feeling somehow as if her happiness were not quite so unalloyed as it had seemed to be a few minutes before.

Her guardian had never so much as named Mr. Kellar to her, much less to tell her that he had invited the gentleman to spend the evening with them; and to invite anybody to Mrs. Denner's, was a most unprecedented thing for Mr. Mallaby to do. Never in her recollection had he issued such an invitation. Then, Kellar's air of familiarity in speaking of Mallaby, the confident way in which he invited himself to Mallaby's room, and his own flashy appearance, all produced an indescribable, but unpleasant effect upon the girl, though less powerful than it would have been had her reflections not been tempered by her happy thoughts of Wilbur.

Her disappointment had curbed somewhat her impatience, and the next time the bell rang, she did

not even leave the seat she had taken in the parlor.
But her heart beat as if it would burst, and her
whole face was suffused with color. How thankful
she was that she was the only occupant of the room,
and how she wished that Wilbur would come before
any of the other boarders took their places for the
evening.

Her wish was granted. He came while she was
still alone, and this time there was no mistaking the
well-remembered voice which asked quite audibly
for Miss Hammond. But she restrained herself
from doing more than rising from her chair, even
when she heard the girl ask him to enter the parlor.
In another moment he was before her, starting and
coloring with pleasure at meeting her so promptly,
and then stopping short in his advance to her, as if
overcome by a sudden fear of his reception.

Agnes instantly dispelled his fear. She rushed to
him, crying:

"Sydney, Sydney!" and then she placed her
hands in his that were widely extended, and she
looked up into his face with intense affection
and delight. He yearned to clasp her to him while
he told her of his fruitless attempt to forget her,
but the remembrance of her exquisite modesty deterred him, and he only continued to hold her hands
very tight, and to return her look with one as fond
and delighted as her own.

How handsome he had grown, and how lovely
she had become, was the thought in the mind of
each; and then, each had so many questions to ask
and so much to tell, that it was a sort of difficulty to
know where, or how to begin. But, Agnes, woman-
like, speedily arranged the matter by bringing him
to the most remote corner of the parlor, and seating
both him and herself in such a manner that only
their backs would be visible to any other occupant
of the room. Then, indifferent as to who might en-

ter, and also to the curious observation of herself
which would be sure to follow, she set the tide of
their conversation flowing. Of course he had to
detail minutely every circumstance of his life abroad,
and to dwell at length upon his recent visit to
Florence and her mother.

"Darling Florence!"

Agnes exclaimed; "I owe everything to her—the
very resolution by which I gave you up, when it became my duty to do so. Yes," she impulsively continued in answer to his look of surprise, "I owe it
entirely to her;" and then she briefly told him of the
influence which Florence had exerted during their
visit to Hubert Street.

"A precious pair you were," he said in pretended
savageness, and having had the satisfaction of delay-
ing my happiness then it becomes your bounden
duty, now to repair the wrong by consenting to a
very early marriage."

She shook her head:

"I must write to Florence first, and ask her if it
would not be possible for her to leave her mother
long enough to come here and to be present at our
marriage; or perhaps her mother could accompany
her."

"I doubt it ; her mother is too delicate to return
for any length of time to our climate."

"But you do not doubt that Florence can be spared, do you?"

"I do most strongly doubt it, and I object also to
our marriage being delayed for any such reason.
Supposing Florence should write that she could not
leave her mother for a month, or two."

"Then we shall cheerfully wait that month or
two, "laughed Agnes.

"We shall do nothing of the kind, "said Sydney
with a lover's impatience, "for directly after our
marriage I shall take you to Italy to visit Florence
and her mother; will that not do ?"

"No; it will not do: I must have Florence if it be possible at my wedding. Do, Sydney gratify me in this. I shall write this very night to her and possibly in a month she will be with us."

"Or possibly in six months," half growled Wilbur rebelling with all his soul at the delay and yet unable to resist the fair pleader. Perchance that which made him more opposed to the plea was a secret, but strong presentiment that any delay would be but the precursor of another and a final separation.

Agnes feeling that she might consider his consent won, and anxious to leave the subject lest he should again demur, said:

"Did you not intend to go to the West? Florence said so in one of her letters some time ago."

"That was some time ago," he answered lightly, "when I did not expect to take upon myself any family ties; now that things are changed, I shall remain in New York, the locality of our residence subject to your desire.

"You are very good, but what will your sister say—and oh," as if suddenly remembering, "what did she say when you told her you had become a Catholic?"

"I have not told her yet. I was too full of you, and I did not want to mar my pleasant thoughts by one of her tirades until I had seen you."

Ten o'clock striking softly from the mantle timepiece caused Sydney to take his watch out with much surprise at the lateness of the hour. It did not seem to him that a half hour had elapsed since his arrival at eight o'clock, nor did the time seem any longer to Miss Hammond.

"I wonder why Mr. Mallaby has not come down," she said, and then remembering his flashy visitor, and feeling that the latter was still closeted with him, she began to look a little anxious. Some of the boarders had entered the parlor, and had glanced with no little surprise at the absorbed occupants of the remote corner, and fancying that they understood the situation had smiled a little to themselves. One of them even, with true feminine curiosity made an excuse to see Mrs. Denner, in order to learn the full meaning of such a confidential *tete-a-tete*, and that being the first account which the good woman had received of it she went to the parlor to behold it with her own eyes. Sure enough; it was exactly as described; Miss Hammond in close, absorbed, and evidently delighted conversation with such an elegant-looking young gentleman; he might have stepped out of one the tailor's fashion books. What did it mean?

Mrs. Denner was as puzzled as her curious informant to explain, and she in turn found an excuse to go to Mr. Mallaby's room, in order to sound him. But, before she reached his door she heard his vioce raised in angry expostulation. Amazement rooted her to the spot for a moment. Never before had she heard Mallaby's voice pitched in such a key or with such anger in its tones.

"I tell you, no, a thousand times no."

Those were the words he used; she could have sworn to them on her deathbed; and then listening further, she heard another voice but one that was too guarded in its tones to enable her to distinguish a word.

Mysteries were thickening; never before had Mallaby a visitor, and that this one should have been admitted to his very room augured something painfully strange. The good woman *must* see him, and she knocked at the door quite boldly.

"What's wanted?" said Mallaby without leaving his seat.

"It's me, Mr. Mallaby; I want to see you;" and Mrs. Denner spoke in a most aggrieved tone. Mallaby went to the door, opened it sufficiently to pass into the hall, and closed it tightly behind him. Mrs. Den-

ner had not obtained even a glimpse of the stranger.
She was indignant as well as aggrieved; it was so
obvious that Mr. Mallaby did not intend to let her
see his visitor.

"I always thought, Mr. Mallaby, as you considered
me your friend."

Mallaby looked at her with the air of one demented.
Still under the influence of the hot emotions roused
by the interview just interrupted, he was in no humor to sympathize with, or even understand this unreasonable whim of his landlady.

"I always thought so, Mr. Mallaby," she repeated,
lifting the corner of her apron to her eyes, "until
this night's doings has proved how a poor, simple,
trusting woman may be mistaken in a boarder as
she's had for the last ten years, awaiting on him,
and a-tendin' on him with her own two hands, and
a-calling of him ever that blessed man."

By that time she had positively worked herself
into a state of tears, and she was sniffling quite audibly behind her apron.

"In the name of God, woman, what have I done to
you?" burst from Mallaby, dimly comprehending at
length that he was in some way to blame for her
emotion.

"Oh, Mr. Mallaby! you're like the rest of the men,
deep and subtle when you're dealing with a poor,
simple woman; and I didn't deserve it, Mr. Mallaby.
I as waited on you, and tended on you these ten long
years with my own two hands."

"Upon my soul, woman; I don't know what you're
talking about," burst from Mallaby again, growing
desperate with the thought of what he had just left,
and what he had again to meet before that interview
would be terminated, and this additional unreasonableness on the part of his landlady.

"It's your unkindness, Mr. Mallaby,—" taking her
apron from her eyes and twirling it between her fin-

gers: "your unkindness in keeping things from me,
as is making me feel bad, and I tendin' on you, and
waitin' on you these ten long years with my own two
hands."

"Good God, woman! will you ever come to the
point?"

"Yes, I'm coming to the point if you'll give me
time, Mr. Mallaby," spoken with as much anger as
grief, for she was fast becoming exasperated that her
boarder should be so obtuse as not divine the matter
from what she already had said:

"I'm coming to the point," she repeated, letting
her apron drop, and fixing herself squarely and reso-
lutely in front of her astounded boarder, "and I'm a-
coming to it in an honest way, Mr. Mallaby. I'm
not coming to it in a way that some people might
do, a-beating around the bush, and a-hemming and a-
hawing from the weight of their own consciences: I'm
coming to it, I am."

A significant cough from the invisible visitor destroyed the remnant of Mr. Mallaby's patience.

"Either tell me immediately, woman, what you
want, or leave me to attend to my business." Never
before had she seen him so angry-looking, and despite her own indignation it caused her to be a little bit afraid—afraid lest she had gone too far with
"that blessed man."

So once more she had recourse to her apron in
order to simulate an appearance of grief while she
said:

"Down in your own heart, Mr. Mallaby, you must
feel as how you're been unkind; a-going and a-having
of a visitor in your own room—you that never had
no such thing these ten long years that I've been a-
tending and awaiting on you, and in your own private room, Mr. Mallaby, where nobody never comes
except the girl to clean it, and your own blessed self;
and then there's Miss Agnes in the parlor with a

strange gentleman, and I ain't told anything about
that.   Oh, Mr. Mallaby, you ain't been like yourself
in a-keeping of these things from one as has the feelings of a mother for you and Miss Agnes."

And once more she was sniffling audibly behind
her apron.

"Oh,"ejaculated Mr. Mallaby, too much amazed
to give utterance to anything more. He was too little
versed in feminine attributes ever to have suspected
Mrs. Denner's curiosity, or even now that he knew
it, to understand it; and the knowledge came upon
him too suddenly and too speedily after his hot interview with Kellar, to cause him even the amusement that it might have done at another time; the
emotions resulting from that same interrupted interview also prevented him from feeling the anger war-
ranted by the seeming impertinence of the woman
as his chief irritation had come from the time she
was unnecessarily consuming, now that grievance
was removed, he could treat her with something of
his wonted gentleness, and he said so quietly as to
astonish her:

"I am glad, Mrs. Denner, it is nothing else I have
done to you."

And without another word he disappeared quickly
into his room, shutting the door as tightly behind
him, as he had done when he came out.

Mrs. Denner was a very much disappointed, and
mortified woman, disappointed that her boldness had
failed to obtain any information, and mortified at
Mr. Mallaby's treatment of her: she felt with a sinking of the heart that she had presumed too much upon her boarder's apparently simple and gentle manners; but with all, she could not yet repress her
desire to learn something, and she lingered, hoping
for a repetition of the high tones which had so startled her a few minutes before.   In that also she was
disappointed, for Mallaby's voice was as subdued as

that of his visitor. But she caught the sound of
Miss Hammond's voice; as if that young lady were
speaking to some one in the hall below, and she hurried down in time to confront Agnes and Sydney at
the parlor-door exchanging their adieus.

"Oh, Mrs. Denner!" said Agnes, catching sight of
her. "This is that good Mrs. Denner, Sydney, of
whom you heard me speak when I was at your house
on Hubert Street; and this gentleman, Mrs. Denner,
is Mr. Wilbur from whose house I came to you nearly two years ago."

Mrs. Denner made her best bow, and smiled with
supreme satisfaction: her curiosity was at last receiving some enlightenment.

"To-morrow evening then, I shall see you again;"
said Agnes, placing both her hands in Wilbur's
while Mrs. Denner a little in the rear, remained to
attend the gentleman to the door.

"Yes; to-morrow evening, "and then he wrung her
hands, said "good-night," quickly, as if did he linger
over the words it would be harder to tear himself a-
way, and departed, Mrs. Denner deferentially opening the door for him.

When she turned back, Agnes was still standing on the threshold of the parlor looking radiant
from happiness.

"Perhaps you guess what I have to tell, Mrs. Denner," she said.

That good woman had been guessing very hard,
and having received the information which had accompanied Miss Hammond's introduction, she was
enabled to guess pretty correctly; but Agnes enlightened her further by telling her of Wilbur's conversion, and of her guardian's entire sanction to their
marriage.

At which annoucement Mrs. Denner could not refrain from saying:

"I cannot understand your guardian, my dear: he's

gone and had a stranger with him all the evening in his room—him that never had as your blessed self to cross the threshold of his door—all the evening he's had that stranger, and they've been a-talking loud and queer—leastwise your guardian has—for I heard him."

She prudently reserved all communication of her effort to gratify her own curiosity.

Miss Hammond's glow of delight faded, and an uneasy expression showed itself in her face; but she said nothing of her feelings to Mrs. Denner. Instead, with a gentle good-night she went to her own room, and began at once a letter to Florence, becoming so happy in the detail of all her glad tidings as to forget her anxiety concerning her guardian.

Long after that letter was finished and the writer of it lay in the slumber of youth and innocence, her guardian was still closeted with Kellar.

An hour after midnight had rung out from one of the city clocks and had chimed from the little time-piece resting on a bracket, before Kellar rose to go.

"I shall not accept to-night, the decision you persist in giving," he said. "You have not had time to consider the consequences of such a decision, nor have you had time to realize what is promised by an acceptance of my proposition—a clear, clean sweep of the past by both Jared, and me; a full release from all your harrowing obligations. I solemnly swear this to you, and in order to convince you that I must keep my oath, I shall prepare in the presence of any witness you choose, a paper which must nullify any act of mine against you, should I ever be tempted to break my pledge. You are mad, Mallaby, if you refuse."

Mallaby had been sitting with his head half drooping upon his breast, and his eyes looking into the space before him with mournful intensity, but at Kellar's last words he rose.

"I may be mad," he said speaking slowly and sadly, "but, I shall not be dishonest. To do as you request, use the trust I have won by integrity, and induce the firm you mention to invest in these bonds issued by this Australian company, would be to sink me lower in my own estimation, than I could ever sink in the opinion of others, by the fulfillment of your threats. That, when the bubble should burst—after having enriched this enterprising Australian company, and you and me—I should be held guiltless as not being supposed to know anything beyond the advantages it promised, does not alter the conscientious aspect of the case. It is a clever scheme, ingenious, and well calculated to entrap and deceive; I have no doubt of the favor with which it would be received, did I broach it to my firm, and recommend you as one of its trustworthy exponents. But, Kellar, it is not an honest scheme, and I shall be no party to it. My answer is final."

His tones increased in vigor and rapidity, and as he finished, he straightened himself, and looked fully and with a sort of defiance into Kellar's face.

That gentleman shrugged his shoulders and smiled.

"In spite of all that, I still hold to my conviction that you will ultimately consent," he said with a covert sneer in his tones. "Sleep upon it, Mallaby, and let your dreams picture to you the consequences of your refusal. I should not have called to-night and thus anticipate the visit you invited me to make to-morrow evening, but, on my return home, finding, as I told you, a letter urging me to hasten matters, I thought it well to lose no time in fully disclosing to you the business upon which I have returned to New York. Besides, I should like to have your final answer to-morrow."

"You have it already," said Mallaby.

Kellar again shrugged his shoulders and smiled;

then, he drew a cigar from his pocket, lit it at the gasjet, and puffed at it for a moment or two, watching Mallaby closely as he did so. The result of his observation seemed to give him some inward satisfaction, for he took the cigar from his lips, smiled again more broadly than before, and said lightly, glancing at the clock:

"Too late I suppose, to see Miss Hammond. Tell her that I deplore the circumstances which prevented my return to her company. As I have told you, already, that brief view of her on my entrance, enchanted me. Lucky fellow, Wilbur is. Probably, I shall drop in to-morrow evening to be properly introduced."

Two o'clock chimed from the bracket.

"So late, or rather early;" laughed Kellar, "well, I must depart if I would give you an opportunity for the dreams of which I spoke. But you'd better pilot me out, Mallaby; your hall-lights must be extinguished by this time."

But neither the light in the hall leading from Mr. Mallaby's room, nor the mellowed light in the hall below had been extinguished. Mrs. Denner had left them both aflame in order to show Mr. Mallaby the attention she was willing to accord Mr. Mallaby's visitor, mysterious though he were, and Mrs. Denner herself, determined to watch the departure of the visitor, and to catch a glimpse of him if possible, had taken a seat in the parlor, just behind the door which she kept partially open. She had extinguished the parlor-lights, so that she found herself quite secure from observation, and, having interrogated the girl who admitted Mr. Mallaby's visitor about the appearance of that gentleman she waited with no small impatience for him to descend. But sitting for three hours solitary and silent produced a most drowsy effect, and long before Mallaby and his company descended, the good woman was as soundly asleep in her chair as she would have been in her comfortable bed, and snoring loudly. Both Mallaby and Kellar heard her as they descended the stair, and the former in no little surprise when they reached the parlor from which the sound came with startling distinctness pushed back the door and entered the room. There was sufficient light from the hall to reveal the sleeping form, the arms folded tight, and the slovenly-looking head almost buried in the ample bosom. Mallaby surveyed it for a moment, and owing to his scene with Mrs. Denner some hours before, he comprehended the situation.

Her feminine curiosity had induced the vigil.

Had he not been filled with far different and more engrossing thoughts, he might have been both angry and amused; but, as it was, with his very soul in the grip of a temptation so strong that it seemed to tax his physical, as well as his mental strength, Mrs. Denner was too minute a matter to give him more than a passing thought. He left the room, closing the door behind him, and without a word went forward to open the hall-door for Kellar.

Nor was Kellar interested enough to ask who it might be; he had no concern but that which had brought him to Mallaby, and once more as both stood for a second on the stoop, he scanned Mallaby's face, the light of the opposite gaslamp made every feature visible. And as before he seemed to be affected by his observation, for he took his cigar from his lips, and smiled as he had done above stairs. Then he said a careless "good-night" and went leisurely on his way.

Mallaby lingered for a moment looking after him, and then there came strangely to his mind the memory of the night when his ward, Florence Wilbur, and he stood on a doorstep exchanging their good-nights. He saw again the kindly look in Miss Wilbur's eyes, and he experienced again the strange feeling which had so thrilled him then. Its dim foreboding was coming so true in his own case, would it be equally verified in Miss Hammond's? Oh God! if it should—he staggered against the railing which supported the stoop and tremblingly held himself there.

The solemn quiet which brooded over the street seemed after a little to descend in a measure upon his own troubled and tempted spirit. Still clinging to the railing he lifted his eyes to the sky. He fancied the stars shone with more brilliancy than usual; and then with a queer retrospection his mind went back to one of the quaint fancies of his childhood, when he thought the stars were the eyes of the angels watching a sleeping world. Now, when he was almost an old man, they seemed again like eyes, but eyes every one of which looked down into his soul: eyes that encouraged him, that plead with him, that exhorted him.

He had repelled with seeming firmness the temptation Kellar had placed before him, but only God knew the grip of the demons in his heart; only God knew the stern fight his soul had waged. Kellar had said to sleep upon his proposal; that dreams sometimes induced subjection, Mallaby almost feared to return to his room lest it might be so; lest the thought of the freedom which was promised as the price of his compliance, might in his dreams overpower him, and cause him to yield in his waking hours. So, he lingered until the policeman of the beat passing the door looked up curiously at the bare-headed man holding with both hands to the railing of the stoop. That made him go within and he closed the door and ascended to his room, the snore of Mrs. Denner accompanying him the greater part of the way, and suggesting to him in a sort of mechanical way, the propriety of extinguishing the hall-lights. Thus, when that drowsy landlady at length opened her eyes a full hour later, she was in total darkness, and it required two or three minutes to enable her to know where she was, and to recollect the circumstances that had brought her there.

She was indignant with herself at having slumbered upon her watch, and though she surmised from the darkness that Mallaby's visitor had gone, she could not retire without obtaining further certainty of that fact. So she groped her way to Mallaby's room, and listened at his door. There was not a sound, nor did there seem to be any light. Convinced that he had gone to bed she went to her own, trying to temper her disappointment and chagrin with the thought that at least, she had gained some important information from Miss Hammond.

XXVIII.

A NERVOUS restlessness and anxiety seemed to possess Deborah Wilbur during the whole day of her brother's return; it had not been apparent to Miss Liscome because that lady had been too much engrossed by her own anxious thoughts to be as observing as usual, and Miss Wilbur herself had striven somewhat to conceal the fact. But when Prudence had taken her departure Deborah's nervousness evinced itself in her inability to remain long in one room, or engage in one occupation, and when the afternoon waned without bringing Sydney home, she became impatient as well as restless.

She was also somewhat uneasy whenever she reverted to the manner with which on that morning, he had received the information of her preparations for their departure to the West; while his answers had been the seemingly satisfactory ones she had repeated to Prudence, there had been that in his manner and in the tone of his voice which did not seem quite to agree with his replies, and which consequently, did not inspire the expectation and cheerfulness Miss Wilbur might reasonably be supposed to feel. All that, however, she had not told Miss Liscome, and now. while she went from parlor to dining-room, and thence to the kitchen to Anne, who was very much vexed that Mr. Wilbur had not come home to his dinner before it was spoiled, her vague, but anxious fears increased.

He had told her upon leaving the house that he was going to attend to some business matters which had accumulated during his absence, and she suppos-

ing his errand would not consume more than a few
hours, had not even inquired the time of his return.

The business matters which he said he was anxious
to settle, were not only matters relating to finances,
and which entailed a visit to his business agent, and
another to his lawyer, but the more private matter of
seeing Mr. Mallaby; and the gracious reception accorded by that gentleman, encouraging Mr. Wilbur to
anticipate a very speedy union with Miss Hammond,
caused him to attend to other business matters the
settlement of which he had only deferred until he
could be assured that he might renew his suit for the
hand of Mr. Mallaby's ward.

All this consumed so much of the day that it was
well-nigh evening, when to his sister's great relief,
Sydney at length returned. But when he announced, almost before he had fairly removed his hat,
that he was going out again in an hour, or two, she
looked at him somewhat aghast.

"It is part of the business on which I have been
engaged to-day," he said with a smile, "and I must
attend to it."

A sudden hope filled her heart.

"Have you been arranging matters for our speedy
departure, Sydney? I can forgive any absence, no
matter how prolonged, if it is for that purpose, and
then, as I told you this morning, *my* preparations
are pretty well completed."

"You shall know in a little while," he answered,
smiling still, "just now I am preparing a surprise for
you, and would rather not be questioned too closely."

"Only tell me this," she persisted, "that we are
going away, and I shall not ask another question."

"*We* are going away," he replied, with an emphasis on the first word that had a significance of
which she did not dream, "and now if you have any
concern for my physical wellbeing, ring for Anne to

bring me something to eat.   I am almost famished."

Miss Wilbur became as hopeful and buoyant as she had been before anxious and uneasy. She felt certain that the surprise her brother intended to give her was an announcement of the very early date on which they were to begin their journey to the West; that he had already secured the tickets, and knowing how complete were her preparations, he felt, of course, no necessity for giving her more time than was necessary to pack her trunk; and even that should be speedily done, she meant to begin it that very night just so soon as he should go out; and she felt equally certain that the business to which he had been attending nearly all day, was negotiations for the sale or transfer of the property from which they both derived their income: it did seem a little strange that the evening must be given up also to the same matter, but perhaps it was necessary in order to meet certain desirable parties.   Thus assured, she bustled about with unusual alacrity, insisting on waiting upon him herself, and all the while maintaining so lively and constant a conversation it taxed him not a little to answer her and at the same time to satisfy his appetite.

As soon as he again went out, she began the packing of her trunk, calling Anne to assist her.

"Are you going away to-morrow, ma'am?" inquired Anne.

"No, hardly to-morrow, out it may be so soon after to-morrow, that it is well to be quite ready. There is nothing like taking time by the forelock, Anne."

But Anne was saying to herself:

"Faith, it's not by the forelock you take it, but by the whole head," a thought in which she might seem to be justified by the preparations for departure began by her mistress over three months before.

and daily accompanied by the observation that it was well to be in readiness.

Deborah took up so much time in the packing of her trunk, holding lengthy soliloquies as to which articles she should pack first, and then when they had been snugly placed, changing her mind, and making Anne take them all out, that it was then ten o'clock before she seemed to have made any progress: and an hour later, when she heard her brother enter the house, her trunk was still in its yawning condition, and her bed was strewn with articles of dress that had yet to be packed. But she was anxious to see Sydney, and bidding Anne to go to bed, she hastened below.

Sydney had gone into his own uncarpeted and disordered study, struck a light, and he was seeking for a chair when his sister entered. He was in such a happy mood that he could not refrain from jesting a little about the absurdity of such a premature upsetting of the household goods.

"You might at least have left a fellow a chair," he said with a ludicrous assumption of ruefulness; "and where in the name of all that's curious, am I to sleep? or do you want me to do penance for my past transgressions by lying on the floor like some of the Catholic saints used to do?"

"I told you this morning where you were to sleep," answered Deborah curtly, and in no way responding to her brother's pleasantry, "and it isn't right for you even in jest to make an allusion to Romish saints, or anything else that's Romish."

"Isn't it?" he repeated laughing, "why my aciduous sister, I thought a man had a right to freedom of speech in this country. I am afraid if you were a ruler, Deborah, you'd be a despot, a petty, wilful, grinding, bigoted awful despot; but show me to my sleeping-chamber: I have no recollection of being told about it this morning.."

"Because you paid no attention when I was telling you," replied Deborah, half disposed to be angry at his banter, "your mind seemed to be on something else."

"It *was* on something else; " he answered, "but lead the way to my room. I am beginning to get sleepy," rubbing his eyes and yawning.

Deborah led the way to the chamber which had been occupied by the young guests nearly two years before, and which was still adorned with the gaudy scriptural texts.

The sight was so ridiculously odd and incongruous, it excited Sydney's keenest humor.

He threw himself into a chair the better to laugh at his ease, saying when he had recovered his voice;

"By all that is funny, Deborah, what's the meaning of that?"

He pointed to the text covered wall opposite.

His sister had become quite angry;she was always annoyed at being made the object of his banter, but now in addition, to have him turn to sport her biblical efforts was an aggravated insult.

"That, Sydney Wilbur," placing herself squarely before him, and speaking with the shrill snap that anger always gave to her voice, "is an effort made by me to bring divine grace into this room; to bring it into this room at a time when it seemed likely to be banished altogether from this house by the presence of those two Romanists you chose to invite here.

"This is the room they occupied, and before they set foot across its threshold, I just fortified the surroundings by pasting up those blessed words of Scripture; and I attribute to their holy influence the way you've been saved from a marriage with that Miss Hammond."

She delivered the last words with an unmistakable air of triumph, and tossed her head until her little corkscrew curls danced upon her forehead. As the room in anticipation of Sydney's occupation of it had been early and amply illuminated, there was suffici-ent light to reveal every change in her countenance.

Her brother laughed again and reclined more comfortably in his chair, but at the same time, he looked very fixedly at his sister.

He had not intended to tell her just yet of his own conversion to the abhorred Catholic Faith, nor of the renewal of his proposal to Miss Hammond but, Deborah herself seemed to drive upon it, and to make an opportunity for the communication. And while he continued to look at her in that fixed way, he was thinking of the improbability of gain-ing any advantage by delay. She would storm as much a week, a month hence, as she would do on that very night, and though he hated to have his exquisitely happy thoughts of Agnes rudely disturb-ed as they must be by the scene his sister would assuredly make, still it would be a relief to know that the dread communication was over. He sat erect and said in a quiet, low, firm voice, so unlike the tones he had used in his banter, as to seem to belong to another person.

"Your scriptural precaution has hardly had the desired effect; I became a convert to Catholicity while abroad, and my chief object in coming home, was to renew my suit for Miss Hammmond's hand. I saw her this evening, and we are to be married I trust at an early date."

Deborah glared at him. Had he gone suddenly crazy? had her senses suddenly left her, or had they both become insane together? Such were her first thoughts, and their tenor gave a sort of terrified look to her face.

"I am sorry that the news should startle you," said Wilbur, "but, it is nevertheless true; and part of the business on which I was engaged to-day, was that of making an entire settlement of this house upon you. That, with your income will support you comfortably, and enable you to live apart from my wife that is to be, and me. Knowing your religious prejudice I could not for a moment subject you to a life with us, Romanists.''

The clear matter and firm manner of his reply convinced her of its truth. She could no longer doubt the horrible intelligence, and disappointment and rage made her speechless for the moment.

Concern that her brother had apostatized from the faith of his fathers was not so keen as that he should have to forfeit the fondly-expected fortune. In that moment of mute fury she mentally cursed Miss Hammond, and she was conscious of a frantic longing to strangle her. Had it been left to her own physical strength to accomplish the task, she felt that she could have done it unaided; rage and hatred had made her so strong.

Her face reflected the passions tearing her soul; it became red and swollen, and every knot and line showed with repulsive distinctness. The fingers of both her hands were rapidly closing and opening and her foot beat the carpet with equal rapidity.

To her brother, abhorring as he did, any exhibition of temper in a woman, it was somewhat of a sickening sight, and he covered his face with his hand to shut it out; she at the moment recovered her voice, the loud, shrill rasping voice from which he fain would have covered his ears.

"You will lose the fortune, Sydney—a half million of dollars—a half million of dollars."

The last words wer fairly shrieked.

He answered, preserving his calmness and speaking very low that the contrast between his tones and her own might recall her to some propriety of accent.

"I can hardly be said to lose that which I never had.'

"But I—your sister, your only sister—you always intended to share it with me."

Her voice had not dropped in the least from its shrill, high key.

"So I should have done; but now not having the opportunity to do so, neither can *you* suffer any loss; and, as I have told you, your future is assured."

She changed her plea to a tirade on his conversion, or perversion, as she called it, flinging at him all the biblical terrors she could remember.

He either smiled, or made some indifferent response. Then she tried tears and hysterical sobs, sinking to her very knees at his feet. He was as little moved, showing not even a change of expression, save a look of utter weariness combined with an evident disposition to go to sleep.

The total failure of all her efforts renewed her rage. She sprang to her feet.

"May you live to curse the day that you ever saw Miss Hammond—may the wrath of Heaven strike her——"

She was not suffered to finish her malediction, for with the last word she found herself caught by her shoulders, lifted from the floor, and put down with no very gentle thrust into the hall without. Then she heard the door locked on the inside, and after that not a sound.

Knowing now that nothing would move her brother from his intention, and still bursting with rage and disappointment, she felt she could not sleep without confiding in somebody, and as her sole confidant was Miss Liscome, she decided to send for that lady. It made no difference that it was after midnight, that Miss Liscome probably would have to be roused from her bed, and that she herself would have to awaken Anne. She aroused Anne at once more to the latter's disgust than to her curiosity, and dispatched her on the errand.

Prudence was not in bed when the summons came. She was just finishing a note to Mr Kellar, in which she gushingly thanked him for his flattering impression of her, admitted with ludicrous ingenuousness a similar impression on her part, and cordially invited him to take tea with her sister's family the next evening but one.

She had begun the note three hours before, but indecision about the style and matter of its intended contents, had made her thus slow in its progress.

"Is it sickness?" she asked of Anne, whom she herself had admitted, being in some alarm that the bell should ring at such an hour.

"Not sickness but temper," answered Anne with evident desire to be brief in her communication. Of the temper of her mistress she felt that she could speak with certainty; Miss Wilbur in dispatching her on her errand had done so with all the asperity of face and tongue usually accompanying one of her tempers.

The heart of Prudence sank a little. Could Deborah's temper have been occasioned by the fact that she had learned the real extent of her (Prudence) acquaintance with Mr. Kellar? Impelled by this fear she summoned courage enough to ask Anne the cause of the temper of her mistress.

"I don't know'm," answered Anne curtly; "such things ain't my business, and I never seeks to find things out that ain't my business."

Which reply silenced all further questions of Miss Liscome, and she briefly desired Anne to wait while she went to get her bonnet and shawl.

Miss Wilbur impatiently awaiting Anne's return paced the hall outside of her brother's room. She hoped that her ceaseless tread which she made as heavy as she could, would annoy him, and she meant when Miss Liscome arrived, to address that lady in such loud tones that even if he were asleep it must

awaken him. He should know that all his perfidy
was about to be disclosed.

But the efforts of her petty malice were without
effect. Her brother, relieved to have the dread communication over and freed from his sister's presence,
had resumed his happy thoughts of Agnes, becoming
so absorbed as even not to hear the quick stamping,
nervous step passing to and fro outside his door.

But when his sister hearing Anne enter, screamed
to the latter over the baluster at the very top of her
voice he started in his chair, and when she continued in tones loud enough to be heard across the
street, he rose angrily.

"Is Miss Liscome with you, Anne?"

"Yes ma'am," answered Anne in a much more
guarded voice than her mistress used.

"Have her come right up to my room; I have a
great deal to tell her."

Every word was fairly shrieked.

Sydney made a sudden stride toward the door intending to give his sister a sharp reproof of her
unseemliness, but he as suddenly checked himself,
feeling that her disappointment had made her defiant
of any reprimand. Then he heard her ascend to her
room, and directly after, he heard Miss Lisome's
skirts rustle in the same direction. Once more he
seated himself unwilling yet to dissipate by slumber the pleasant thoughts of his betrothed. But he
had taken a different seat; one that was almost in
front of the ample fire-place with its fully exposed
hearth, and from at first looking in a sort of vacant
way before him, he became gradually conscious that
his eyes were resting more particularly on something
that seemed to jut up between the bricks. A sort
of childish curiosity impelled him to examine it;
he did so, finding a very much tarnished little met-
al case; it was partly open and the equally tarnished crucifix of the tiny rosary that nestled within

hung quite outside of the case. Surprise that so Catholic an emblem should be found in that room exceeded for a moment his curiosity to examine it closely; then it flashed upon him how there had been Catholic occupants of that room, and he held the case directly under the light and polished it with his handkerchief. The name Agnes in tiny letters appeared, and he knew then it was her rosary; he raised it in rapture to his lips, then put it into one of his inner breast-pockets; he regarded it as a sort of talisman, and he meant to keep it as a precious little secret until after their marriage.

It was well that the curtain of his future veiled from him the time and the circumstances when that rosary should meet the eyes of his betrothed.

Above stairs Deborah was pouring forth with wild gesticulation, and wilder utterance, the awful things her brother had told her, breaking down in the end by a very storm of crying.

Prudence was amazed; amazed at what she had heard, and amazed at Deborah's most unusual conduct; but, accompanying her amazement was a little thrill of thankfulness that her fear produced by Anne's message was utterly unfounded. And, owing to the matrimonial hopes afforded by Kellar's flattery she was not so dismayed at the renewal of Wilbur's suit to Miss Hammond as she would have been some time before. But it was necessary to assume the indignation and sympathy which Deborah evidently expected; so she lifted her eyes and her hands in a sort of righteous horror, and, presuming Miss Wilbur's greatest concern was for the loss of her brother's faith, she said with severe sanctimoniousness:

"His soul, Deborah, his poor, poor misguided soul."

But, to her further astonishment Deborah stopped her tears to answer sharply;

"Don't be a fool, Prudence Liscome, lifting your

hands about his perfideous soul; it's his fortune that he'll lose by marrying that jade— a half million of dollars-oh-o-o-oh!" moaned Deborah.

"I don't understand," replied Miss Liscome, thinking the opportunity a good one to be enlightened about that much quoted fortune. "How does marrying Miss Hammond deprive him of a half million of dollars!"

Deborah was too much enraged and disappointed to care to preserve her mystery any longer so she told in a brief snappish way about her Uncle Derwent's will.

"Dear, dear;" said Miss Liscome, " but it's dreadful. And now you can't go to California, and with the house upset as it is, I don't wonder you're just beside yourself; I'm so sorry for you, dear Deborah."

She leaned forward to accompany her words of condolence with an action of endearment, but Deborah who had always a contempt for such softness, sprang away from her.

"Keep your hands to yourself, Prudence Liscome," she said crossly, "I have no need of being whinnied and coddled by you. Thank Heaven I'm strong-minded enough not to want the ways of other women folks with their kisses and slobbering."

Prudence fell back with a little rise of color betraying itself through her rouge.

"I'd like to have that creature here this minute," pursued Deborah, sitting very erect and squeezing one hand within the other, "I'd fix her beauty; I'd teach her to bring dissension and loss of fortune in to a family—I'd—I'd tear her to pieces!" —the last words were uttered with such a sudden and vehement burst of passion that they fairly frightened Prudence, and she hastily pushed her chair back. And thus Deborah continued her tirades until the dawn glimmered through the windows, varying them only by fits of crying, or by rapidly pacing the room.

Prudence, taught by her recent experience refrained from any attempt at either sympathy, or consolation; but she was solacing herself, however, by thoughts of Mr. Kellar, at one time becoming so absorbed in deciding what she should have for the supper to which she had invited him, that she did not even hear Miss Wilbur when that irate lady addressed her.

"Are you asleep, Prudence Liscome, or are you a stick or a stone?" she shrieked, when for the third time she had spoken to Prudence without receiving a reply. And then she continued while she began to pace the room furiously:

"It seems to me *some* people would be ashamed to be ungrateful in the face of all the friendship that's been shown them in this house; but, that's just the way of women like you, Prudence Liscome," stopping short in her walk.

Prudence, roused to a sense of her position attempted to disclaim the charge, but she was cut short:

"Don't talk to me—if you had any feeling, you'd find a way to help me out of my trouble— you'd think of some means to prevent Sydney making this horrible marriage."

But Prudence was unable to reply to that speech. She could only look with a sort of blank helplessness, at which Deborah disgusted, threw herself on the bed and buried her face in the pillow. Exhausted from her violent bursts of temper, she soon fell asleep, seeing which, Miss Liscome sought the most comfortable easy-chair, nestled within it, and was also speedily slumbering.

XXIX.

KELLAR chuckled when he received Miss Liscome's note of invitation to tea; she had addressed it to Mallaby's office, and it was that gentleman who handed it to Kellar. After his hasty and chuckling perusal of it he threw it to Mallaby to read.

"I told you I should follow her up," he said laughing; "this proves that I have done so."

But Mallaby did not reply, nor did he make any comment when he had finished the note.

"She's so easily flattered and so shallow I shall not have much difficulty in finding out how much she knows," continued Kellar.

But Mallaby with perfect or well-simulated indifference, turned to a packet of letters and began to open them.

Kellar burst into one of his loudest guffaws.

"You're a game one, Mallaby," he said, when his mirth had subsided, "trying to make me think because you've stuck to the answer you gave me last night, that things have lost their terror, or their interest for you. You're a living lie, Mallaby, and you know it. You're as keenly alive this minute to every terror of your position as you have been any time these ten years past, and you're a fool trying to cheat yourself into the belief that you will adhere to your first impulsive decision. You will yield at the last minute, or, if you do not I shall be merciless. Remember, this is *my* game, and it is all, or nothing with me. On your word hangs *my* fortune. Refuse to speak that word, and I shall not show you a shred of pity."

"I have already told you to do your worst," Mal-

laby answered without looking up from the letter he
seemed to be reading, but a word of which he did
not understand, for Kellar's threats alone looked up
to him from the paper.

"I shall wait twelve hours longer for your answer,"
resumed Kellar, " and in that time use your re-
flection to better advantage than you seem to have
so far. This evening I shall give myself the pleasure
of seeing Miss Hammond, and after that, before
I leave the house I shall expect your final decision.
Should it be unfavorable, it will lead me to utilize
against you, even the secret knowledge Miss Liscome appears to hold. So, hoping that you will
digest these interesting, and vital truths, I shall
say, *au revoir*, until evening."

He laughed again and went out whistling.

The digestion of which Kellar spoke had been
going on from the moment that Mallaby had awakened that morning. He had slept barely two hours
after the interview in his room, and then fearing to
meet his ward while the traces of his vigil and his
agitation were so unmistakably visible, he had taken
a hasty breakfast and was half way down town before she had opened her eyes. He had not even
seen Mrs Denner, and being so pre-occupied, he had
forgotten to leave any excuse for not meeting his
ward at breakfast. On his way to his office he
wondered if the date of her marriage were appointed,
and now, when Kellar left him, he wondered about
it again, hoping ardently that it was, and that the
date was an early one. Had he *his* way the marriage should take place that very evening. As Wilbur's wife, she would, she must be safe from the
doom that was surely approaching her guardian.

The thought of her safety nerved him. He bent
to his work at the desk with a courage for any fate,
and thanking God in his heart for the opportune
arrival of Wilbur. Had Wilbur not come, then in-

deed would his resolution not to assent to Kellar's proposal need all his strength to sustain it. Now, trusting that Miss Hammond would be safe, Kellar might do his worst; the answer to his offer should continue to be the firm, honest one it had been at first. Miss Hammond was surprised that her guardian had left no excuse for not meeting her at breakfast; never since she had been at Mrs. Denner's had he failed to join her at that meal, save the occasions on which his business took him from the city; and now to learn from the waitress that he had taken only a cup of coffee, and that, two hours before his wonted breakfast hour, caused her no little anxious conjecture. Her anxiety was increased by Mrs. Denner's remarks made later in the day, when that solicitious woman found an opportunity of speaking privately to Miss Hammond.

"Your guardian's visitor did not leave him, my dear, until it was nearly morning as well as I can calkilate: because feeling as how Mr. Mallaby mightn't think about locking up, I sat in the parlor waiting for his friend to come down. He didn't come down at all as I could see, and I got that tired waiting, I fell asleep. And then you know yourself, the way that blessed man shot off this morning with nothing on his poor stomach but one little cup of coffee. What do you think of it, my dear?"

But Miss Hammond was not disposed to tell her thoughts, and Mrs. Denner having said so much only because she presumed on the young lady's communicativeness of the night before, was disappointed at receiving in reply no more than:

"I suppose he had some engagement which took him away this morning, and the hour was such an early one he had little appetite."

"Fudge!" thought Mrs. Denner, though she was careful to give no voice to the thought, and then, to impress upon Miss Hammond that she had no fur-

ther curiosity in the matter, she left the room without saying anything more.

Her remarks however *had* caused Miss Hammond
to become exceedingly anxious; she thought of the
flashy appearance of her guardian's strange visitor,
and that thought in connection with his visit which
Mrs. Denner said had been so protracted, together
with her guardian's early and mysterious departure
that morning, all seemed like links in a chain of
curious and perhaps not creditable proceedings.

Her former suspicion and distrust of him returned;
the feelings with which a few months before she had
learned his inability to defray her expense to Italy,
the doubt so often engendered by his own shy, timid
manner, all came upon her now with new force and
pain. And still, singularly enough there blent with
these unhappy feelings a sort of pity for him that
was almost akin to affection; it accompanied every
emotion of distrust and it seemed almost to reproach
her for her doubts. She sought relief by turning her
conflicting thoughts to Wilbur, but even then, through
their happy tenor, there seemed to run an undercurrent of inexplicable fear and pain. She was almost
glad that it was one of the days on which she gave a
number of music lessons, hailing the occupation as of
beneficial distraction. But, even through the five
finger exercises of the most elementary of her pupils
there seemed to run a perpetual reminder of her
own vague and mysterious uneasiness.

When she met her guardian at dinner in the evening, he did not refer to any of the events that had so
disturbed her, and though she endeavored to watch
him without being herself observed, she saw nothing
in his manner or appearance to indicate any secret anxiety upon his part; there seemed to be even less
traces of care and concern than she had seen on frequent other occasions, and she felt a momentary relief. Thinking that he might after dinner refer to

his hurried departure of the morning, and determined if he did not do so to make some playful allusion to it herself, she was somewhat anxious for the conclusion of the meal. But just as they rose from the table Wilbur's card was presented. Mallaby smiled as he saw it, a heartier smile than perhaps Agnes had ever seen him wear before.

"Of course you will go to him immediately," he said, continuing still to wear his hearty smile, and even actually looking at her, as he opened the door of the dining-room for her to pass out.

"Of course I shall," she replied laughing back at him as she passed into the hall and then she turned again to say:

"And you—are you not going to see him?"

"After a little," he answered, and then he closed the door, and followed her to the stair.

"One moment," he said, as she was about to ascend. "Does Mr. Wilbur wish the marriage to take place soon?"

"He had become suddenly flurried, and he had spoken with unusual quickness as if it were only by speaking very quickly he had the courage to speak at all.

She had turned, surprised at being detained, but she was still more surprised at his question and the manner that accompanied it, but, she did not suspect that his inquiry was prompted by any other motive than a sort of kindly curiosity to know how soon he must yield his care of her, and she answered with a blush:

"He asked me to let it take place within a fortnight, but—"

He interrupted her:

"That will do; that was all I wanted to know."

The genial smile had broken out all over his face again, and the flurry had gone from his manner. He had no wish to hear her buts; for he felt confident that such constant and ardent love as Wilbur had shown, together with his determination of which Mallaby felt equally confident must break down any barrier of objections she might interpose. The fact of Wilbur's present early visit was a proof of the impatience which would certainly break no delay, and though on the evening before with becoming maidenily bashfulness she might have hesitated to assent to so early a date, he was sure that on this evening Wilbur would win her consent. And to prevent her speaking further he turned back to the dining-room.

She lingered on the stair, wondering at the delight her guardian seemed to manifest at her answer. Could it be, that she was still a financial care to him and that he was glad at the prospect of so soon being freed from the burden? That thought caused the blush called up by his question to mantle her whole face. She almost regretted not having assented to Wilbur's wish; even yet she might do so but for the letter mailed that very morning to Florence. With a sigh that her happiness should seem to be so alloyed she turned and went up to the parlor to Wilbur, feeling the moment she entered his presence a sense of rest and protection that made her after the manner of her sex, feel, in her very relief, like bursting into tears. His lover's eyes were sharp and he detected the slight quivering of her lips, and other signs about her face which manifested inward trouble.

"What is it?" he said, refusing to relinquish her hands and looking down into her eyes with a very anxious earnestness in his own.

She refused to answer, and only laughed at his questions declaring that his imagination must be playing some very strange tricks, and when he found that she *would* not reply, he said with a tone of entreaty:

" Recall your decision to put off our marriage, Agnes. As my wife, whatever little annoyances you may be subjected to now, must cease. You will, you must be *quite* happy then."

''I cannot recall my decision for my letter went to Florence this morning," she answered with forced gayety, and then to end entreaties that because of her own longing to respond to them, were agonizing, she drew him to the corner they had occupied the night before, and began to talk on all sorts of topics. Her very wilfulness seemed to be an additional charm and he listened, more intent upon watching the play of her animated features than upon his answers. He regretted having been cajoled into an assent to her wish the night before, and he ardently hoped that Florence's answer would say she could not come; in that case the marriage could and *must* take place immediately that her reply was received.

"Your sister is glad to have you home, is she not?" asked Agnes, driving in her random way upon the very topic on which she felt somehow that Sydney might be anxious to say least; to her surprise however, Sydney manifested more interest in that topic than he had done in any of the others. He roused himself and answered with a smile:

"I fear her joy has turned to gall and wormwood—I told her everything last night: my conversion to the Catholic Faith, the renewal of our engagement; it caused a sort of tableau, and the result is that I have taken all my meals out to-day, and this evening, I mailed to her a note stating that I have engaged board at a hotel, and shall continue to do so until she promises not to refer in any, but the most amicable way to what has occurred. I suppose her disappointment was the greater that she expected to go West with me, and in anticipation of our removal had the house completely torn up."

The hall-door bell had rung while he was talking,

and as he finished, they heard the door opened, and immediately after a voice which Miss Hammond instantly recognized as Kellar's inquiring for Mr. Mallaby.

Wilbur looking at her saw her start slightly and a momentary look of pain came into her face; then, as if conscious that he had observed her, and desirous of obliterating the impression her start and look might have caused, she began to question him about Deborah; to question and in the same breath to pity her.

"Was she very angry? well it *was* a dreadful blow to one of her strong religious prejudices. Was she much incensed against me? I don't blame her, poor creature; it must have seemed very hard. Did she say cruel things to you, Sydney? but of course you were very patient with her."

And thus she continued, while Wilbur finding that she did not wait long enough for him to answer, was content to let her continue; it gave him an opportunity to think. He too felt that he had heard that voice before, but he could not recall where, and now, linking the troubled signs that Agnes had shown on her entrance to the parlor with her too evident desire to conceal by volubility the agitation of the present moment, he was confident there was some secret unhappiness, or unpleasantness in her life. He ascribed to her maidenly delicacy her unwillingness to confide in him, but it made him all the more eager to extend to her speedily a husband's protection. Urged by the warmth of his feelings he was about to make another appeal to her to yield to his wish regarding the time of the marriage, when the door opened and Mallaby and Kellar entered.

The sight of the latter sent an unaccountable chill through Wilbur, and with a sort of disgust he recognized now to whom belonged the voice he thought he had heard before.

Kellar seemed to be more flashily dressed than ever; the bosom of his shirt sparkled with diamond studs; a massive watch-chain adorned with almost as many charms as it had links, stretched more than half way across his breast, and on the little finger of each hand scintillated an immense opal. He came in with the same confident, patronizing air that had both surprised and repelled Wilbur, on the first occasion of their meeting, and that was now in marked and strange contrast to the half-drooping, hesitating manner of Mallaby

Miss Hammond, of course, did not rise at the introduction somewhat tremulously given by her guardian, and the slight inclination of her head betrayed a hauteaur and dignity that augured ill for her favorable impression of Mr. Kellar. But that gentleman with supreme assurance bowed very low, making at the same time a complimentary reference to their accidental meeting on the evening before ; then he turned and saluted Wilbur with a familiarity that astonished Agnes, and irritated the gentleman into saying with stinging curtness:

"I met Mr. Kellar yesterday in Mr. Mallaby's office. We were not introduced."

"What a stickler for the proprieties," said Kellar, with one of his guffaws, "but you are none the worse for it, Mr. Wilbur, only you must make allowance for an old stager like me. When a man has passed a good part of his life in the company of rough miners he isn't supposed to know much about the proprieties. But, introduce us now, Mallaby; comply with all the forms of etiquette. You used to be good at that sort of thing — don't you remember, in the *old* times?"

The emphasis on the old was both marked and peculiar, and for the moment of its utterance he looked full and significantly into Mallaby's face, but

Mallaby's eyes had dropped. Then Kellar turned back to Wilbur.

"I told you yesterday, Mallaby and I were old friends—so old, our friendship dates before Mr. Mallaby's ward here—with a bow to Miss Hammond—"was born, It was the remembrance of that old friendship that brought me back to New York a month ago—the longing to see my old friend, Matthias Mallaby. Come now, introduce us."

Mallaby seemed to brace himself, and he said, trying to speak playfully, but betraying despite his effort, the evidence of feeling that caused Agnes new wonder and pain, and that caused Wilbur an astonishment amounting almost to resentment against Mallaby himself.

"Your own introduction has been so complete, I don't know what there is left for me to say. I can only repeat that you are Nathan Kellar; that I knew you first, a great many years ago. Mr. Kellar, Mr. Wilbur." And then Mallaby fell back to a chair beside Agnes, and he seemed to drop at once into his first half-shy, half-embarrassed manner.

Wilbur had bowed with freezing dignity to the introduction, but it had no effect on Kellar. He drew a chair into the centre of the little circle, and began a sort of monopoly of the conversation. No one seemed to care either to stop him or to answer him. They appeared to listen, but it was with such divers and antagonistic feelings to the speaker in the breasts of each, that their silence was not complimentary.

Yet, Kellar talked well; and introducing subjects with which he was thoroughly familiar, he spoke with a flow and elegance of language that could only come from early and considerable culture. He seemed to know every item of interest connected with mining, and to be an authority on the causes which militated against the successful working of a lode._ He developed plans of syndicate in mining interests that caused Mallaby to raise his head suddenly, and to flush with new floridness, and he depicted and deplored the workings of mining monopolies, with an appearance of severe rectitude.

The boarders who according to their custom had dropped into the parlor after dinner, stopped their own conversation to catch the fragments of this speaker's interesting remarks. Sometimes, he pitched his voice a little higher as if in forgetfulness, and then there was a quiet and sort of sly drawing of chairs nearer to the party in the corner.

Wilbur, though sometimes interested in spite of himself, was still secretly chafing at it all; he was disappointed and angry at having his visit to his betrothed so interrupted, and he was annoyed that she should be introduced to Kellar. He was even indignant at Mallaby for having introduced her, and he became more determined to use every means in his power to hasten his marriage, when with a husband's right he could remove Agnes from all the influences by which she was now surrounded. Mallaby was only her guardian; surely, her husband would have the right to remove her entirely even from him.

Agnes owing to her dislike for Kellar, and her uneasiness regarding her guardian, was hardly interested at all; and her eyes more frequently turned to the drooping figure at her side, than to the speaker, or even to Wilbur. She wanted to feel indignant at Mallaby for having such a man for a friend, and for introducing him to the little home circle, but, up with her indignation there sprang a most inexplicable pity for Mallaby himself; and while she seemed to listen politely to Kellar's well-turned and fluent sentences, she was mentally questioning the source of her strange compassion for her guardian. She could assign no cause other than her gratitude for the ed-

ncation he had given her : and yet, did she fully believe the statement he had made regarding that, or
was there not still in her heart a doubt of his honesty?
Agonized by her conflicting emotions she turned
involuntarily, and took a longer and more searching
look at Mallaby. As if he felt the gaze, he
lifted his head suddenly and looked full into her eyes.

Had he read in her face the emotions which in that
involuntary moment she had hardly repressed, that
he should flash upon her an answering glance com-
bining at once pain, tenderness, pleading and reproach; and for the instant that it lasted, it so changed the whole expression of his face, that Agnes visibly started.

Her start drew upon her the attention of Kellar
who stopped short in his account of the wonders of
a salt mine, to ask her if she had been affected by
anything he had said.

"Oh no!" she answered hurriedly, and blushing
like one detected in some guilty act. And then her
eyes met Wilbur's fixed upon her in pained surprise;
he had observed both her look, and the one with
which Mallaby had responded to it, but the impression made by the latter was in a day, or two, to be
singularly, and most unhappily revived.

It was a relief when Kellar at length seemed to
arrive at the end of his topic, and he rose to go.
There was no pretence of asking him to prolong his
call, nor regret at his comparatively early departure;
nor was there a hint at an invitation to repeat his
visit. Both Wilbur and Miss Hammond said good-
night coldly, and Mallaby accompanied him from
the parlor.

In the hall Kellar lingered, a self-satisfied smile
upon his lips. Seeing no disposition on the part of
Mallaby to speak, he said somewhat curtly:

"Shall we go to your room for that answer? The
utmost limit of the time I gave you is reached."

"It is not necessary to go to my room. I can give you your answer now, here—the answer that I gave you before—the answer that any honest man *must* give—No!"—

And Mallaby drew himself erect, and looked at Kellar with a steadiness and fearlessness of mien that surprised and exasperated that gentleman.

"You are prepared to accept the consequences," he sneered, every vestige of his wonted affability gone, and its place taken by a savage aspect.

"I am prepaerd for the worst that you can inflict," replied Mallaby, still maintaining his firm mien.

"Wait till the grip of my worst closes on you, Mallaby," was the hissing retort, and then Kellar laughed contemptuously, and strode to the door; Mallaby followed, but before he could overtake him, Kellar had opened the door, slammed it behind him, and descended the stoop. Then, Mallaby's fearless mien deserted him; he seemed suddenly to collapse into a cowed, and miserable creature, and it was well there were none of the curious boarders about or there would have been strange comments on his drooping figure, and the painful, heavy way he ascended to his room.

One hope alone nerved him; the hope of his ward's early marriage. Did it take place in a fortnight, as Wilbur desired, no shadow for his doom might fall upon her; unless, indeed, Kellar, to make his vengeance more malicious should traitorously unburden himself to Wilbur. Mallaby groaned. What in that case would be Wilbur's course of action? what must be his own? Could he longer keep his pledge to the dead? But, surely in that event, Wilbur's magnanimity would show itself—his ardent love for Agnes would surmount even the horror of her guardian's doom—he would save, he would protect her, and somewhat assured Mallaby lifted his head from his breast, wiped the perspiration from his face and breathed a little more freely. But he was restless, and he was so anxious for the termination of Wilbur's visit in order to learn if there had been a definite date set for the wedding, that he kept constantly wandering from his room to the hall.

On the lovers in the parlor there seemed to have fallen a sort of shadow; it evinced itself in the silence which was maintained on the departure of Mallaby and his visitor. Wilbur felt that it was his right to have some confidence from Agnes; a revelation at least of the impression made upon her by Kellar, and how she regarded the seeming intimacy of her guardian with him. Agnes waited for Wilbur to speak—she had a vague misgiving that he was displeased, but she had not the courage to probe his displeasure, still less could she bring herself to a revelation of her own conflicting thoughts about Mallaby. And thus they sat for a full quarter of an hour, Wilbur looking fixedly and gravely at his betrothed, and she at intervals shyly raising her eyes for an instant to his face, but neither saying a word. Her silence angered him at length, and he suddenly rose to go. Even then she did not speak; a lump which rose in her throat at this seeming unkindness on his part, prevented her, and proudly restraining her tears, she accompanied him to the parlor-door, and there extended her hand.

"Good-night," he said, his voice softening, though he had striven hard to keep it stern.

"Good-night," she quiveringly replied, without raising her head, and the effort to speak, sending the tears with a rush to her eyes, a drop fell upon his hand. That completed the softening of his feelings, and to escape the curious stares of a couple of the boarders who still remained in the parlor, he drew her into the hall, closing the parlor-door behind them; then he said very gravely but at the same time with great tenderness:

"Now tell me what is the matter, Agnes."

She looked up trying to smile through her tears.

"You seemed displeased."

"So I was at your want of frankness; surely I have a right to your confidence."

"My confidence," she still tried to smile though she was inwardly as disturbed as ever, for that same mysterious compassion for Mallaby strongly checked her impulse to unburden herself regarding her guardian. The unburdening must in some measure reflect upon Mallaby, and perhaps cause Wilbur to be unpleasantly affected to him. So she only continued to smile in a sort of troubled way, and to repeat:

"I have no confidence to give."

Wilbur began to be a little bit provoked; he fancied her firmness and her reserve were entirely too unfeminine, and that with all his admiration of and love for her, she lacked the pliant qualities which as *his* wife she must, and ought to possess. But, as he continued to look at her, he again softened, and he said with more tenderness than he had first spoken:

"Perhaps I am hasty, Agnes, but I feel you have something on your mind which I ought to know. However, when you have given me the dearest right of all you will I am sure, have no reserves from me. Make me happy now by hastening that time. Write, or permit me to write to Florence telling her that we have decided not to wait, and let our marriage take place as I proposed first, within a fortnight."

"I could not do that, having written to Florence as I did; it would be positively unkind when I owe so much to the dear girl. Do be more patient, Sydney: the time will pass quickly."

He saw that it was useless to plead longer, and though secretly he was still uneasy and dissatisfied, he was anxious not to part from her in any seeming displeasure.

"I am going a little way out of the city to-mor-

row," he said, speaking in his kindest tone, "in order to confer with a party about the sale of some
property, and, I doubt my return before a late hour
to-morrow night; so I may not see you until the
next day, when I shall call immediately that I get
back."

"You forget, I have told you that I give music
lessons; I shall not be at home until late in the
afternoon."

Wilbur ground his teeth in the effort to suppress a
savage exclamation. Then he said with something
like temper:

"Have I not rights as well as those music scholars
of yours? Cancel your engagements at once, Agnes.
Surely it is not necessary for you to continue to teach
music up to the very day of your marriage."

"Not exactly necessary for the sake of my purse
but very necessary for the sake of my conscience:
those people have paid me in advance, and even to
refund the money to them would be hardly the correct thing so long as I have the leisure to fulfill my
part of the contract."

"You are the same incorrigible puritan that you
were a year ago," retorted Wilbur half playfully,
but still with unmistakable evidence of being annoyed. Her conscientious firmness excited his admiration, but, at the same time it irritated him, and
made him more fiercely eager for the day when it
would be his right to command her.

They parted at length, and Agnes ascending
slowly to her room was confronted on the stair by
Mallaby.

"Is the date of your wedding fixed?" he asked
abruptly.

Surprise at his abrupt question, and his excited
manner of asking it, kept her silent for a moment.
Then she answered with mingled astonishment and
displeasure in her tones:

"We are going to wait to hear from Miss Wilbur; if she can come to be present at our wedding it will be deferred."

"Good God!"

And Mallaby seemed to fall against the baluster, his hands hanging helpless at his side and his head dropping upon his breast.

Indignation mastered Miss Hammond. "Is it such a disappointment to have the care of me so long? Am I so great a burden?"

He saw with fresh sinking of his own heart the mistaken impression she had received, and obeying the first impulse that came to him, he put out his hands in a sort of appealing manner while he said piteously:

"Not that; it could never be that!"

"What then is it?"

Her indignation was suddenly modified, for he presented such an utterly dejected appearance. He felt that he must give her some explanation if he would not have her divine the actual truth, and he began, the desultory, whispered manner of his sentences telling more of his inward agitation than did the words themselves.

"I expect a reverse—a reverse of fortune—a great reverse—it may come in a few days—it will take from me everything except the consciousness of my own rectitude," raising his head and straightening himself for an instant, as if the action arose from some involuntary impulse of his manhood — "and I thought—I hoped to witness your marriage before that would happen. Were you provided for I could go away to bear alone my losses and my poverty."

Not once had his voice risen above the lowly whisper that obliged her to bend her head to catch his words, but it was such a painful, sad voice that her own heart seemed to beat in very response to it. The

touching gentleness that was so potent on other occasions was irresistible on this, and for the moment
every doubt of him vanished; to her he was what he
appeared to be, a most touching object of compassion.

"And you would want me to forget what I owe to
you," she said, impulsively and forgetting to lower
her voice until a warning motion from him recalled
her, "surely in the case of your poverty, it would be
part of *my* duty not at least to desert you. I doubt
my right to marry if my marriage is to prevent my
helping you."

"Don't talk so wildly," he whispered, a sort of dismay coming upon him that she should thus interpret his words, and in order to take her thoughts out
of their undesirable channel, he continued:

"I have been too premature in telling you what I
have for there is still a hope that things may not be
so bad. And I would not have told you at all but
I could not bear to have you think you were a burden," he spoke with the same touching sadness of
manner he had used at first.

Then he seemed desirous to leave her, and he turned to continue his ascent of the stair.

But, so many questions crowded upon her mind she
put out her hand instinctively and held him, and yet
she did not know quite how, or what to ask; she only
knew that she must ask something to quiet the hot
turmoil of her own thoughts.

"Has this Mr. Kellar, anything to do with the reverse you expect?" she blurted out at length, when
he had waited more than a minute for her to speak.

He could not say "no" without telling an absolute
lie, and more than that he felt that Miss Hammond's
own observation of his manner with Kellar, would
cause her to doubt such a reply.

So he answered briefly "yes," and turned once
more to leave her.

But, she must know more, and again she caught him saying with a sort of breathlessness:

"What is the reverse you expect—who is Mr. Kellar? what has he to do with you?"

Whatever replies he might have made to her rapidly-uttered questions were stopped before he could even form them, for they both heard Mrs. Denner's voice in the hall below; and hearing it in a manner which seemed to herald her presence speedily in their company, Mallaby gently detaching himself from the grasp of his ward, whispered:

"Good-night, my dear," and hurried to his room.

Miss Hammond went to her chamber but in a frame of mind that prevented sleep until it was nearly dawn.

XXX.

Miss Liscome was in a fever of delighted expectation.   Mr. Kellar had written his acceptance of
her invitation to tea, and she was so eager for the
hour to arrive, and so full of preparation for it, that
she had hardly time to respond to a summons from
Deborah which came that same morning.   But, the
summons was imperative, and, Prudence though
rendered bolder than usual owing to the prospect of
speedily having a suitor, hardly dared to disobey it.
   So she caught up her bonnet and tripped across,
determined however, to make her call very brief.
   Deborah had not seen her brother since the night
of his dreadful revelations; he had left the house on
the succeeding morning, before either his sister or
Miss Liscome had awakened from their slumber of
exhaustion, and he had not returned since; nor did
she receive any message from him until this letter
that came by post, and which was brief, curt and
peremptory.   She held it out to Prudence.
   "He thinks he's going to subdue *me*," she said,
her little black eyes flashing, "but I'll show him
that I can bite as well as bark. I'll yield to no such
terms as he dictates—I'll say just what I want to say
and what I ought to say, about his outrageous conduct; and if he won't hear it here in this house, I'll
go to the hotel where he says I'm to send my answer to. I'll be a thorn in his flesh for depriving me
of *my* share in that half million. I am going there
now to find him, and I want you to accompany me,
Prudence."
   Miss Liscome was a little bit aghast; she had neither the time, nor the inclination for such a jaunt, and

she protested mildly, alleging her invalid sister's need of her at home.

"Bosh!" replied Deborah, contemptuously, and proceeding to array herself in her out-door garments, as if there were no notice to be taken of Miss Liscome's objection.

"But I can't go—I really cannot—," protested Prudence, nerved to desperation when she thought of how many hours she might be detained with Miss Wilbur and all there was yet to be done in preparation for the evening.

"And why not, pray," snapped Deborah, turning from the dressing-case in front of which she had been tying her bonnet strings, and fixing her eyes piercingly on her visitor as if the latter had as yet given no reason for refusing to go.

Miss Liscome quailed: no amount of courage could sustain her against such a look; it seemed to go through her, and to ferret her most secret thoughts.

"Don't tell me again it's your sister," continued Miss Wilbur—"your concern for her is too sudden. It's something else—out with it, Prudence Liscome."

Prudence fairly trembled, and a blush was showing through her rouge."

Deborah waited, both of her hands still up to her throat grasping her bonnet strings and her eyes fairly flaming into Miss Liscome's face.

"My sister *is* sick as you know," tremblingly began Prudence, and with a sort of injured, reproachful air, "and we are to have company to tea, and I must go home to prepare for that."

"*Company for tea,*" repeated Deborah while a sudden light flashed upon her mind.

"Is the company that friend who you were so secret about—that man Kellar, that called here?"

Miss Liscome hung her head in affected bashfulness, and lisped:

"Yes."

"Umph!" said Deborah removing her hands from her bonnet strings, and fairly glaring at Prudence, "and you're going to try to catch *him*, are you? If he has the proper amount of sense he'll not be caught by the bait of an old maid like you. But go; Prudence Liscome you are no more capable of gratitude than a pig's ear is capable of being made into a silk purse. Faugh, I hate such people."

And hastily finishing the tying of her bonnet strings she swept past Miss Liscome who was too crestfallen to utter a word, and in another moment she had left the house, giving the hall-door a bang behind her that made Prudence shiver.

There was nothing for Miss Liscome to do but depart also, and that she did, but in rather a slow, and dejected manner, meditating as she crossed to her own house, whether she should ever be able to reinstate herself in Deborah's favor, and if she should care very much should she not do so, since she had Mr. Kellar's friendship. In that thought was a balm for everything, and she continued to solace herself by pleasant imaginations of his approaching visit. It was a little alloy in her anticipated bliss that he must meet at the tea-table her sister, her brother-in-law, and her nephew, but all three had been instructed not to inflict their presence afterward upon the visitor, so that she looked forward to an uninterrupted tete-a-tete in the parlor.

Mr. Kellar arrived punctually at the hour named in his invitation. His dress was in the flashy style of the preceding evening, but that with Miss Liscome passed for a mark of his means, and it was with very conscious pride that she introduced him to her relatives.

His gushing response to the introduction ravished Miss Liscome, and won Mallary and his wife; the nephew, Malliflower Mallary, was too much absorbed in either contemplating his exquisite feet, or looking for specks on his clothes, to seem to pay at first much attention to the guest.

At the table, Kellar displayed his conversational gifts. The little family speedily felt that it was in the presence of a very superior man, and each member was silent from awe and wonder. Prudence was so nervous from pride and delight that she could hardly steady her hand to pour out the tea, and when she asked Mr. Kellar if he would have more, her voice trembled.

"I must take more," responded Kellar, "if it were only for the charm of receiving it from so fair a hand, Madame."

At which speech Prudence hung her head and simpered some inaudible reply.

"You can hardly form an idea," resumed Kellar, as he received his second cup of tea from the hand he had so fulsomely praised, and looking round with a benign air, "of the pleasure it is to be with such a home circle as this, and to me who have been the greater part of my life a camper out, it is particularly refreshing. I was talking about it to my friend Mallaby—Matthias Mallaby—to whom I owe the exquisite privilege of knowing you, Miss Liscome," bowing to the lady.

Malliflower Mallary straightened himself at the mention of Mallaby's name, and he fixed his pale blue eyes on the speaker with an interest he had not shown before.

Kellar noticed the sudden attention and wondered a little.

"I was telling Mallaby about it," he continued "about the pleasure I expected to have this evening, and—"

"I say boss, you're talking about Mr. Mallaby, ain't you?" interrupted Miss Liscome's nephew, to the mortified astonishment of his aunt, and the exceeding surprise of everybody else.

"Yes, young gentleman, I was talking about Mr. Mallaby," and Kellar bent toward the youth with a very fatherly air.

"And you prefaced your remarks by saying he was your friend."

"I certainly did, my young friend," responded Kellar in greater astonishment than ever, while Miss Liscome in her effort to extend her foot far enough to give him a touch with it nearly slipped off her chair. But young Mallary according to the peculiar formation of his mind, was not going to be turned from the one idea he had suddenly caught by any warning look or motion from his aunt. He did not even once turn his eyes to her, as he continued:

"As he's your friend does he get angry and blow out at you if you preface your remarks?"

Kellar began to think the youth slightly demented, but he had no objection to humor him, and he answered with an increase of paternal benignity in his manner:

"No, my young friend, he does not."

"Well, he roared at me when I prefaced my remarks."

Miss Liscome in her horrified emotions upset the teapot.

Mr. Kellar began to think there was some method in the youth's madness; his apparent insane remarks were evident cause of his aunt's agitation, for she so far forgot herself as to openly glower at her nephew, and to answer half angrily to her sister's exclamations of dismay at the rivulet of tea on the snowy cloth:

"There is no need, Precilla, for *you* to trouble yourself."

"And was there an occasion, my dear young friend, on which *you* experienced Mr. Mallaby's brusqueness?"

Kellar's voice was as soft and persuasive as a woman's, and he leaned toward Malliflower as if he were utterly oblivious of the accident at the other end of the table. Perhaps it was that seeming obliviousness on his part that made Miss Liscome so bold as to glower at Malliflower, and to show her temper a little to her sister. She did not dream that the visitor was reading her as surely as he was probing her nephew.

Young Malliflower was assured and emboldened; it was rarely that he was the object of so much attention and deference, for his propensity for prefacing his remarks together with his love of showy dress made him the butt of his companions in business and not infrequently an object of ridicule even to his most friendly acquaintances; now under the genial influences of Kellar's manner his wonted habit of prefacing every account that he was called upon to give came up with renewed intensity.

He straightened himself in his chair and dropped his knife and fork in order to place his long, bony hands on his knees: he could talk better when he had thus spread himself:

"Well, boss, I'll just preface my remarks, by stating to you that my motives on that occasion were entirely good, entirely good, sir, which goes to prove that I had the right to preface my remarks, and let me just here further preface my remarks by telling you that it was with no idle curiosity I at that time prefaced my remarks to Mr. Mallaby."

Kellar began to wonder when the preface would end; and Miss Liscome was wrought up to a fever-heat of fear and anger. Her sister and her brother-in-law were too much accustomed to Malliflower's idiotic oddities, to be amused at him, and not knowing the little secret underplot which agitated the breasts of others at the table, they were not even curious.

"You are talking nonsensically, Malliflower, I

am sure Mr. Kellar must think so," burst from
Prudence who could endure the situation no longer.

But Kellar was not going to be baffled.

The youth might have useful information under-
lying his many prefaces, and his questioner determined that he should have ample opportunity to impart it.

"I assure you Miss Liscome, that I am charmed.
Your nephew is an extraordinary young man; so
novel and entertaining. Please do not hint at the
discontinuance of his conversation."

And Kellar smiled fascinatingly at Miss Liscome.
Then he turned back to the nephew.

"Go on, my dear young man; you were saying that
you had prefaced your remarks to Mr. Mallaby by—"

Young Mallaby straightened himself more than he
had done before, and fondled his knees with his bony
hands; never was he so full of importance: the interest and attention of this elegant and cultured
gentleman caused him to swell with conceit.

"I tell you, boss," he said, turning in his chair
so that his back was squarely presented to his
aunt, "but let me just preface my remarks by saying
that a letter came to me one day, and Aunt Prudence
found out that it wasn't for me, but for that friend
of yours, Mr. Mallaby."

"How did she find out? did she read the letter?"
asked Kellar so softly, that his words were almost
whispered, but they sounded as loud as if they were
shouted to dismayed and horrified Miss Liscome,

"Read it, you bet, boss, she read it," answered
the youth betrayed by the consciousness of his importance and his self-confidence into an unusual
vivacity of manner.

"She read it, and I read it, and we all read it, and
I'll just preface my remarks by saying it was a very
odd letter —it was all about a man named Jared."

Not a muscle of Kellar's face moved, nor did he make the slightest change in his attitude. He did not even raise his eyes to Miss Liscome. She was ready to faint from confusion, anger, and fear, and the natural color in her cheeks was brighter than any rouge she had ever put on. Her nephew continued:

"I'll just preface my remarks again by saying that I couldn't think what I had to do with any one named Jared, but Aunt Prudence found out that it was for that Mallaby, and she made me take it to him."

"And was that the occasion on which my friend, Mr. Mallaby, treated you so gruffly?" asked Kellar in the same persuasively low, gentle voice.

"That was the occasion, boss; I just went to preface my remarks so that he'd understand what I wanted to see him about, but he wouldn't listen, and I had to give him the letter before I had time to tell him anything."

"And did he not thank you, my dear young friend, for the time and the trouble you had taken? and was he not glad to get his letter?"

Kellar's voice was tender as a lover's.

"No; he did not thank me. He took the letter and read it, trembling all the time as if he had the ague, and looking at me when he got through, as if I was a wild animal that he'd like to shoot. And then he went into his office."

Kellar turned upon Miss Liscome fairly beaming upon her.

"My dear Miss Liscome, may I trouble you for another cup of that delicious tea?"

He extended his cup as if he did not know that the tea had been spilled, and that the teapot had not been replenished.

Prudence took the cup without well knowing what she should do with it, being assured there was no more tea on the table, and in doubt of the temper of the kitchen fire. Probably the overworked domestic as it was a warm evening had let it go out. She could not risk a truthful answer by summoning the girl, and with a brief excuse for leaving the table she went herself to the kitchen.

The interval of absence was somewhat of a relief to her; it enabled her to think for a moment; but, her thoughts were almost sickening, and as she waited while the girl endeavored to rekindle the fire sufficiently to boil some water, she was bitterly reproaching herself for not having taken some means to prevent her nephew's revelation; but she never dreamed of *his* reference to the letter; indeed, she had not thought him intelligent enough to attach any importance to the matter, nor even to remember the fact that a letter had come to him which had been intended for Mallaby. That Kellar knew now to what her secret knowledge of Jared amounted, she was quite convinced, her conviction nothing shaken by the composure he had maintained during her nephew's account.

In her vain and shallow-mindedness, she feared the effect of the disclosure upon Kellar's friendship for herself, and she was more disappointed and chagrined at that, than at being detected in any untruthfulness. She tried to think of some plausible explanation, of her unwarrantable use of the name of Jared, but her efforts served only to make her thoughts more intricate and distressing, and in her perplexity she poured half-boiled water on the already well-drained tea-leaves having utterly forgotten to put more tea into the vessel.

But Kellar heroically drank the watery stuff, declaring to Miss Liscome's apology when she saw how absolutely colorless it poured out, that it was more for the pleasure of being helped again by her fair hand he had asked for another cup. And the silly creature believed him, and in her pleasure at his flattery she became less fearful of the conseq:ences of her nephew's garrulousness, and consequently less agitated.

Mr. and Mrs. Mallary, simple people that they were, being little more than older editions of their ridiculous son, saw nothing in what was going on about them, to arouse either their wonder or suspicion, and remembering as they rose from the table, Miss Liscome's instructions, they managed to leave the visitor's presence without even the form of an excuse. Mallary having been encouraged by Kellar, to feel as it were, the importance of his own powers, was little disposed to do likewise, and he lingered, even following his aunt and her guest to the parlor-door.

"Mr. Kellar will excuse you, Malliflower, " said his aunt with exterior sweetness, but an interior exasperation that made her voice tremble a little.

And Kellar feeling there was no more important information to be gained from the youth, hastily interposed:

"Certainly, my dear young friend, I know how precious are the evening hours to youths like yourself. By all means leave us. Your charming and estimable aunt will entertain me."

While he was speaking Prudence had partially withdrawn into the parlor, and directly that Kellar followed her, she shut the door unceremoniously upon her nephew.

The visitor's continued flattery increased her confidence; in her egregious vanity she felt that his regard for her was great enough to condone any fault, and she turned to him with an air meant to be arch and coy, but which was only ridiculous.

He understood it all, and the smile with which he beamed upon her was but the outcome of his secret mirth and satisfaction.

"I congratulate you, my dear Miss Liscome," he

said, pretending to survey her with an air of admiration, "I congratulate you," he repeated, "on the possession of qualities most rare in your sex. You have shown a masculine judgment, penetration, and wit, in your use of the contents of that letter for Mr. Mallaby which fell by mistake into your nephew's hands. No doubt, you had read Mr. Mallaby's odd, timorous character, and could not resist amusing yourself a little with it."

"Oh, Mr. Kellar," she remonstrated, lifting her hands to him in a sort of deprecating way, and affecting to be exceedingly abashed.

He caught her hands and held them, doing so without difficulty for she did not make the least motion to withdraw them, while he resumed:

"My friend Mallaby is a little morbid on a subject connected with this name Jared, which you have used with such admirable cleverness, my dear Miss Liscome; just a little morbid, but his morbidness is of such a nature, that I fear for the happiness of your friends, the Wilburs, should Mr. Wilbur marry Mr. Mallaby's ward, Miss Hammond."

In her astonishment Prudence actually jerked her hands from their captors.

"My goodness! Mr. Kellar," she exclaimed, "you don't say so."

"I do say so, Miss Liscome, and stick to the fact after saying so."

"And it was only this morning I left Deborah, Sydney's sister, you know, in a dreadful state of anger, because, I would not accompany her to see him in order to give him a talking to about his marriage. Deborah was in such a rage about it when he told her, that he has left his home these three days past and is boarding at some hotel."

It was Kellar's turn to be surprised; he had not dreamed that Miss Hammond's engagement would cause a rupture between Wilbur and his sister.

"I intended to call on Mr. Wilbur some time to-morrow, and thought of getting you, my dear Miss Liscome, to arrange with him the time of an interview with me. I think I have some things to tell him which may make him hesitate to marry Miss Hammond."

Prudence was trembling from sheer delight. Here was a prospect at once of dashing the happiness of the hated Miss Hammond, and of making her own peace with Deborah.

"I shall arrange it all with Sydney's sister," she said, "I shall see her this very night, and she, I know will contrive an early interview for you."

"Thank you, my dear, dear Miss Liscome, and may I rely upon you to get me early word to-morrow? I must see Mr. Wilbur to-morrow."

"Yes; I shall get Deborah to telegraph to Mr. Mallaby's office for you."

"No; not to Mallaby's office: send it to this address," giving her a card with the number of his boarding-house upon it.

He staid a full hour after that, pretending to grow both communicative, and confidential, and winning with little difficulty the whole story of Miss Liscome's secret knowledge of Jared—all but her matrimonial overtures to Mallaby; that she had not the hardihood to reveal; she even told him the contents of the letter —she remembered them exactly, and his secret anxiety lest the letter had contained more than it did, was quite removed. And she, in her gushing delight did not notice his omission to confide to her the cause of Mr. Mallaby's morbidness. Indeed, she was so full of her guest's attentions to herself, that she almost forgot her satisfaction at the threatened blight to Miss Hammond's prospects. She was trembling with the momentous thought of offering him the little golden heart. Her better sense whispered that there was nothing in the occasion to warrant such a proceeding

on her part, but on the other hand her ardent gratitude
for his flattering attention was urging her to show him
in some way how warmly she responded to it. Her
impulse prevailed, and when he rose to depart, she
excused herself, and left the room for a little. When
she returned, the heart in its wrapping of tissue paper carefully in her hand, she found the task of actually giving it to him harder than she had anticipated. It was only at the last minute, when he was
saying another good-bye on the stoop, and promising
himself the pleasure of speedily seeing her again,
that she slipped it to him and then said in a confused
way:

"It is only a little token of gratitude, dear Mr.
Kellar; you have been so entertaining."

And then she retreated to the hall, and he flashing
back one of his broadest smiles at her went slowly
down the stoop and slowly up the street, trying to
guess by feeling of it what the token might be, and
laughing gleefully at the old maid's folly and weakness.

Being barely ten o'clock, Prudence nad no doubt
of finding Deborah up, and she hastened to don her
bonnet and shawl and run across. She was still
thrilling with exultation and delight, and she felt as
she pulled the bell with unusual force, that her present good spirits would amply sustain her should
Deborah, despite the tidings brought to her, still refuse to be appeased.

Deborah was in little better mood than that in
which Prudence had left her in the morning. Her
visit to Sydney's hotel had resulted in disappointment; he had left a half hour before her arrival and
would not return until an early hour the next day.
She glowered at Prudence when she saw her and
snapped out:

"What do you want?"

Prudence lost little time in making known her

errand, and she dwelt so much on what Kellar had
said of being able to tell Mr. Wilbur that which
would make him hesitate to marry Miss Hammond,
that Deborah was mollified at once. Prudence had
told the whole story so skillfully suppressing all the
facts which bore upon herself, that Miss Wilbur
supposed it was only that evening Prudence had
learned of Kellar's acquaintance with Mallaby, and
that she had made the discovery in a most accidental
manner.

"And didn't he hint at what he has to tell Sydney?" questioned Deborah.

"No; he did not; but, it's something weighty you
may be sure, or he wouldn't speak in that confident
way. So you'd better arrange about the interview;
for Mr. Kellar wants word sent him as soon as possible to-morrow."

Deborah pursed her lips together and began to
think. If this man really did have information
powerful enough to avert that horrible marriage, it
might be wise policy for her to seem to have become resigned to the present situation. It would
mollify Sydney, and in the event of the engagement
being broken, cement him more firmly to her. She
was secretly glad to have a pretext for yielding
to him, her hostility having gained nothing. She
would write to him at once in a sort of penitent
spirit, and promise compliance with all he asked;
and in order to prevent him from being suspicious
of the motive of her submission, she would put in a
postcript—as if it were an unimportant matter and
almost forgotten—the fact that some one wished
to see him and desired a time appointed for the interview. She was confident that Sydney would come
home immediately on the reception of that message
and she thus informed Prudence when she had detailed her plan.

"So, I shall not be able to give you an answer

much before noon, to-morrow," she added, and
Prudence, on the whole, well satisfied with the result of her mission, bade Deborah good-night, and
hastened home.

Miss Wilbur's note dispatched at an early hour the
next morning, arrived almost simultaneously with
her brother's arrival from his suburban visit. He
smiled when he read it; he had not expected to have
her yield so easily, and then as he read it a second
time, smiling more broadly at the stiff penitence it
expressed, he thought it well to be a little slow in
accepting her compliance. He would defer for a day
or two longer his return to Hubert Street, the party
wishing to see him could call at his present address.
He was so indifferent about the solicited interview,
that, in answering his sister's note he did not assign
any hour for it, and Deborah was disappointed and
chagrined that he did not reply in person to her
message. She sent curt word to Miss Liscome, and
that lady learning from it nothing more than Wilbur's address, and the fact that he had just returned
to that address after an absence of several hours,
took it upon herself to telegraph the same to Mr.
Kellar.

Mr. Kellar frowned when he read the telegram.

One object of asking Miss Liscome to prepare the
way for his interview with Wilbur, was, as it were to
avert the disagreeableness of ushering himself into
Wilbur's presence. With all his assurance he quailed secretly before the unmistakable dislike and distrust of him evinced by that gentlemen.

He had thought first of seeking Wilbur's sister,
and asking her to arrange the matter of the interview.
But the tea at Miss Liscome's seemed to present
even a more opportune means, and being the friend
of the family that she avowed herself to be, her
services could be as effectually used. He did not
doubt that with the garrulous tendency of her

sex, she would repeat every word he said in reference to the communication he had to make to Wilbur and while he felt that Wilbur's first emotions on hearing such a reason for the interview, might be those of indignation and distrust, he was equally certain that they would be succeeded by such curiosity and interest as would at least insure him a civil hearing.

The telegram announcing no hour for the interview puzzled and disappointed him. Had neither Mr. Wilbur's sister, nor Miss Liscome been able to see him, or had his consent to the interview gone no further than this vague message?

He put on his hat with a savage thrust, and took his way to the hotel where Wilbur was temporarily sojourning. Then having ascertained that the gentleman was in, he sent up his card, first writing on the corner, "Pressing and confidential business."

Wilbur's first impulse was to return a decided and emphatic refusal to see the man, but the phrase in the corner of the card checked him. His curiosity was excited, and he gave a curt order to show the gentleman up.

Kellar bore his wonted air, an easy swagger but it was a little less dashed with the familiarity which was so hateful to Wilbur; there was even something of a respectful reserve in his manner that won a readier attention than Wilbur thought at first to give him. That attention was increased by the promptness and brevity with which Kellar introduced his business, and it was painfully riveted as Kellar continued. He might have been a lawyer for the careful, exact, bare way in which he made his communication, and when he had finished, Wilbur staggered to his feet like a man who had received a deadly blow. He thrust his hands out before him as if he would push Kellar away, and then without speaking—his lips seemed to be glued together—he paced

the room. Kellar watched him without moving a
muscle of his own face, or changing his easy position.

The first effect of the shock passed, Wilbur's judgment asserted itself. He stopped short in his walk,
and asked, speaking between such compressed lips
that the words had a startling sharpness:

"You claim to have given me facts, facts to which
you have been an eye-witness. Give me your proofs."

"My first and best proof is that Mallaby himself
will not deny what I have told you. Tax him with
it, or even hint at it, and see how his guilt will betray itself."

"Your motive for telling this to me now," the words
still came from tightly-compressed, and bloodless
lips.

"My motive: I don't know that I am bound to tell
you that, it is sufficient that I have given you the
information which in justice you ought to know. And
knowing it, it lies with you to make it serve you. If
in defiance of what I have revealed you will proceed
to make the connection you contemplate, you will
be prepared of course to bear your share of what the
future may bring. I at least have done *my* duty."

He rose to depart.

Wilbur's brain was in a whirl. Had some inexorable fate from the first decreed that Agnes Hammond
was never to be his wife? Was this the reward for
his ardor, his constancy, his sacrifice, to be met at
the end of his weary months of wandering, regret
and doubt, with a revelation which made it impossible for him to marry her? He wished that Kellar
had not told him; that he had been suffered to walk
unknowingly into the trap prepared for him. The
discovery afterward would be horrible, but then he
would not be deprived of Agnes. Now, he himself
must resign her, that is if Kellar's story were true.
He jumped at the doubt, and hugged it, but in a

moment it was dissipated by the remembrance of the proof which Kellar had adduced. He had said that Mallaby would not deny it—what stronger proof could there be? and then a shiver broke over him as he thought of telling to Mallaby what he had heard and receiving in reply a horrible confirmation of its truth. And as a further confirmation there flashed upon him Mallaby's own manner with this man, Kellar; his shyness, his ill-concealed fear, his silence, the expression of his face in response to a look from his ward two evenings before, all these bore out the awful things he had heard. Then Miss Hammond's inexplicable agitation on the last evening he saw her—her reserve with him—surely he needed no more to prove to him what she knew, and knowing, what she must be. He groaned audibly and covered his face with both his hands. Then remembering the presence of his visitor, who, though he had risen to depart, had been too intent on watching Wilbur's evident agony to make any further motion to do so, he took his hands from his face, and said with forced calmness:

"You have finished your business with me, I believe."

Kellar bowed.

"Then good-day," and Wilbur turned haughtily on his heel and threw himself into a chair in a remote corner of the room.

Kellar went out with a broad smile. He had acted to his own satisfaction *his* part in the first act of the drama of Mallaby's doom.

XXXI .

NOT once during the day succeeding the last visit of Wilbur had Agnes been able to see her guardian. As he had done on the previous morning, so did he on this morning, depart before she had even awakened from the feverish slumber into which she had fallen about dawn, and as on the former occasion he left neither excuse nor apology. And at dinner he was not present, nor had he come, Mrs. Denner said, to lunch, causing that good woman to express an anxiety about him apparently second only to Miss Hammond's own concern, save that the young lady gave no voice to her feelings. Wilbur had said not to expect him that evening so there was nothing to distract her from her nameless trouble, and it grew in proportion as she dwelt upon it, assuming its size from the very vagueness by which it was surrounded. She tried to pray, but the words seemed to be only words with little meaning to them, and then she wandered from her room to the parlor, and back, lingering in the hall and on the stair hoping to catch the sound of his key in the lock.

She was determined to make him reveal the mystery that seemed to surround him, the secret of Kellar's influence over him, and for that purpose she would not retire until she saw him. She could not carry the burden of his mystery another day. When midnight chimed without bringing him, her fears took a new shape. Some accident might have befallen him; she started in affright and pain at that thought, for his unselfish kindness, his many little acts of affectionate regard came to her, and as she pictured him borne to some hospital, or worse to the *morgue* with the unknown dead, she burst into tears.

She was alone in the parlor, even Mrs. Denner having retired on the promise of Miss Hammond to extinguish the light, and see that the door was properly secured so soon as Mr. Mallaby should come in, and she wept without restraint. She sought to quiet her fears by thinking he had business which would detain him all night, but he had never remained from home for such a period without leaving, or sending word. No; it must be something had happened to him, and she burst into a very paroxysm of weeping.

At that instant, there was the sound of a key in the lock of the hall-door. Everything was so still she heard it distinctly, and hastily drying her eyes she hurried from the parlor, meeting her guardian just as he had softly closed the door behind him.

She forgot everything but her relief at seeing him, and she extended both hands to him, smiling through the tears still wet upon her cheeks;

"I am so glad you have come, Mr. Mallaby—I was afraid something had happened to you."

He put down his umbrella, and took her hands, clasping them tightly enough to make them ache, and his worn, anxious face seemed fairly alight with the smile that overspread it.

"I am sorry to have caused you any anxiety but I had some business matters to attend to, and I did not dream you'd stay up for me. Good-night."

He had spoken with the sad gentleness that was so touching, and having dropped her hands, he was turning to ascend to his room. The feelings that had caused her to wait for him assailed her anew, though they were mingled with and tempered by the inexplicable sympathy he inspired. She sprang after him clasping her hands about his arm, and forcing him to turn with her to the parlor.

"I must ask you some questions to-night and you must answer them," she said.

His face blanched until not a trace of its wonted floridness could be discovered. His knees shook, and his breath came in labored grasps. It was as he had feared. Kellar had taken his revenge. She knew it all. It was owing to his fear of that, that he had not come home earlier, in order to avert as long as possible the moment of seeing her, and the relief he had experienced when he so unexpectedly met her and was assured by her manner that his fear had been groundless, seemed to make the dismay and horror of this moment all the deeper.

He could not answer her as she drew him shivering and gasping into the parlor, and when she relinquished his arm for the purpose of closing the door behind them, he sank into the nearest chair.

When she turned and saw him—saw the death-like face, the grizzled head sunk low upon his breast, the whole form so utterly collapsed, shrinking and trembling, a sort of voiceless horror took possession of her for a moment; for a moment, until it was tempered by the same inexplicable sympathy which of late seemed to permeate all her emotions.

"Tell me what is the matter." she said, in a subdued, but excited voice.

He answered in a trembling whisper without looking up:

"Tell me what you know, how much you have been told."

"What I know —how much I have been told?"

The horrified astonishment in her tones made him look up, without, however, lifting his head.

"I don't know anything; I have been told nothing. What could I have been told? who would tell me?"

He raised his head from his breast the florid color coming partially back to his face. She had not been told then; she did not know yet. He felt like one

who had received a reprieve, though to-morrow the
finger that was so inexorably tracing his doom might
bring its characters into her sight. Under the influence of that feeling of respite he tried to look at
her steadily while he said:

"What are the questions you would ask of me?"

"In what way has this man Kellar come to be such
an intimate acquaintance of yours? What is the
mysterious anxiety you are so frequently betraying?"

Made desperate by the emotions excited by his
manner, she had spoken almost fiercely. He put his
hands out before him in that deprecating way he
seemed to use so much of late; it was as if he would
make some mute appeal before he spoke.

"I have nothing that I can tell you."

The accent of his voice belied his words; and his
ward, again a prey to the old emotions of doubt and
distrust and yet at the same time torn by that singular pity and sympathy, could restrain her feelings
no longer.

She laid them all before him: her doubts of him
engendered by his own manner, her pity evoked by
his evident anxieties, her desire to symphathize with
and comfort him, aroused by his gentle kindness
and now her utter disbelief in what he had averred
that he had nothing to tell.

"You asked," she continued, her breast heaving
with every word, and the color deepening in her
cheeks, "what I had been told; that proves I
might have been told something; why then, if another might have told me, cannot you tell me?"

At the last her voice had taken a pleading tone
that cut him to the heart. He rose slowly from the
chair, so slowly that he seemed like an utterly brok-
en old man. In a queer, incongruous sort of way he
wondered if the dead pitied the agony of the living, if
the mute cold lips of the phantom he so often fancied.

near him, would have blessed or cursed him—could it but have whispered one word in his ear, willingly, gladly would he accept every future consequence. But there was nothing only the painful silence with which his ward waited for his answer. And he felt that he must answer her.

"When I said there was nothing I could tell you, I spoke truly. I am not at liberty to tell you, nor to tell anybody. Another might tell you; that is beyond my control; and when that happens, as it may now at any moment, I have only to ask that you judge me by the instincts of your own tender charity—that even while your belief in what may be told to you may be strengthened by my own refusal either to deny, or to admit it, you will temper your conviction as much as you can, remembering that circumstances sometimes belie us.

"When you are married I shall go away—far away, and then if it be too hard to have a kindly memory of me, you can forget me."

"When I am married!" she repeated, wrought to such a pitch of feeling she could hardly pronounce the words distinctly, "will it be the proper thing for me to marry without telling Mr. Wilbur something of this? He seemed to feel the other evening that I was wanting in confidence with him—that which I would like to have confided to him were my feelings about you. He saw the agitation which I could not conceal after my interview with you, and he was wounded at my reserve."

Mallaby inwardly groaned : to have his secret before its revelation casting its shadow on the path of the lovers smote him to the soul. Yet what could he do? He sank again into the chair, and let his head drop upon his breast.

Miss Hammond's temples were throbbing so furiously she bound both her hands about them.

For one whirling moment the thought came to Mal-

laby of seeking Wilbur, and telling as much as
he dared to do without violating his conscience : but
the thought was discarded in the instant of its conception, for his revelation must be followed by questions from Wilbur which could not be satisfactorily
answered. ·Unless indeed, that Kellar already had
told Wilbur, but even then Mallaby could neither
deny, nor admit Kellar's disclosure. But at least
he must tell this excited girl something to avert the
shadow which otherwise might come between her and
her betrothed.

"Tell Mr. Wilbur," he said, " that your guardian
has a secret which troubles him—which has troubled
him for years—but he cannot tell it because he is
bound by an oath—but even could he do so he would
hesitate lest—" he paused, showing plainly his painful doubt of what his next words should be. His
ward, her hands still pressed to her temples, was looking at him with widely distended eyes—"lest the
memory of another should suffer."

She knew not whether it were the look in his face,
the quivering something in his voice, or the mysterious intuition which at times seems to be borne from
the very air into sensitive souls, that caused an utterly unexpected and horrible thought to flash into her
mind.

Flinging her hands from her temples she took a
step forward. It brought her so close to him, he could
feel her hot, labored breath upon his face as she
said with the air of a passionate demand:

"Is the other whose memory would suffer *my
father?*"

He averted his face.

"Tell me!" she commanded grasping his hands.

He felt the fever of her touch through his own
veins, for his blood seemed to have turned to ice at
her utterly unexpected question.

"Tell me!" she repeated.

It was useless to try to withstand, or evade her, and he turned back to her, his face as bloodless as that of a corpse. His lips hardly opened to emit his reply, and she caught it more from watching his mouth than from actually hearing it, and it confirmed her fear. She dropped his hands, putting her own again to her temples.

"Tell me *something* more," she pleaded, "all at least that you may without violating your oath—to whom did you give that oath—and how did your affection for my father come to be so strong that you would save his memory at the risk of your own happiness?"

"Your father and I were old and tried friends— bosom friends—for years we had not a thought from each other—our joys, our cares, our griefs, were the same. Why should I not love him more tenderly than even many brothers love, and when the trouble came which blighted his life why should I not be eager to do for those whom he had left. My oath was given to your mother to assure, and to save you from any blight upon your future life."

Again her hands were flung from her temples, but only to be clasped over her eyes while she thought wildly, feverishly of what he had said. Everything about him seemed to proclaim that he spoke the truth, and if so what did she not owe him; not alone gratitude on her own part, but on that of her dead parents. He had served them all, and he was still a martyr in their cause.

Mallaby, expecting her to answer and finding she did not, resumed:

"Since, as you say, Mr Wilbur seemed to expect you to tell him some of the feelings you have communicated to me, perhaps you had better confide to him the portion of this interview which revealed to you that I held an anxious secret; you need not state anything further, for the rest does not concern

him, and would not have been made known to you,
had you not divined it as you did. You may add,
however, to your statement to Mr. Wilbur, that I
shall go away directly after your marriage. Being
only your guardian, there ought to be little regret,
or thought about any course I may pursue."

The phrase, "being only your guardian," struck
even through the wildness and anguish of her
thoughts, bringing back with a painful bitterness the
frequent occasions on which she had so slightingly
spoken of him.

He deemed the interview ended and he moved toward the door. She looked at him as he went, wanting to speak, to stop him, but knowing not what to
say, and he went out leaving upon her mind and
heart a picture of him that was finally to surmount
by its pathos and dejection every other thought.

If she could only think clearly, but her thoughts
were so confused and conflicting; one moment she
almost doubted all that Mallaby had told her, and
wondered whether his story might not have been in-
vented to conceal the betrayal of his trust as her
guardian, and the misappropriation of her money;
the next she rejected every suspicion and severely
condemned herself for having any. One instant she
questioned if Mr. Kellar, being the old friend of
Mallaby that he termed himself, would not know if
what she had heard were true, and whether he
would not reveal to her what her guardian had withheld. The latter had said that she might be told
something at any moment. From whom was the revelation more likely to come than from Kellar. But
her repugnance to the man was too great to permit
her to seek an interview. .

What should she do? Tell Wilbur only what her
guardian had advised her to tell, and suffer the latter to go away after their wedding as he was plan-
ning to do; that would be an easy course to pursue,

and if what he had told her had only been an in-
vention to hide his own dishonesty. it would be
the best and most feasible course. But, if on the
other hand, his statement were true, her duty was
plain to tell Wilbur the martyr her guardian. had
made of himself for her sake and for the sake of
her parents, and to insist that Wilbur should unite
with her in preventing Mallaby's departure. Surely, in return for his self-sacrifice it would be little
for her to soothe his declining years as much as
she might do. And then for the first time it flashed upon her that her affianced might hesitate to
give his name to a woman whose father's memory
was shadowed by such a secret as her guardian
seemed to carry. For aught she knew it might be
a secret relating to some crime. Why had she not
thought to ask her guardian that? but even as she
regretfully put the question to herself, she felt he
would not have answered her. Wilbur no doubt in
his masculine judgment and penetration would be
sure to feel that the secret could pertain to nothing
else than a crime of some sort, and knowing as she
did his high sense of rectitude, his pride in his own
unstained family name, how could she dream that
he would fulfill his engagement with her.

Oh God! how hard it was. To give him up again
when already she had suffered so much, and then,
Mallaby's story might not be true, and she should
have sacrificed her happiness for naught. But Mallaby's drooping, pathetic figure as it looked a little
while before when he was leaving the room, rose in
very protest. She could not withstand its mute, and
sad plea, and she sank to her knees clutching the
scapular beneath the bosom of her dress and praying wildly for help and strength.

Above stairs her guardian was on his knees also,
his head sunk in his hands and through his fingers
oozing at intervals drops of moisture that might be

tears, or the perspiration caused by his burning thoughts. At times he muttered:

"I have not broken the oath—but *he* will tell her; he will tell Wilbur—then for her the flight—for me the doom, and afterward—oh God, afterward."

XXXII.

FOR three hours after his interview with Kellar Wilbur sat in stern and agonized commune with himself. Should he question Agnes of *her* knowledge of what had been told, and read from her manner—though her lips denied it, that she *did* know, his affection for her must turn to scorn. Should she, feeling that longer concealment was useless, confess to her knowledge, even then his love for her must receive a fatal blow. Her confession would stamp her not as a victim, or a dupe, but as an accomplice and a deceiver. As the other alternative, should he force himself to believe that she did not know, and acting on that belief make her promise to break completely with her guardian, pledging herself never to see him again, he would even then be making an alliance against which every principle of his family honor and every tradition of his family name sternly set themselves. But he could not give her up, and almost unconsciously his hand sought her little pearl rosary that he had found, and which he carried constantly in his inner breast-pocket.

He had to determine on some course before he saw her, and when at length he resolved on the latter alternative which he had proposed to himself, he did not doubt for a moment her willing assent to it.

What then were his surprise and anger when he found his proposition met with a firm refusal. His manner on greeting her had seemed like a foreboding of something unusual and unpleasant, while her pale face and agitated air had told equally of her own trouble. But he would not give her an opportunity to impart it, and thus perhaps seal his doom; he would tell at once frankly what he wished and why he wished it, —reports had reached him that were not creditable to her guardian, and that made it impossible for the wife of Sydney Wilbur to have any connection with Mr. Mallaby, or even ever to see him again.

"Such a request I ought not, and I shall not grant," she had answered, without a moment's hesitation, though her heart sickened and her knees trembled.

"He is only your guardian," said Wilbur, indignation at her unexpected obstinacy mastering everything else in his tones. "It is a little strange that you should choose him rather than me."

"Only my guardian," she repeated, "but I owe to him more than most wards owe to guardians," and then, her voice becoming tremulous and tearful, she told him all that had passed in her last interview with Mallaby.

"The confidence you accused me of withholding," she continued, "I have given you now, and knowing as you do my feelings, my obligations in this matter, you surely will not persist in your request."

He did not answer her, but he only continued to look at her, while he rapidly thought,

Was she acting a part—a part that had been prepared for her? Had Mallaby learned that Kellar had informed, and had he in accordance, drilled his ward or had she in her own cleverness made the part? If so, she was acting it well, with all apparent ingenuousness, and Wilbur found himself touched and softened while he looked. It was impossible to believe that she knew more than she had told, and if so could he have the heart even in his anger at her determination, to tell her the awful things which Kellar had revealed? But it was also impossible to marry her unless she would consent to be severed from her guardian whom Wilbur now hated and detested. He did not believe a word of his story of self-sacrifice which he had told Miss Hammond.

"Why do you look at me in such a manner?" she asked, as he making no attempt to reply, continued to gaze at her, "and what have *you* heard about my guardian, and who has told you—was it that man, Kellar?"

Her last question seemed to indicate that she *did* know more than she had told, else why should she mention Kellar's name? It was sickening that she should be such a deceiver, and yet the expression of her face, her manner, her voice, all belied the thought. He turned away for a moment to think what he should answer. If she did not know, how could he be the first to tell her, and what might be the consequence of that awful revelation?

He turned back to her.

"Agnes!'

His voice had never sounded so sorrowfully tender, but, somewhat it seemed like a knell—the knell of their final parting.

"It is not necessary for me to tell from whom, or what I have heard, it is enough to say that it is different from the confidence you have given me—but it is necessary for the happiness of us both, for the honor of the name that I would give you, that you consent to resign Mr. Mallaby entirely and forever. He is only your guardian."

"If it be necessary for the honor of your name," she repeated, "that I should give up Mr. Mallaby, then is it still more necessary for the honor of your name that you should cancel your engagement to me. I have already told you that my guardian's secret trouble is because he would shield my father and would save me."

"But I do not believe Mr. Mallaby's story," blurted out Wilbur with new indignation.

"And I *do* believe it," responded Agnes, her tones all the more firm that in her heart the old doubt was beginning to struggle.

Once more he resumed his wonted tenderness as he pleaded with her: as he begged her to resign her guardian—it could be managed so easily; he would take her on a long wedding-tour—he would even permit her to write once; and he would see that Mallaby did not want.

She prayed with her heart while he was speaking. Remembering the former occasion when she would have yielded but for Florence, it seemed as if this were an opportunity to atone for her weakness then; and the anguish of that occasion was not so poignant as her suffering was upon this. She thought of her duty to poor, broken Mallaby, broken from the weight of his sacrifice made for her and hers, and she thought of her duty to Wilbur not to suffer him to marry one upon whose name there rested a suspicion.

Perchance also the discipline of prayer and patient endurance of the past months had made her strong for the present trial.

"Do not press me further," she said, "I cannot consent to what you ask."

"And you will let me go—you will say good-bye forever?"

"Not forever! there is another world in which we will meet."

He turned from her and went to the door—his face set in an appalling expression of indignation and grief.

She did not move, not even the hands that hung limp by her side, twitched as they had done a moment before. She seemed to herself to be set in some frozen mould unable to make a sign that would show her anguish. Nothing that she had suffered at their former parting equalled the dumb agony of this. He looked back and saw her standing like a statue; her face as colorless as one. It recalled with a sickening sense the pain of their former separation; he had little reason to suppose that her determination would yield any more now than it had done then. He wanted to hate her for preferring her guardian to him, to hate her for her firmness, to feel that her affection for him was not sincere when she so readily yielded him; to think that he had been mistaken in her character; to believe that the qualities which she affirmed bound her to Mallaby, were only assumed, now that she was aware Wilbur knew something of her family history; and he wanted to rejoice that he had so good an opportunity of escaping from an alliance which might sully the honor of his name; but all were only struggles that seemed to gain nothing while she stood there in her pale, sad, touching, pleading beauty. Then he felt that he too must be firm; as before when he would not yield his religious convictions, neither would he now sacrifice his family honor; from the old Puritan times his family name had descended, and it had ever been the synonym for rectitude: surely he had condescended much, and incurred no little risk in being willing to marry her with the condition of giving up Mallaby —but in that case he could remove her where no breath of dishonor might reach either of them; but, to marry her, consenting to retain her obligations —as she considered them—to Mallaby, would be to invite upon his own head a share in the awful things that Kellar had told him. He shuddered slightly as they reproduced themselves for a moment, and then while their influence was strong upon him he walked back to Agnes, took one of her limp, cold hands in his own, and said hurriedly:

"Reconsider your refusal; think of all that I have

promised; remember *my* happiness that you are blighting; and then answer once more—whom do you choose, Mr. Mallaby, or me?"

The answer was low, but steadily delivered: "I cannot give up my guardian."

He threw her hand from him, and without another look strode to the door. In a moment he had reached the street-door; she heard it close upon him and then she rushed to the window half expecting that he would look back: but he walked rapidly on; she watched him until she could see him no longer, and then she turned away from the window and went wearily up to her room. She had not Florence now into whose arms she might throw herself and sob out her grief and desolation; there was no one to speak to ; not even her guardian, for he had left word in the morning that he would not be home until midnight; and now it wanted an hour of the evening dinner time.

She had such a tired, numb feeling—almost as if she were too fatigued to cry, though there was a gulp in her throat. And how changed everything appeared; even the familiar furniture in her room seemed to have undergone some alteration during her absence, and the noises of the street incident to a summer evening that came in at the window, had a strange, gloomy sound. She stood looking in a sort of dazed manner until her eyes fell upon a little statue of the Blessed Virgin which her own hands had set up in a corner of the room and around which she had improvised a sort of shrine. She threw herself on her knees before it, and the lump in her throat dissolved into relieving tears.

"Mother of God pray for me, help me; my trial is greater than I can bear."

XXXIII.

It was so long past midnight when Mallaby returned, that his ward did not see him, but she was up
early enough in the morning to meet him, confronting him at the parlor-door as he came down from
his room. The hour was so early that no one in the
house was stirring save the help.

"You are ill," he said, his tones betraying more
his anxiety because of her pale, tired look than even
surprise at her early appearance.

"No; not ill," as she drew him into the parlor,
"but I feel that I ought not to defer telling you the
engagement between Mr. Wilbur and myself is brok-
en."

"My God!" he staggered from her, and tottered
helplessly into a chair.

"He has heard something about you, he would not
tell me what—" she continued, speaking with a sort
of breathless haste— "and I, not knowing but this
secret which you bear for my father's sake was perhaps a criminal one felt it to be my duty to let him
cancel our engagement lest a marriage with me
might bring to him any dishonor."

A sense of delicacy regarding her own sacrifice, and
hesitation to wound Mr. Mallaby, deterred her from
telling how Wilbur would have fulfilled his engagement on one condition. But Mallaby seemed to divine more than she told.

"Did you tell Mr. Wilbur?" he asked, "that I intended to go away immediately after your marriage?"

"No!" she replied, "why should I tell him that;
and why should you go if, as you say your secret
trouble concerns my father, and if it be anything to

bring dishonor must I not feel that dishonor reflected upon me, his child, though you were thousands of miles away?"

"If, as you say your secret trouble concerns my father," he mentally repeated experiencing as he did so a new degree of anguish because that sentence told so plainly her doubt of his truth.

"Tell me," she resumed, in her intense feeling unconsciously raising her voice,

"Does this secret pertain to crime—was my father dishonored?"

"My oath forbids me to tell anything," he answered. And as if he feared her pleading he dragged himself up from the chair and over to a remote corner of the room. She did not follow him.

He had little need to ask if Wilbur had mentioned the source of his information; too well he knew that it was Kellar, but he was surprised that Wilbur had withheld from Miss Hammond what he must have heard from Kellar.

To know that he had withheld it however, made his breath come freer.

Perhaps Kellar had after all, been merciful, and had contented himself with causing the engagement to be broken. Perhaps he had even bound Wilbur not to tell Miss Hammond any of the dreadful particulars, and now that he had so far satisfied his revenge, perchance he would cease to hound Mallaby to his doom. He took new heart at the thought, and he turned back to his ward with a less troubled face than he had turned from her.

"My dear, I shall see Mr. Wilbur, and perhaps a satisfactory settlement of all this may yet be made."

Then he shot from the room, and was out of the house before she could stop him. He would not delay for any breakfast lest she might put more embarrassing questions to him.

Her spirits rose a little: his promise to see Wil-

bur gave her sudden and unexpected hope. Perhaps
after all the secret was not such a criminal one, and
sufficient explanation would be made by Mallaby to
enable her marriage to take place. That Mallaby
would tell Wilbur of his intention to go away she
did not doubt, and that Wilbur would accept that
as being the same as if she had consented to give
up her guardian, she equally believed, and though
she sighed at the thought of his voluntary departure, and felt that in consenting to it she would
be abandoning the very duty she had been striving
to perform, her human nature was strongly incit-
ing her not to oppose such an arrangement.

She strove to justify herself by thinking that she
had already given proof of her gratitude to Mallaby
and her devotion to duty; that it would not be in
her power to stop his departure, and that after all
he might not have told her the truth. By such
sophistries was her conscience torn, causing her one
moment to thrill with hope and a delighted assurance
of her reconciliation with Wilbur, and the next, to
reproach herself as a weak, wretched ingrate.

That very morning Mallaby went in search of
Wilbur, going direct to his home on Hubert Street,
and giving his card to Anne who instantly remembered him as the odd-looking man who had caused her
such merriment on the occasion of his former call two
years ago. He was the same comical-looking figure
now, with his short plaid pantaloons, long light coat
and the identical green cotton umbrella under his
arm. But there was something in his florid face
that spoke of trouble and anxiety, and Anne fancied
that he had grown thinner and in her sympathetic
heart she was more inclined to pity than to laugh
at him.

She told him that Mr. Wilbur had been from home
for a few days, but that he had returned the evening before and had gone out again that morn-

ing. She knew nothing of the time of his return,
but Miss Wilbur could probably tell him. He decided to see Miss Wilbur, and Anne ushered him into the disordered parlor, and took his card to Deborah.

Deborah was in the most exultant spirits. Sydney had returned the night before, inquired if she
could be ready to start for the West on the following evening, but at the same time sternly commanded her not to ask a single question. Feeling that
his engagement with Miss Hammond must be broken,
and knowing that she was aware of much more than
he thought she knew, she could easily obey him, and
in her delight she was more agreeable and submis-
sive than she had been for years. She could not wait
for the morning to see Miss Liscome, and so soon as
Sydney shut himself in his room she had dispatched Anne for Prudence, and that lady had remained
with Deborah all night, sharing in the latter's joy and
receiving with immense satisfaction her expressions
of gratitude to herself and Mr. Kellar. In the morning Deborah contrived to get her away early and
secretly lest Sydney should see her. Knowing his
aversion to her she felt that her presence in the house
might annoy him. Of course she had told Anne,
immediately that she heard the news herself, of
their intended departure, and cited its suddenness as
an instance of her wisdom in being ready so long.

The unexpectedly fortunate turn that events had
taken seemed too good to be true—her brother going to
the West to claim that fortune—he had told such was
his intention—his engagement with the hated Miss
Hammond broken, their departure to take place so
soon, all seemed like a delightful dream, and she was
impatient for the hour at which they were to start,
lest anything might happen to prevent them. Thus
her brow clouded when Anne brought her Mallaby's
card; she felt that his visit had something to do with

the broken engagement, that he perhaps had come to repair it, and her first impulse was to refuse to see him; but she hesitated to send that message: it might precipitate the very thing she was anxious to avoid, his interview with her brother; for he might await the latter's return especially if he knew that they were going away that evening.

She asked quickly of Anne:

"Did you tell him that we were going away?"

"No ma'am; I told him nothing but that Mr. Wilbur was out and you were in, and I didn't know when Mr. Wilbur'd be back."

Still, the reply did not convey much assurance, for, how did she know but that Sydney himself had told Mr. Mallaby or his ward, that he was going away. She decided to see the gentleman.

Mallaby met her with the same old-fashioned courtesy that had marked his former visit; while she was cold and prim, conveying in her manner her little desire to see him; it abashed him somewhat, making him think that she knew of the rupture between the lovers, and threw the blame of it upon him. He did not know of her bitter opposition to the engagement.

"I called to see Mr. Wilbur on very important business," he said, hesitatingly, being disconcerted by the piercing look of her little sharp, black eyes, and shifting his umbrella as if there were some connection between it and the business he had to communicate.

"My brother is out," answered Deborah through her pursed lips, "on business that may keep him very late. I don't think it would be possible for you to see him to-day."

He looked blank, and in his dismayed preoccupation shifted the umbrella again, and shouldered it as if it were a fire-arm.

Deborah felt sure that he did not know of their

approaching departure; but, in order to test his
knowledge, she said:

"Could you come to-morrow?"

"Yes, certainly I can come to-morrow," replied
Mallaby, brightening, and removing his umbrella
from its military position. "At what hour shall I
call?"

"You can come at any hour you like to-morrow."

And Deborah silenced her conscience by thinking
that she had told no lie, and that her equivocal answer was justified by the cause in which she had given
it.

And Mallaby thinking that one day could make
little difference, and sanguine of being able to restore
his ward's happiness, thanked Miss Wilbur, and
bade her a very courteous adieu.

"I am to see Mr. Wilbur to-morrow," he said to
Miss Hammond that evening, "I called upon him to-
day, but he was not in."

Miss Hammond felt that she ought to protest
against his seeing Wilbur if he intended to purchase
her happiness by any further sacrifice of himself; but
her heart was crying out so for another sight of Wilbur, that the words stuck in her throat; and again
she appeased her conscience by thinking, it would
not be too late to oppose his departure after his interview with Wilbur. Nor would she ask a question
of where Mallaby had sought him. She knew that
up to the day of their last interview he had been living
away from Hubert St. She would ask nothing until
he had seen him.

The next morning, so early that he was in some
trepidation about the propriety of the hour he had
chosen for his visit, Mallaby was ringing the bell of
No. —— Hubert St. There was no response, and
then he noticed the closed and deserted appearance
of the house. Every blind was fastened so tightly
there was not a chink for the faintest ray of light to

enter. He rang again, a strange foreboding entering
his heart as he did so. The same silence alone responded. Could it be that everyone in the house was
still in bed? He looked at his watch; it wanted a few
minutes of eight; they must be exceedingly late
sleepers; but willing and glad to give them the benefit of the thought, he went away determining to
come back a little later. When he returned it was
the same; no one responded to his frequent rings.
He looked about him making up his mind to seek
information at one of the neighboring houses, when
he saw Miss Liscome coming down the street. Her
juvenile attire was positively jaunty and set about an
old face flaringly red with rouge, it presented a rather
ludicrous sight. She saw him even before his eyes
rested upon her, and remembering his positive refusal to accept her heart, and knowing the object of
his presence on that particular stoop, for Deborah
had told her of his call on the previous day, she resolved to avenge herself for his slight. She knew
that he would hail her appearance expecting that
she was able and would be willing to give him some
information. So, holding her head very high, and
making her mincing steps more measured, she was
passing on, deliberately and pointedly ignoring him,
though he had descended the stoop and stood directly in her way.

"Miss Liscome," he said, his surprise at her manner so great that the umbrella actually slipped from
under his arm to the pavement, and for an instant
he seemed too dazed even to pick it up. She stopped and looked at him; a supercilious look that took
him all in from the grizzled hair escaping from his
broad brim straw hat, to the bony ankles protruding
from the short plaid pantaloons.

"What is the matter with you, ma'am? have I
changed so that you don't know me?" burst from
Mallaby, exasperated by her look, and her pretended

Ignorance; and then he picked up his umbrella, and thrust it under his arm in a manner that made Miss Liscome appear to be a little bit afraid, for she retreated a few steps.

"I believe you are Mr. Mallaby," she simpered, "really, when one has so many friends as I have, it is difficult to remember a casual acquaintance such as you were."

"Casual acquaintance," he retorted, with a savage shift of his umbrella to the other arm, "faith ma'am, you didn't treat me as a casual acquaintance when you used to come to my office so frequently — but that's neither here nor there—can you tell me anything about these Wilburs who live here, I can't get anyone to answer the bell."

"Yes, Mr. Mallaby; I can tell you everything about the Wilburs," simpered Prudence again, " but I do not choose to tell you more than they have gone away, very far away, and are not going to return. "

Mallaby felt that it would be useless to attempt to extort anything more from her, and disappointed, sick at heart, and disgusted, he turned shortly, with a curt,

" Good-morning ma'am !" and went rapidly down the street.

Later in the day he returned asking the immediate neighbors of the Wilburs for information; but they could tell him no more than the brother and sister had gone away the evening before, no one seemed to know where, but as they were accompanied by a quantity of baggage it was presumed they were to make an extended stay. Then he instituted inquiries in the business circles in which it was likely something might be known of Wilbur's movements; but even there all were in ignorance, save that Wilbur had made a hurried sale of some property. Nor had Kellar once turned up since the night on which Mallaby had given him his final answer. Mallaby was

puzzled; more puzzled even by the fact of not seeing
Kellar, than by Wilbur's strange and hasty departure. And though Kellar's absence might be portentous of a further instance of his vengeance, it might
also be a sign that contented with the unhappiness
he had brought to Mallaby's ward, and the disappointment to Mallaby himself in preventing an alliance so much desired by him, Kellar would be satisfied
to pursue his vengeance no further. And Mallaby
tried to incline himself to the latter thought, though
the hunted look in his eyes, and the nervous start
when anyone spoke to, or touched him suddenly,
was an evidence of his little ease of mind.

When he returned again to Agnes without having
seen Wilbur, and having nothing to tell her but his
fruitless search, and the strange reply of Miss Wilbur
implying that her brother would be at home on the
next day when she must have known they were both
going away, Agnes got up suddenly from her chair
as if she could listen to no more. Her whole face was
crimson from the haughty spirit that rose within her.
Alas! pride could make her do without a struggle,
what duty required such an effort to perform.

"Do not attempt to learn where he is gone," she said,
hotly. "Let him go. His sister was bitterly opposed to our engagement, and put you off in that manner
to prevent you from seeing him. He must have told
her that we had broken with each other, and yet he
was so angry with her because of her dislike of me that
he had been living away from home. Since they
have gone away together as the neighbors informed
you, he must have become friends with her again.
Well, she will console him."

"I might have suspected," soliloquized Mallaby,
"that they were preparing for departure, for the hall
and the parlor looked as if people were either just
moving in, or moving out."

"Yes, Deborah expecting him to go West as soon

as he should return from abroad had everything in
readiness to start, even before he left the other side;
nor would she restore the house when he informed
her of the change in his plans, and up to the time of
his leaving home a few days ago everything was in
the same upset condition. Wonderful prescience
on her part; her preparations were useful and in
time."

The last words were spoken bitterly.

Mallaby had caught little of what she said more
than that which referred to the West.

"It is likely then that they have gone West," he
said, when she had finished; "do you know to what
part of the West?"

"If I did, I should not tell you," she answered,
"and you must promise me now, absolutely and solemnly promise, that you will not attempt in any way
to find him; that, should you learn by accident his
whereabouts you will not communicate with him in
any shape. He has severed himself from us, and my
duty is here—with you. We can live as we have
lived, our fortunes and our cares. bound together.
Promise me!" extending her hands to him.

He little knew as he looked up at her what wild,
burning, agonizing feelings were tearing her soul;
how one moment she felt this sudden and total departure of Wilbur to be a means taken by God himself
to punish her for her weak coquetting with the hope of
regaining him through a further sacrifice of Mallaby;
how the next moment she doubted the whole story
of her guardian's sacrifice, and regretted the sacrifice
she herself had made in not giving him up, and how
in still another moment, in her pride and disappointment at not receiving some little last message from
Wilbur, she wanted to dislike him and to stamp him
utterly from her memory: and yet that fighting with
every one of these thoughts were the pious instincts of
her religious training, and the naturally noble im-

pulses of her nature urging her to make her sacrifice now complete and true, by discarding every thought save that of submission, patience, and a filial grati- tude to Mallaby.

"Promise me!" she repeated, the fiery color deep- ening in her face, and her hands still extended.

Something about her, and something in his own heart made him powerless to resist her. He got up from his chair, his eyes recalling the look which had so singularly thrilled her on the night two years ago when he and she and Florence Wilbur stood on the stoop of Sydney's home on Hubert Street.

"I promise you," he said, taking her hands for a moment, and then without another word he turned away and went out. She still saw that peculiar look in his eyes, and experienced again the thrill it gave her. How many times she was to see it before the end came!

XXXIV.

FLORENCE'S letter arrived; the letter which from having been so ardently and joyously expected, was now sorrowfully dreaded. It was brief and had an undercurrent of sadness that seemed in strange sympathy with Miss Hammond's melancholy, but was at the same time inexplicable, for there was no hint at the reason of it, and the fact that she could not come to the wedding was certainly not sufficient cause to produce its sad tenor. She could not come, she said, because the physicians had ordered her mother to the northern part of Italy, and she was obliged to accompany her. Still, she did not imply that her mother's health gave her new anxiety, and more singular than all, while the letter closed with the fondest wishes for the happiness of Agnes and tender remembrances to be given to Sydney, it did not breathe a wish for a reply. Indeed, as Agnes repeatedly read it there seemed to be a studious absence of any desire to receive an answer. Could it be an oversight on Florence's part? that was impossible, for every letter Agnes had ever received from her was wont to be filled with commands for a speedy response. What did it mean? Could she have heard of the rupture, but in her pity for Agnes, pretended ignorance, even though she had determined to drop all future correspondence? But that could not be, for though Sydney had written to her, she would not have received it in time to answer it with the present reply. She crushed the letter in her hand while tears of wounded pride rose to her eyes. "They are all alike," she said, bitterly, "easy and eager to renounce their attachments when the clouds come.

She need not fear, however, I shall not trouble her
with any further correspondence. The implied wish
in her letter shall be strictly regarded. I shall not
write a line to her.''

But even while she thus fiercely determined, something in her secret heart was pleading for Florence;
only Agnes would not listen to it.

Days passed during which Mallaby saw nothing of
Kellar, nor did he hear from him. He tried to exult at
the fact, but he could not divest himself of the secret
fear that this singular silence was more ominous than
all else had been. And the fear increased as time
wore on until it culminated in a restlessness and
suspicion that made him frequently change his office quarters, and strongly desire to change his old
residence.

For Agnes, life had never been so dreary, or vacant; it held out no interest to her beyond that of
trying to fulfill patiently her monotonous round of
daily duties. She was sick of the drudgery of her
employment, and even the hours which she sought
to beguile by a practice of the music that hitherto
she had loved were filled alone with melancholy rep-
etitions of mournful chords. Her one daily comfort
was stealing to some church which she might chance
to find open, and there in solitude and silence pouring out before the Blessed Sacrament her griefs, her
doubts, her desolation. There seemed to be something in those visits when it often happened that she
was alone in the church exquisitely consoling; as if
the very solitude drew her nearer to the Heart of
Him to whom she prayed, and inclined that Heart
more eagerly to hear her petitions.

Mrs Denner was the most puzzled woman of the
age; to see Miss Hammond's handsome suitor come
no more to the house, and yet to hear not alone
no reason given for his absence, but not the slight-

est reference to the wedding, the time of which she had supposed was fast approaching, were mysteries that threatened to interfere with her appetite and her slumber. If she had only dared to do so, she would have bluntly asked for an explanation, but Mr. Mallaby maintained such an absolute silence on the subject that she feared that his very meekness might turn to wrath did she assail him, and Miss Hammond bore such an air of proud reserve it was positively awe-inspiring. Her curiosity was to be further incited, while at the same time her spirits were to receive a totally unexpected blow. Mallaby and his ward were going to leave her. She was prostrated at the information; it was only after a little that she could recover herself to speak, and then she hastened to say that which might cause her curiosity to be enlightened at least on one point.

"Was Miss Hammond going to be married?"

"No;" Mallaby replied shortly, and even somewhat testily, for he had dreaded a little this interview with his landlady, and he thought it better to assume more crustiness than he felt.

"And I'd like to impress upon you, ma'am, that I'll consider it an obligation if you'll ask no questions."

"But I must, Mr. Mallaby," interrupted Mrs. Denner in such a sharply aggrieved voice, it set his teeth on edge. "I must ask if it's dissatisfaction with my house, or my table, or my beds, or my boarders? to be sure, I've always done my best to humor you and Miss Hammond, but, if there's anything more in the way of softer beds, or giving other seats to the two old deaf creatures that bother you at the table, or seeing that you get the tenderloin —"

"Heavens and earth! ma'am, will you hold your tongue?" burst from Mallaby; "it is no dissatisfaction with anything, but a desire on the part of my ward and myself to live in another part of the city;

and as I said before, I'll be greatly obliged if you'll ask no questions."

"No questions—oh, Mr. Mallaby; and you the decent, quiet boarder that you were; no questions, and you like a father to my poor fatherless little ones,"—evidently ignoring the fact of her second husband—"no questions, and I as has the heart of a mother for Miss Agnes—oh, Mr. Mallaby! Mr. Mallaby! Mr. Mallaby!" His name uttered in a higher key each time, and more prolonged, sounded at the last like a wail, and then, as a climax, she threw her apron over her head and seemed to be sobbing behind it.

Feeling there was little use to try to appease her, and anxious to end a scene that exasperated him, he turned away without another word and left the room.

"The old fool," she said, peering out at the side of her apron, with perfectly dry eyes, "does he think as a woman can't find out a thing when she wants to, and that the more a man tries to baffle and hide, the more a woman's bound to know what he's keeping back. He won't be gone from here two hours before I'll know where he plants himself."

XXXV.

MISS HAMMOND had made no opposition when her
guardian proposed to leave Mrs. Denner's. In fact she
rather hailed the change; it would remove her from
objects that seemed to have a strange, persistent, unhappy way of reminding her of Wilbur; for the rest,
all places were alike to her now; she had no concern
for, nor interest in any of her surroundings. She
was hardly surprised when she found that Mallaby
had selected a home for them very far down town,
and almost in the centre of a business quarter.
It was one of the few eminently respectable board-
ing-houses to be found in the lower part of the city,
and the house from its simple, antiquated structure
seemed to date from the time of the old Dutch burgh-
ers. The boarders were entirely business people,
the women seeming to have masculine professions,
and to be too full of their work to have time, or
thought for any feminine weakness.

It was the unhomelike, unsocial air of the place
that had commended itself to Mallaby. He imagined he would be safer there; freer from criticism,
from notice; and yet he felt in his secret heart the
utter futility of it all. His doom was coming; Kellar's strange absence and stranger silence only por-
tended its greater certainty, and the spirit that was
urging him to the frequent changes which he made
in his office quarters was only a mocking delusion,
for where could he hide when the end came?

He would have left the city had he other means
of support, and he did at times contemplate a flight
to some remote corner of the earth, but he dreaded

to subject Miss Hammond to the hardship of such a change, and he could not flee without her.

Miss Hammond saw daily how his nervous, haunted manner increased, but she never commented on it; and yet he felt that she knew it, that she was getting to live almost in the atmosphere of suspicion and fear in which he dwelt; that she would hardly be surprised when one day a hand should be laid on his shoulder, and a stern voice should say to him: "You are wanted."

They had few conversations with each other, and those never referred to the thoughts that lay so heavy on the mind of each; but, there were frequent occasions in which Miss Hammond caught her guardian looking into her face with an indescribable wistfulness, and there were times when Mallaby found the eyes of his ward fixed upon him in a sad questioning way that harrowed him.

Occupied and circumspect as were the noarders, they still had some time and inclination to admire the beautiful girl, and a few of them might have attempted a passing acquaintance, had she not chilled every approach to such by her ice-like reserve. Her guardian was a puzzle, and to those who had a sense of humor, extremely amusing. His dress out of proportion as to harmony of color or propriety of fit, his green cotton umbrella carried equally when there was not a cloud in the sky, and when the rain came heavily down made him such a prominently funny figure. Then the relation that he bore to his lovely queen-like ward made him a still more conspicuous object. People wondered why she had not transferred to him for appearance's sake, some of her own tasteful appropriateness in attire, and whether she were not ashamed of his oddities. But no trace of such a feeling ever appeared in her manner. She was quietly attentive to him, and indifferent to everything else; while for him, even those who were the most inclined to laugh at him found their hearts strangely touched as they watched his manner with her—the total change in the expression of his face; it showed such a patient, tender, mournful wistfulness.

Agnes continued to give her music lessons, her little circle of scholars increasing and taking her some days to homes so remote from her own abode that the journey fatigued her; but fatigue had grown to be somewhat of a blessing; it kept her wearing thoughts at bay. On one of these days that she had made the long journey and was returning from it, slumber overtook her in a Broadway stage; though so gentle as to attract no attention it was deep enough to enchain her until she had gone some distance beyond the point where she was wont to alight. Then she saw that she was not far from the Battery green. Being August, the foliage was in a state of mellow luxuriance, and not being disfigured as the place is now by an unsightly elevated road, it seemed peculiarly inviting to her tired heart and mind. She strolled toward it rather than to her home, and entered one of the walks that led to the water. Something in the summer odor recalled St. John's Park—recalled the evening on which Wilbur had ask her to marry him, and recalled it all so distinctly and painfully that she seemed overpowered. With all her struggles she had been unable either to cease to care for, or to forget him, and now for an instant she was utterly powerless to stop the tide of bitter anguished thoughts and doubts. The one doubt more poignant than all the others, and that never failed to surmount and permeate every thought, was her doubt of Mallaby. If only she *knew* that be had sacrificed himself for her father, then could she crush every feeling save that of devotion to him; but might not the restless, haunting fear which he was betraying more and more every day, be caused by the fact that when that should happen which he so mysteriously dreaded, it would reveal to her his utter duplicity? and then she would discover that she was herself only the victim of a cruel fraud, owing not alone no duty to her guardian, but even no gratitude, since all his kindness to her had been well remunerated by his own dishonest personal use of her fortune? And it would be for this that she had made *her* sacrifice. These were the thoughts which so often troubled her, and which were torturing her now as she walked on slowly with her head bent. It needed all her faith, all her resolution, all her prayer, to keep her from yielding to a very abandon of grief. She tried to comfort herself by remembering what her Confessor had said, when in the beginning of her trial she had disclosed her feelings to him; that her sacrifice at the first had been made from a true sense of duty, however imperfect her motives and incomplete her renunciation might have been afterward, and that God would surely bless her, no matter how seemingly futile it might prove to be; and then she turned to the picture he had drawn for her of Christ's renunciation and agony. At that stage of her thoughts, she reached the end of the path on which she had been walking, and lifting her eyes to determine which direction she should take next, she saw a few yards ahead of her, Mallaby. He was standing on the walk that skirted the water, and evidently gazing seaward. How stooped he had become! His shoulders rose until they seemed little less than a hump, and his long, light coat hung on his form as if it were much too large for him. Even his pantaloons seemed to have shrunken away more than usual from his ankles leaving those bony members in a very much exposed condition. His umbrella was held behind him, the knotty protuberances of its huge, horn handle which she could plainly distinguish from where she stood, sticking up with a grotesque look. The

memory of the feelings with which she used to regard his appearance during her schools days, rushed back to her, but they excited neither mortification nor amusement. She had gotten beyond all
vanity now and thought but alone of her duty.

While she stood looking at him, she saw approaching from the other side a very slender young man
dressed in a bright blue suit; even his hat was of the
same azure hue, and it cast a sort of blue hue over his
beardless, stupid-looking features. That which attracted her attention more even than his appearance
was the hurried manner in which he walked until
he arrived within a half dozen yards of Mallaby.
Then he stopped abruptly, thrust his hands into
his pockets, put his head on one side and began to
stare intently at Mallaby who ignorant that he was
the object of any observation continued to gaze out
to sea. Miss Hammond became uneasy as she
watched the protracted stare of the stranger, — a
proof of her inoculation with the mysterious fear of
her guardian—and she started toward him with unwonted speed. Having reached him she gently touched his shoulder. He turned as suddenly and fearfully
as if her touch had been the hand to summon him to
his fate, and beholding her hardly reassured him, for
what could have brought her? she had never been in
that place before. Seeing his agitated surprise she
hastened to explain.

"In coming home I rode further than I intended to
do, and seeing this place I was attracted to walk
here. I caught sight of you, and while I was looking
at you, that young man seemed to set himself deliberately to watch you."

Mallaby turned in the direction she indicated and
saw the youth still surveying him.

"I shall find out what he wants," he said, trying
to make his voice firm and calm, and with Agnes beside him, he approached the stranger, recognizing

as he did so, the queer youth who on a memorable occasion had returned a letter to him.

The recognition—potent as it was with all the youth *might* have discovered from the perusal of that letter, though Mallaby remembering distinctly its contents felt that it had revealed nothing—rather added to Mallaby's fear. Had it not been that Agnes was beside him, and that for her sake he felt he must assume a confidence, and even an indignation he was far from feeling, he would have gone his way and left the spy undisturbed. He knew nothing of Miss Liscome's relation to the youth, for Kellar, owing to reasons of his own, had never told the result of his acceptance of that lady's invitation to tea; how it had revealed to him the incident of the miscarried letter, and the amount of Miss Liscome's knowledge of Jared.

Before they reached the young man he turned and absolutely ran away, not relaxing his speed until he was quite out of sight.

"Some demented creature," said Mallaby, looking after him, and wiping the perspiration from his face, though there was neither sufficient heat in the day nor hurry in his walk, to have caused it.

"Perhaps so," Agnes answered wearily. She was so tired of it all: the fear, the suspicion, the restlessness in which they lived; the mysterious secret that haunted his life; the horrid doubt that tortured her own.

XXXVI.

On other occasions Miss Hammond saw the singular youth; she saw him when she went to take an
omnibus, or a car, on her daily journey to the homes
of her pupils; twice she met him directly as she left
the house, and he was always in a sort of frantic
hurry either absolutely running, or walking with
such extraordinary speed it was little less than a run,
and so far from seeming to maintain any watch of her,
he hardly appeared to see her. That he was watching her guardian she felt certain, and that her guardian must know of this singular espionage, she felt
equally sure; since, however, he forbore to speak of it
she also was silent. But when he came to her one day
and asked if she would mind going up town to live
she knew then that he was aware of the spy at their
door, and he knew by the manner of her ready assent, that she was also aware of it. Yet neither referred to it. Nor was the change to up-town quarters permanent; for though released apparently from
the vigilance of the blue-dressed youth, they saw no
more of him, Mallaby seemed to feel an ever-urgent
necessity for frequent removal. Further up town,
then to the east side, again to the west, they went,
Agnes never protesting, never hesitating, never
questioning, and Mallaby, never excusing, never
explaining, never alluding to the mysterious source
of his restlessness. He knew in his heart there was
little use in it all, for if there were spies upon his
track he would be found when he was wanted no
matter where he went, and it was not so much to flee

from that espionage as it was to escape from the curious observations which his own nervous, haunted manner brought upon him from the people of every house in which they took up their abode.   He had grown to be painfully shy of it, and just so soon as it began to be marked the landlady was told that he and his ward would engage board in another part of the city.

Thus more than a wretched year passed leaving traces of its misery in the increased furrows of Mallaby's face, the diminished corpulence of his figure, and the death-like pallor and the worn look of his ward.   She was still bound to the wheel of her monotonous and laborious employment, and painfully realizing that its proceeds were actually necessary. Her guardian's frequent change of office quarters together with his diminished energy were sensibly lessening his business profits, and he could no longer conceal the fact.   She strove to redouble *her* energies, seeking more pupils, and wondering if she could not utilize her evening hours in some way.   Filled with the idea she answered one of the advertisements for a female copyist, the work to be done at home, and saying nothing of the matter to Mallaby in order to spare his feelings.

She received an answer desiring her to call at an office on Reade Street.   Responding to it she ran across her guardian just as she was turning into the street from Broadway.   He was evidently collecting bills, and he seemed to have something of his old-time energy and briskness; but he turned ghastly when he saw her.   The slightest untoward incident might be so full of portentous meaning now.   She had to explain, but she ended with a sort of plea to be permitted to fulfill her intention.

The color came back to his face, but the large, freckled hand that held sundry papers shook as if it were palsied.

"Things have not come to such a pass that you must work day and night," he said, speaking with the air of one who had received a cruel blow, and then he turned in an opposite direction to that she had been pursuing, evidently expecting her to accompany him. She stood wavering between her anxiety to secure the work seemingly within her reach, and her desire not to widen the wound she felt she had already given him. He looked back at her motioning her to follow. She obeyed, expecting him to say something when she reached him, but he was silent walking on with his head drooped, his umbrella held very tight under his left arm, and his right hand seeming to clutch, rather than hold some papers. They turned out of Reade Street into bustling, crowded Broadway. It was almost the hour of noon, a time when business seemed to be at its greatest rush, and people were hurrying as if cases of life or death depended on their steps. The autumn sun was shining brightly, giving a sort of cheerful beauty to the human picture.

"We shall go home," he said, when they reached Franklin Street, and he paused to wait for a stage. She felt that he was taking her home to show his utter disapproval of what she had contemplated and to prevent the execution of her intention, but she did not answer. The stage was in sight; Mallaby stepped closer to the curb, Agnes followed him while the crowd surged about them.

Suddenly the crowd seemed to part for some one who forced his way through it; some one who reared himself before Mallaby like a great black shadow sprung out of the sunshine, and a hand was placed on Mallaby's shoulder, while a voice said with horrible distinctness:

"Matthias Mallaby, you are my prisoner!"

And Mallaby looking round with a gasp and a shiver saw the hand, and looking up he met the strong, stern face with its triumphant eyes, and he knew that his long dreaded doom had found him. He turned to Agnes—white, horror-stricken Agnes —the look in his eyes that recalled the evening when he, with her andFlorence, stood upon the stoop on Hubert Street; but, he only said in a husky whisper: "My dear, it has come."

XXXVII.

It had come. The fate that Mallaby had been
so sickeningly expecting, the mysterious something
that Miss Hammond had been dreading, and it was
a charge of murder, a murder said to have been committed by Matthias Mallaby in California twenty
years before. That much knowledge Mallaby could
no longer conceal from his ward, and that much
knowledge made her frantic with the thought if
what Mallaby had told her in the past were true, it
was *her* father who was guilty of this crime of murder.

Unmindful of the presence of the officer who had
accompanied them home and who would not leave
them until he had his prisoner safely on a westward-
bound train, she knelt at Mallaby's feet clasping his
knees with her arms, and crying through her streaming tears:

"What shall I say to you? what shall I do for you
—I, the daughter of the murderer whom you have so
nobly shielded!"

"Hush!" he said, stooping to her and trying to
raise her, his face as ghastly as her own, and his
voice tremulous and husky.

"They will let me go with you?" she continued,
turning with a frightened, questioning glance to the
officer, who smiled grimly, but did not answer, at
which she bounded to her feet, repeating wildly:

"They will not prevent my going with him, will
they?"

"No one can prevent your traveling on the same
train, young lady," he answered with a sort of kind
evasiveness: but the answer did not satisfy her.

"He is my guardian," she said, with simple touching earnestness, "and it is my father who is guilty; my dead father, to save whose memory, and to save me from the dishonor, Mr. Mallaby let himself be charged with the crime. I must go with him to do as I would do for my father for whose sake he suffers, and to tell those who will try him that he is not the guilty one."

Mallaby, too much overcome to try to stop her had buried his face in his hands, while the detective touched in spite of himself by the beauty, grief and simplicity of the speaker, answered very kindly:

"If you can prove that on the trial it will be well; but the simple fact of your saying so will not make the jury believe it."

"But he, Mr. Mallaby, must tell them, as he has told me," she said, at which a queer, skeptical expression came for a moment into the detective's face; and then remembering suddenly the oath which Mallaby had told her, she turned to him and whispered:

"Are you so bound by that oath that you will not be able to tell everything on your trial?"

He took his hands from his face and nodded. He could not trust himself to speak. If only he could have uttered one word; but the phantom seemed to stalk between him and the face of his ward, and the lips that once had shrieked after him the very words he had used in the taking of his oath, now seemed to open again as if to curse him did he betray an iota.

"Then *I* shall plead to the jury," said Agnes wildly, her eyes streaming with tears; "*I* shall tell them of your care of me, of your devotion to my father, your long suffering for his sin. I shall touch their hearts—I—"

She could say no more for the sobs that choked her, and she fled to an adjoining room to give vent to her grief in solitude.

Mallaby by an unwonted grace, was permitted two days to arrange his affairs, but he was everywhere either accompanied, or shadowed by the officer; Miss Hammond also, with a strength of will that surmounted every emotion and every doubt, made the arrangements for *her* departure. In addition to the strain of her position, she had to bear the impertinent and unfeeling curiosity of the people of the house, for the presence of an officer of the law, having been found out by some means, both she and her guardian were the objects of most trying scrutiny; and aware of that, she schooled her face into an impassable expression—beyond its pallor it told nothing. But never was her soul so torn by emotions. The daughter of a murderer—well was it that her engagement with Wilbur had been broken, for, keener than any anguish of her own, would have been the disgrace she would have inflicted upon him; then the prospect of either the extreme penalty of the law, or a life imprisonment for Mallaby to whom she owed so much— oh God! how could she live on and know that he was suffering for her father's crime? and again the horrid doubt that Mallaby might not have told her the truth. If only she could be quite sure of that; would his trial make it clear? would it do anything but prove him guilty of the crime with which he was charged, and so leave her in the same horrid, torturing, awful uncertainty?

What prayers and tears she poured out in her hurried visits to the Blessed Sacrament, and what acts of renunciation she made!

Mallaby betrayed outwardly as little as his ward did, the conflicting emotions of *his* soul. Now that that which he so long dreaded had really happened, a pressure seemed to be removed, and he would have felt thankful and relieved had it not been for Agnes. She was so utterly unprovided for. All the means that he could furnish would pay little more than

the expenses of her journey. And he had no friends
in California to whom he might intrust her. He
groaned when he thought of it. He had tried to induce her to return to Mrs. Denner, whom, despite
her faults of curiosity and inquisitiveness, he knew
to be kind-hearted, and there remain until the end
of his trial; but Agnes would listen to nothing save
accompanying him. She would earn her living in the
west as she earned it in the east, she said, and he
was forced to be silent.

Some of the morning papers of the day on the
evening on which they were to depart, contained a
sensational account of Matthias Mallaby, and his
arrest for murder. How, or who furnished the account it was difficult to say, for even the officer who attended him, and who courted as much quiet as he
could do seemed to be very much annoyed by it.
The writer of the article, however, knew little of
Mallaby's antecedents, for nothing was told further
than Mallaby had come from California to New York,
several years ago, and since in his business avocation
had borne an unblemished reputation. That article
met Mrs. Denner's eye, or rather her ear through her
husband's eye, for he reading it, told her. She
was making sauce for a pudding and she had been
carefully managing the ingredients so that they
should not depart from the narrow way of the bowl,
but, at the news about Mallaby, she let the spoon
which she held, flop into the mixture, and sent the
latter streaming over the vessel and down on the
spotless table.

Another time, and the sight would have harrowed
her, both, because of the loss of material and the
stains that were made; but on this occasion she was
too much astonished, and to do her justice, in too
much grief for Mr. Mallaby to care about trifles.

True to her promise to herself when Mallaby left
her, she had discovered where he had gone, and

when he again changed his residence she managed
to find that out also, though she failed to learn the
locality of his second removal. The fact, however, of
his frequent changes had given her intense satisfaction; it was an indisputable proof of the superiority
of her house.

The article in the paper gave Mallaby's address and
stated that he would start that evening for the West,
and those facts determined Mrs. Denner to prompt
action.

"That poor child, Miss Agnes," she said, "may
need something I can do for her. I shall get ready
this minute and go to her."

In the natural kindness of her heart she had forgotten her former anger at Miss Hammond's reticent
leave taking when that young lady was going away,
not a word having been imparted to satisfy the good
woman's devouring curiosity regarding the strangely
absent suitor. She tortured herself with conjectures
about the sudden cessation of his visits, and at
length she felt certain that the departure from her
house with Mr. Mallaby and his ward, was due to the
breaking of Mr. Wilbur's engagement to Miss Hammond. As everybody in the house knew of that engagement it would be of course too mortifying to the
young lady and her guardian to remain after it was
broken. Now, as she bustled about her preparations
for immediate departure, there came to her mind
thoughts of the mysterious letters Mallaby used to
receive, and later, the mysterious visitor who had
the extraordinary privilege of going to Mallaby's
room and who remained there so long.

"There was some heavy trouble on his mind," she
soliloquized, "but, he's innocent; I know he is, that
blessed man!" and then recurring to the numerous
kindnesses of which her children and herself had
been the recipient from him, she burst into tears,
still, however, continuing to soliloquize, but in a

manner as if she were defending Mr. Mallaby from
visible accusers.

"I tell you he wouldn't hurt a cockroach," she
said, trying to make the skirt of an old-fashioned dress
meet round her corpulent figure, "much less as kill
a man; why, I've known him to save a half-drowned
fly, saying, to let the poor little thing enjoy its life;
and then to tell me that he's a murderer—Mr. Mallaby as is the gentlest, kindest, sweetest, modestest
man the Lord ever made," and her tears streamed beyond all control. She was obliged to cover her
face with a veil, and thus screened, but with her
tears still flowing she set forth.

Miss Hammond had closed all her engagements
with the parents of her pupils, and as her engagements were closed before the appearance of the article in the paper, none of them knew the cause.   They
wondered at the suddenness, and deplored the necessity, but Miss Hammond's own reserved manner
seemed to forbid even the proffer of friendship
which some of the mothers, in admiration of the music teacher's beauty and accomplishments, might
have been disposed to make.   The next day, that on
which they were to start, Miss Hammond packed her
trunk.   So far she had endured the strain with a
strength and coolness that surprised herself; but now,
when the trunk,—the same little modest article that
had accompanied her from the Convent—was locked
and ready to go into the expressman's arm, a sudden sense of her utter desolation of female friends
seemed to overpower her.   Most girls had somebody;
a mother, sister, or companion; she had no one.

True, she remembered her kind teachers of the
Sacred Heart, but in the beginning she had neglected
to maintain a correspondence with them, and afterwards she was too proud to reveal to them her hu-
miliations.   She threw herself sobbing into a chair.
Just then there was a knock at the door, and the

tow-headed servant without waiting for a response thrust her fluffy locks within the room.

"There's a lady to see you, Miss, and as she said she was an old friend of yours, and as the parlor's taken up with men to see that officer, I thought you wouldn't mind if I just brought her up—she's out in the hall."

Agnes arose in a sort of mute, but indignant protestation, knowing no lady to whom she would have accorded the privilege of a visit to her bed-chamber; but, Mrs. Denner quite unveiled, and with her eyes still streaming, and her whole face showing a sincere sympathy and grief, had followed the girl to the doorway. Her presence seemed almost like an answer to Miss Hammond's longing for some one, and remembering only the motherly interest which Mrs. Denner had always tried to show, Miss Hammond rushed to her, threw her arms about her, and continued upon her breast the sobs that had only been interrupted by her entrance.

Within the room, with the door closed upon the fluffy-haired domestic, Mrs. Denner told how she came to make her present visit. Then Agnes told in return all that *she* knew of what had happened to Mr. Mallaby, her account comprising the fact he was suffering for her father's crime. In justice to her guardian she told that, and Mrs. Denner instead of being shocked as Miss Hammond had expected her to be, put her arms the closer around the young lady, and said:

"You poor, dear, darling child: it's little wonder your heart would be broken—but maybe it won't come out so bad after all: it's not at the blackest side we ought to look."

And then they cried together, and it was only after a little that Agnes was enabled to tell she was going to San Francisco with her guardian.

"San Francisco!" repeated Mrs. Denner. " I have

a sister there; it was only last week I had a letter
from her, and I'll tell you where she lives, and give
you a bit of a note to her—maybe it would serve
you if you wanted a place to stay in when you get
there.''

And Agnes thankfully accepted the proffer.

XXXVIII.

MRS. DENNER made one of the strange little party which, a few hours after her meeting with Agnes, alighted from a cab at the Jersey City ferry-house. The officer, fearing that the notoriety given by the newspaper article might lead to the discovery of their presence and make them objects of morbid observation, hurried his prisoner to the boat in waiting, Agnes and Mrs. Denner quickly following.

That their presence was known and had been even awaited, was evident from a group of people who followed them from the moment of their alighting from the cab, and who persisted in following and staring until the little party had actually boarded the train. How thankful Agnes was for the companionship of a female, as the ill-mannered and morbid group of spectators, finding that she was with the prisoner pressed close to her, and even rudely attempted to penetrate beneath her veil. Not a word was spoken until they were on the car and it was time for Mrs. Denner to go. She had given Miss Hammond the letter she had promised, and now, to avert the scene she felt she would be sure to make, did she begin at once to say good-bye, she said instead:

"You will go at once to my sister, dear, and of course, you will write to me how you like San Francisco;" speaking as if Miss Hammond were starting on the most ordinary journey in the world; but then her eyes fell on Mallaby's drooping figure, the old, familiar umbrella lying across his lap, and she could carry her stoicism no further.

"Oh, Mr. Mallaby!" she cried, stooping toward him, and taking his big, freckled hands in her own: "You poor, dear, blessed man!"

"It is time for you to go," said the detective, apprehensive of further notice being drawn upon them by the woman's outburst, and Mrs. Denner having no small fear of this officer of the law, drew back immediately, Mallaby looking at her the gratitude he did not express, and smiling upon her in that touchingly sad manner which, as she expressed it afterward, made her want to cry her heart out."

Miss Hammond went to the door of the car with her, giving her a last embrace on the very platform, and then hurrying to her seat, she saw her still near the track when the engine having shrieked its warning whistle, the train started on its way. Mrs. Denner could hardly tear herself from the spot even when the cars had whirled entirely out of sight, her heart was so filled with the unhappy travelers. Her grief and sympathy had excluded for the time even her curiosity to know about Wilbur; why his engagement to Miss Hammond had been broken—the young lady had not once mentioned his name, and Mrs. Denner had been too full of the dear child's present trouble to ask a question about him. Now, however, as she looked along the track over which the train had passed, she thought of him, and stigmatized him as a dastard, "for," she soliloquized, "all this wasn't in the paper without his knowing it, big gentleman as he is, and why, even if the marriage was broken off, couldn't he at least come forward to ask to do something for her. The Lord help us, how it's the way of the world to leave us when we're in trouble."

That strange wretched journey! How often during it Agnes recalled the longing of her school days for travel; to behold the scenes of which she read with such interest and delight; now, they whirled by her without arousing a gleam of interest, or curiosity. She seemed to herself as she looked listlessly from the car window, like one in a nightmare, wondering when she should experience the relief of awaking. Objects lost their picturesqueness in the thought of the guilt of her father, the fact that Mallaby was suffering for it, and the constant, but futile endeavor to think what *she* could do in the interest of justice.

Though permitted to see Mallaby frequently she rarely spoke to him. What could she say that she would have said in the presence of the officer, or that she could say to Mallaby himself at such a time? And he had as little disposition to speak; had he trusted himself to do so, his overcharged feelings might have betrayed him into some violation of his oath, and now, that in spite of him, his trial might reveal what he had so solemnly sworn to guard, he was more painfully anxious to have no mark of a broken pledge upon his conscience. He seemed to be wonderfully calm; no trace of agitation, nor anxiety, at any time in his manner, and his eyes constantly fixed upon the scenes which they passed, with the air of a man engaged in some earnest retrospection.

As they neared the end of the journey he referred with a sort of mournful satisfaction to the letter of introduction Agnes held to Mrs. Denner's sister.

"She will be kind to you, I am sure," he said, " kind, while I am in prison; "and then his eyes that had seemed to leave the exterior view in order to seek her face, but which had looked beyond rather than at her, resumed their mournful, preoccupied observation.

It was well that on their arrival in that utterly strange, unfamiliar city the young woman had a letter of introduction; it was a sort of sheet anchor in the gale of utter desolation that overtook her as the time neared for her parting with Mallaby. He was to be taken immediately to prison, and all that could be done for her was to consign her to the care of the driver of one of the public cabs, giving him instructions where to take her.

"They will let me in to the prison to-morrow to see you?" she asked, addressing Mallaby, but seeming to expect an answer from the officer, and that person compassionate from two sources, a naturally kind heart, and his sympathy for the unprotected girl, answered kindly:

"There will be no doubt about that—I shall see that permits are sent to you to enable you to see him, if possible every day."

"Thank you," murmured with a half sob, for she was trying so hard to keep her tears back, and then she turned entirely to Mallaby.

He was standing in his old, familiar attitude, his umbrella under his arm, and evidently, endeavoring to preserve a sort of indifferent composure, not looking at her but up at the cloudless, California sky.

Taking one of his hands in both of her own, she clasped it very tight.

"I shall go to see you to-morrow, Mr. Mallaby, and every day—I shall pray for you, I shall think of you and love you for what you have so nobly done; but more than all I shall pray to God to have justice done you."

She had succeeded to the end in controlling all e-motion save a slight tremulousness of voice, and for an instant he let his eyes meet hers; they had the expression which recalled the evening in Hubert Street; then he looked again towards the sky, and she dropped his hand and turned away. He wondered with a sort of inward shiver what change her feelings would undergo when she knew.

XXXIX.

MRS. SIBLY, Mrs. Denner's sister, unlike Mrs. Denner, was small, slender, pretty and refined-looking. She was a childless widow having a little means to which she added by renting furnished rooms. Her quiet manner and neat appearance were in favorable contrast to her sister in the East, and they prepossessed and even in a measure refreshed the tired, desolate girl seeking not alone acquaintance but a home.

She was also kind-hearted and sympathetic, and having read the letter—an extravagant account of Miss Hammond's many virtues—and having heard Miss Hammond's own brief, simple account of the cause of her presence in California, she seemed to take the young lady to her affections at once, but in an exceedingly quiet and gentle manner.

Thus, Agnes found herself comfortably domiciled and with the unexpected companionship of a sympathetic friend on her daily journeys to the prison, for Mrs. Sibly would not suffer the young lady to go out alone, even when the latter became sadly familiar with the route. Then, Mrs. Sibly was a devout Catholic, and embraced with the same eagerness that Agnes did, opportunities to visit the Blessed Sacrament, and to pour out before it long, fervent prayers. With Agnes the burden of every petition was, as she had said to her guardian it would be, that justice should be done to him—that everybody should know how he had sacrificed himself, and that it was her father who was guilty. She crushed the thoughts that rose of the obloquy which would attach to her, as the daughter of a murderer, the thrice bitter

thoughts of Wilbur's satisfaction in having missed
so disgraceful an alliance should he hear the true
facts in the case as he could hardly fail to do, when,
if the justice she craved were granted, the papers west
and east would be full of it. She heroically struggled against every feeling but that which seemed to
be her present duty, absolute devotion to Mallaby.
Her doubt of him grew less with every visit to his
prison-cell—he was so gentle and uncomplaining, so
courteously thankful to the officials about him, so
calm in his manner at all times. All was a proof,
Agnes thought, that the story of his sacrifice must
be true—it was the consciousness of his innocence
which made him thus patient and resigned; were it
not so, some agitation of his guilty conscience must
betray itself. And each time she left him it was
with a burning desire to have some opportunity to
sacrifice herself for his sake.

The trial began at length—the trial of Francis
Forrester, Alias Matthias Mallaby, for the murder of
Reuben Turner in the gold mines in 18—.

Owing to the attention which the press had been
drawing to the case, the court-room was crowded,
not a few being ladies, and these concentrated their
observation on the slender, veiled figure of Miss
Hammond. The papers, according to their sensational wont, had discanted on the devotion which she
showed to her guardian, and on her arrival in the
court she was immediately pointed out. Mrs. Sibly
accompanied her, and the two had places almost directly opposite the prisoner.

Confinement had told upon him in the attenuation
of his figure, and his big, white, freckled hands seem-
de to be constantly in uneasy positions as if they missed their usual care, the umbrella. His grizzled hair
showed far more white than red, and his brown eyes
from the worn pallor of his face seemed to have become larger and brighter. For an instant he turned

them about the court-room, and Agnes feeling that
they were in search of her threw up her veil and met
them; Mallaby smiled in response——a smile of such
unutterable kindliness and gratitude, her tears came
and she hastened to cover her face again.

That first day consisted of little more than impan-
elling the jury. On the next, the prisoner pleaded
"Not guilty."

"Thank God!" said Agnes, beneath her veil. She
had feared that his sacrifice would go even to the
extent of accusing himself in court of the crime.

Then the examination of the witnesses against the
accused commenced, and the first one called was
Nathan Kellar.

Agnes started and threw up her veil. It was he,
the mysterious acquaintance of her guardian, and
he took his place with a brisk step in the witness-
stand,—looking as large, portly, and flashily and ex-
pensively dressed as when she had seen him in New
York. His manner was that of confidence and
triumph combined; he had even the effrontery when,
having ascended to his place he stared quickly, but
cooly around the court-room, to bow slightly to Miss
Hammond, She colored with indignation and dropped her veil.

The substance of his testimony was, that twenty-
three years before he had met the prisoner, Francis
Forrester, in New York. Forrester had just arrived
from England, and was anxious to make a fortune
in America. He, Kellar, in company with a cousin
since dead, induced him to accompany them to
California intending that all three should try their
luck in the gold mines. But, Forrester becoming ill
in San Francisco remained there. Two years after,
Forrester accompanied by Reuben Turner, went to
the mines, and meeting again with Kellar and
Kellar's cousin, resumed his acquaintance with
them. The four became close companions, the com-

panionship being marred alone by the frequent quarrels between Forrester and Turner. The quarrels
seemed to spring out of some inexplicable dislike of
Turner entertained by Forrester, and were always
provoked by the latter; that on one occasion, he,
Kellar, and his cousin were obliged to interfere to
save Turner from the summary wrath of Forrester;
that, on that occasion Forrester was heard to say
he would fix Turner some day. That, on a certain
night, when Kellar, and the deceased cousin of the
latter, and Turner, were sitting together playing
cards, Forrester suddenly drew a pistol on Turner;
that Turner fell, exclaiming :

"Forrester has killed me!" and that at the moment of his fall and exclamation, another of the
miners had come upon the scene, a man named
Wildred Everley. That Kellar's cousin having conceived a liking for Forrester, and now pitying him
because of the consequences that would ensue from
his crime, insisted to have it given out that the murdered man had committed suicide; that he induced
Kellar despite the latter's conscientious protest to
consent to the plan. That Everley also was won to
the same view. That the plan was fully carried out.
Everybody supposed that Reuben Turner, from his
despondency at his ill luck, had committed suicide.
That Kellar and his cousin accompanied Forrester
when the latter took the body of his victim to San
Francisco there to be interred by relatives.

That Kellar and his cousin waited for the interment. That they then parted with Forrester and
went East, and after some time went to Australia.
That conscientious scruples had not ceased to torment
Kellar, but that they were always temporarily allayed by his cousin's compassionating arguments. That
on one occasion, about eight years after the murder,
having business which recalled him for a short time
to New York, he met Forrester, the latter having

assumed the name of Mallaby, and admitting to Kellar that he had assumed it in order to conceal his identity should any question ever arise of his part in the shooting of Reuben Turner.

That Kellar returned to Australia, and lived there with his cousin nearly eight years, when his cousin died. That Kellar's conscientious scruples regarding the murder, tormented him anew, and having no one to allay them as formerly, they kept increasing in vigor, until they compelled him to return again to New York and seek Forrester, or Mallaby. That he did so, and frankly told what had brought him.

That Mallaby defied him, saying that the lapse of so many years would make it difficult to prove the murder. That Kellar's testimony alone would not be sufficient, and that the man named Everley who had heard Reuben Turner's last exclamation, might be dead, or in some other way not accessible.

That Kellar, having seen in the papers occasional mention of John Turner, a rich and influential Californian, he conceived him to be the brother of the murdered man, and the same whom he had met in the home of Reuben Turner on his first visit to San Francisco, though at that time John Turner was a mere youth.

That, to ascertain the correctness of his surmise, he came to California, and finding John Turner absent in Europe he waited his return, ascertaining in the mean time, however, that he must be the Turner of whom he was in search.

That, on the return of John Turner from Europe, Kellar recalled himself to Turner's recollection, and laid before him the whole story of the shooting of his brother. That, John Turner, bitterly disliking Forrester in the past, was intensely imbittered when he found that the blood of his brother was on Forrester's hands, and that he swore to bring him to justice should it cost every cent of his immense fortune.

That John Turner immediately filed his accusation with the authorities, and placed his means at their disposal in order to ferret out such witnesses as would be necessary in the case.

During the delivery of Kellar's evidence he did not look toward the prisoner, but at its conclusion he turned and faced him, with a cool, leisurely stare of triumph.

Mallaby seemed to receive it with the utmost composure; not a muscle of his face moved, not a change of color came into his worn features.

The next witness summoned was Prudence Liscome. Miss Hammond with a gasp threw up her veil and leaned forward with total forgetfulness of the observation she was attracting to herself. Having seen, nor heard nothing of Miss Liscome since the day on which she bade her farewell at Mrs. Denner's door, she could not imagine what *she* should have to do with her guardian, and it seemed to her as she watched the woman ascend to the witness-stand, as if some fantastical labyrinth were closing about them all.

Prudence, though somewhat abashed by her elevated and exposed position, was still endeavoring to smirk at everybody, and that fact together with her gay and ridiculously juvenile attire, and rouged face presented a sight that caused an audible titter. That she was uncomfortable was apparent from her awkward attitude, and that she was confused, was equally apparent when she began to give her evidence; she interspersed it with so much she need not have told, and that made it necessary for the counsel to remind her frequently she was straying from the point.

She knew Mr. Mallaby; he was at one time so intimate a friend that on every occasion she called him "dear," at which ingenuous statement many in the court-room laughed audibly. She had so much trust in him, (looking at the jury with an expression that seemed to say: "and he was one of your sex, gentlemen,") that she applied to him for advice about the investment of her money, and, in her gratitude she tendered to him a souvenir, which he in a sort of savage manner refused to accept. At this point she was sternly admonished to keep to the point, and not introduce irrelevant facts, whereupon she bowed, smirked more broadly than before, and said her only object was to make known what a heartless man Mr. Mallaby was, at which some of the people laughed again so loudly that they were called to order.

Miss Liscome continued, how, by accident having read a letter intended for Mr. Mallaby, but which seemed to be directed to her nephew, she found in it mysterious allusions to some one named "Jared." That, after the letter had been returned to Mr. Mallaby, without letting him know how it had been read, she, conceiving, from the account given by her nephew of the agitation with which Mr. Mallaby had received the letter that he must have some fear of this "Jared," used to mention the name as if she had been in secret communication with the person so named, and the mention of it invariably produced in Mr. Mallaby signs of an extraordinary fear and agitation.

But all this was not told without more stern admonitions to keep to the point, and when informed that she might leave the stand she seemed inclined to make further communications of her personal feelings for the prisoner.

Mallaby had not been able to repress a start when he saw Miss Liscome, and he flushed with astonishment and indignation when she referred to the incident of proffering him a souvenir; but what were his feelings when he learned the source and extent of her mysterious knowledge of "Jared." He knew now

for the first time that the young man who had made
so ludicrous a scene when returning the letter was
Miss Liscome's nephew, and the same who had been
a spy upon his track in New York.   Then, he remembered how Kellar had accepted her invitation to
take tea with her, and how silent he had been about
her after.   So, it was all Kellar's work; the bringing
of such a witness to California, the secret espionage
kept upon Mallaby prior to his arrest; he wondered
if Kellar would be able to produce Everley as a witness, and if he would be able to produce another witness whose testimony in mercy to himself Miss Hammond ought to know.

Malliflower Mallary was next summoned, and to
the intense, though partially suppressed merriment
of most of the spectators, a tall youth whose attenuated proportions were more prominently set forth by
a bright blue cloth suit, seemed to shoot up into the
stand.   He was in such a frantic hurry to respond
to his name that he nearly had knocked down two
persons who were a little slow in getting out of his
way, and by his whirligig movements when he reached the stand almost rendered breathless the official
who had attempted to guide him.   He looked as if
he apprehended some injury, and at the first question of the prosecuting-attorney, he wheeled around
and faced that gentleman with the air of one entirely
on the defensive.

He would just "preface his remarks," his voice
pitched in such shrieky tones, that it reached to
every part of the court-room, by telling "the judge,
the gentlemen of the jury, and the ladies and gentlemen of the court," that it was with "no idle curiosity" he had come there as a witness.

His odd appearance, his queer voice, and his utterly unexpected and ridiculous language, caused
laughter that it took some minutes to subdue; and
in his subsequent testimony he would insist on pref-

acing his remarks, and reiterating that he was prompted by no idle curiosity, until the amusement of the court audience became almost beyond control. It was only when the prosecuting-attorney assumed his most stern manner that he could elicit from the witness how he had returned the letter intended for the prisoner, but which had come to him by mistake, and the agitation which the prisoner had manifested on that occasion. When told that he might leave the stand, he did so with a jump, and he dashed through the laughing spectators back to his place.

His testimony concluded the evidence for that day and Mallaby rising to accompany his guard back to prison, cast a quick timid glance at his ward.

She was still leaning forward in that attitude of strained and painful attention that the announcement of Miss Liscome's name had caused, but her eyes were fixed upon her guardian with a look that expressed doubt, anguish, and even a sort of terror. He understood the look. Miss Liscome's testimony had been a strange revelation to her, for he had been so silent about her visits to him. Oh God! must his fate continue to be in the blackness that shrouded it now, with even *her* heart doubting him, closing to him ? A film seemed to gather over his eyes; he was obliged to clutch the officer's arm for support and he turned away seeing nothing but that white face with its awful expression. She also turned away, dropping her veil, and catching Mrs. Sibly's arm.

"Get into the air quickly," she said, " my breath seems to have gone."

They took their wonted course to a church. At the door, Agnes said:

" Don't wait for me; I shall remain here a long time."

"But soon it will be the hour for your visit to Mr. Mallaby." answered Mrs. Sibly much surprised.

"I do not think I shall go to the prison to-day. I shall stay here instead."

Without another word she passed up quickly to one of the pews near the altar; there she dropped upon her knees, bowed her face in her hands and was motionless.

Mrs. Sibly very much astonished, and even somewhat anxious, waited in one of the rear pews, saying some prayers on her own account. To her, there did not seem to have been anything in the evidence thus far, to call for such strange deportment on the part of Miss Hammond; she had never before omitted her visit to her guardian.

But Agnes was plunged into a more raging sea of doubt than ever; a sea into which also came up all the distrust she had ever held of Mr. Mallaby. Why had he never referred to Miss Liscome's visits to his office, when he knew that she, Agnes, had met Miss Liscome at the Wilburs? How did Miss Liscome come to know Mallaby so well as was set forth in her deposition? why should she conceive the idea merely from reading the contents of a letter if those contents were so mysterious — of using the name of "Jared" as a weapon of terror over Mr. Mallaby's head, and why, if Mr. Mallaby were really innocent of the crime imputed to him, should he have shown on the return of the letter opened by another in mistake, the terrible agitation described by the witness, Malliflower Mallary? Then she remembered the letter which once had come to him in her presence, at the foot of Mrs. Denner's stoop—his agitation and perspiration at its reception, though the day was cold enough to make her shiver under her heavy cloak. And, everything else about him that had ever tended to her doubt, distrust, or suspicion, seemed to come up furiously, causing her to forget the arguments she had so often used in his favor. Then remembering all that she had sacrificed for him, she felt as if she fiercely hated him; not even the fact that the full revelation of his duplicity would relieve her from the obloquy of being the daughter of a murder- er, seemed to assuage her feelings. She could not go to him in such a state of mind; and she contin- ued to kneel, silent, motionless, but waging a fierce, inward battle with herself. She tried to pray, but, it was only after hours of that fierce struggle that her prayer became calm and resigned. She had tak- en no note of the lapse of time, and she was astonish- ed when Mrs. Sibly touched her on the shoulder, and told her it was almost evening. That good lady had gone home, but becoming anxious as the day wore on she had returned to look for Miss Hammond. She was surprised to find her still in an attitude of devotion.

XL.

The counsel engaged for Mr. Mallaby, had the reputation of gaining cases on the most slender threads of evidence. He worked up forgotten, or obscured clues in a manner that shamed the detectives, and he turned the quibbles of the law to the favor of his client in a way that amazed the jury; but, in the present case, the chief obstacle to success, was the client himself. He had positively refused to disclose anterior circumstances that might help to prove his guiltlessness of intention in committing the murder, and the utmost the attorney could get from him was the name of a woman who knew these anterior circumstances, and who would violate no pledge, as Mallaby would do, by disclosing them. But Mallaby had neither seen nor heard from her for over twenty years, at which date she was somewhat past middle age, and a childless widow

The attorney had gone to work on this slender clew, inserting advertiseiments in the papers east and west, and offering large inducements for the appearance of the woman. Each day, however, found him unsuccessful; the woman was evidently, either dead, or, possibly having merged her identity in a second marriage, was hidden away too securely to be found. And yet, this witness might be so necessary for the cause of his client.

Chafing under his failure to find her, and, as he regarded it, the insane refusal of his client to tell more than he had told, he said with a manner that betrayed his irritation:

"You are either an extraordinary character, Mr. Mallaby, or a very great fool."

Mallaby made no reply. He was sitting as he always sat since his incarceration, with his hands clasping his knees, and his head bowed down upon his breast. It was the evening of the day on which had been given the first testimony against him; that testimony which had caused such a look of terrified suspicion in Miss Hammond's countenance, and this was the first day on which she had failed to visit him. He had seen nothing since his return to his cell but her face; even when he glanced up at the attorney it was she who seemed to look at him rather than the determined countenance of the lawyer.

How much *he*, the wretched prisoner, longed for the finding of the woman who could tell all the circumstances without violating any pledge. Her testimony, at least, would make his honesty clear to Miss Hammond; without that testimony, Miss Hammond's doubt, suspicion, and horror, must remain, together with the additional pain of what *might* be disclosed during the remainder of the trial. He wondered, since Kellar had broken faith in so much, why he had not made one other revelation; it were better for the prisoner's sake that he had made it.

"You see, Mr. Mallaby," broke in the attorney again, "Mr. John Turner is savage about this case, and he is to go on the stand himself, to-morrow, and take up everything that can in any way tell against you. It is absolutely necessary that I should be in possession of every fact anterior to the shooting in order to show that, at least, it was not premeditated."

"I am sorry that I cannot help you, Mr. Fullerton," replied Mallaby, with the air of one denying a favor that was to benefit another than himself--"but my oath is more sacred to me, than what the consequences of this charge may be."

Fullerton, disappointed and irritated left his client.

The next day, the court-room was more densely crowded than ever, the press having given sensational accounts of the trial, and having accorded great prominence to the fact that John Turner, the influential millionaire, known the whole length of the Pacific slope, would testify against the prisoner.

The poor, drooping prisoner had but one thought, Agnes. All night he had slept but little, being haunted by her face as he had seen it last, and the moment he had taken his place within the bar, he looked for her. She was not there, nor anywhere in the court-room that he could see, nor could he distinguish the little veiled woman in black who always accompanied her. His heart gave a bound and then seemed to sicken with a sort of despairing reaction. Had some one anticipating the remaining testimony of the trial, told her? was that the cause of her absence? if so, what hope had *he*.

His head sank lower upon his breast; he hardly heard the buzz of the people about him, nor did he seem to be aware when his counsel whispered to him —not until in startlingly loud and distinct tones, the name, John Turner, was called. That aroused him; he lifted his head, straightened a little in his chair, and looked at the witness, wondering in a sort of vague way, if that stalwarth, heavily-bearded, and almost fierce-looking man, could be the pale, slender youth whom he remembered as John Turner.

There was an impassioned energy about every movement of the witness, and an emphasis in his tone that told unmistakably of the fierceness of his hatred for any one. He wasted no words in his evidence, every phrase was cut like his own character, with determination, accuracy and directness.

He knew the prisoner, Francis Forrester, alias Matthias Mallaby, when the latter was a member of the household of his brother, Reuben Turner. He knew him afterward as the husband of Reuben Tur-

ner's only child, Millicent. He knew him again as
the partner in a mining enterprise of his brother,
Reuben Turner, and in both of the latter relations he
knew him to be the cause of great unhappiness. He
had read letters from his brother, Reuben Turner,
to the latter's daughter complaining of the unkindness and unfairness of his son-in-law; he had listened to statements from his niece, Millicent, of her
dislike for her husband because of the latter's treatment of her father. On one occasion, when, goaded
to madness by these complaints, he sent an indignant letter to Forrester, he received a reply from
Forrester in which the latter threatened to fix his
father-in-law some day, and the witness having preserved that letter, as it was always his habit to preserve every letter, it was read before the court, and
there was no mistaking the threat. It was there in
the prisoner's large, old-fashioned penmanship, following indignant denunciation of the inexplicable
and unjust dislike of his father-in-law. And John
Turner further deposed that he was at the home of
his employer, ill, when the news of his brother's
suicide came, that he insisted on returning to see
his brother, and on beholding the ghastly sight, and
witnessing the grief and horror of his niece, Millicent, he had a relapse of his illness and was borne
back again to the house of his employer. His relapse
was so severe that he became delirious, and he did
not recover entire consciousness until several weeks
had elapsed. Then he learned that his niece was
dead, and her husband had gone no one knew whith
er.

That he heard nothing of his brother-in-law until
on his recent return from an extended tour in Europe he found awaiting him Mr. Kellar, who easily
recalled himself to the recollection of the witness,
and who told to the witness the facts pertaining to
the shooting of Reuben Turner. That Mr. Kellar

declared to the witness he made such disclosure solely to satisfy his conscience; because he scrupled
going to his grave without telling the truth to Reuben Turner's brother; that Mr. Kellar did not hint at
a wish to bring the murderer to trial; that he did
not even say that he knew the whereabouts of the
murderer. But, that the witness, John Turner, was
indignant to think that the stigma of suicide should
rest upon his brother, and he determined to bring
the facts to light, and the murderer to justice, though
it should cost his whole fortune. With that view,
the witness obtained all the information Mr. Kellar
could give, acting upon it accordingly. As he ended his testimony he seemed spurred by his vindic-
tive feelings to add:

"Investigate the trust he has held for the ward to
whom he is guardian; learn if it has been marked by
the treachery he pursued toward my niece and his
murdered victim, her father and my brother."

Mallaby lifted his head high at that speech, and
gazed with unflinching look at the witness; but, at
the same time he was thanking God in his heart that
Miss Hammond was not present. It would have
been another shaft of distrust in her soul, and a
shaft that he had no means yet of displacing.

Wildred Everley was next summoned, and despite
his effort at composure, Mallaby started. What fate
had kept Everley, who, twenty-two years before was
a man varying on old age, still vigorous enough to
ascend to the witness-stand with the agility of forty
instead of seventy years, and to give his testimony
in a sharp, brief, straightforward manner.

He recognized the prisoner, despite the changes
that time had wrought in the appearance of the latter, as Francis Forrester whom he knew as a miner.
They had worked together in the mines for a short
time previous to the shooting of Reuben Turner.
On the night of the shooting hearing a scuffle in the

cabin occupied by Forrester and his friends, he rushed in, but only in time to see a pistol in the hand of Forrester turned toward Turner, to hear its report, to see Turner fall, and to hear him exclaim that Forrester had killed him.

Immediately, Forrester was caught by his two friends, Kellar, and the latter's cousin, and hustled away from the fallen man, while he, Everley, examined the body of Turner to see if he were quite dead. He was dead, and Everley straightened his limbs, and laid him out on the floor of the cabin.

Then Kellar came to him, telling what his cousin proposed; that the shooting, for the sake of Forrester, and his poor young, friendless wife, be given forth as a case of suicide. Everley feeling that it made little difference to him, consented to say nothing about the matter and the next day, Forrester and his friends carrying with them the body of the supposed suicide left the mines.

After that he, Everley, was too much absorbed in his efforts to make a fortune for his own family, to give the matter any thought; and, having after the lapse of a few years made a moderate fortune, he went to reside in Southern California. There in recent years he frequently heard, and read of the millionaire, John Turner, but it never entered his mind to connect him with the Turner who had been so summarily shot in the mines, years before—not until a neighbor brought to him a newspaper containing a paragraph asking for information of one Wildred Everley, who had been a miner in early years, and who could give to John Turner some information of how his brother, Reuben Turner, had died.

That testimony closed the evidence for that day. It was said, that on the next day there would be taken the testimony of one more witness for the state, and then would begin the little evidence that could be adduced in favor of the accused.

As the court adjourned, the prisoner wondered who the witness could be who was to give testimony on the next day, and then he relapsed into his thoughts of Agnes. Would she come to-day?

When he returned to his cell, instead of taking his usual seat, he walked about uneasily, and at the slightest noise in the corridor glancing anxiously at the door. As the hours wore on without bringing her, he threw himself on a stool, and in utter dejection leaned forward until his face nearly touched his knees.

Miss Hammond had been so prostrated by her e-motions of the previous day, she was unable on the next morning even to leave her bed; successive attempts to do so but sent her back in a state of great-er weakness to her pillow. Mrs. Sibly, much alarm-ed, would have summoned a physician, but Agnes begged her to wait; she would be better as the day wore on. Her prediction was verified, but not to the extent of either going to the court, or to the prison. She was hardly sorry to be obliged to absent herself from the latter place, for how could she meet her guardian while her emotions about him were still so conflicting. With regard to her absence from the court-room, she hardly knew—whether to regret it. Might not the evidence as on the day before adduce things about Mallaby that would harrow her further? and she was so tired and so weak, she only craved a truce from every thought.

Early the next morning, finding Miss Hammond strong enough to prepare for her visit to the court, Mrs. Sibly would have read to her from the "Morning Chronicle," the testimony of the previous day; but, she was checked at the first word by the hand of Agnes laid heavily on her arm.

Don't, Mrs. Sibly; since I was not present yesterday, to hear it, I would rather not learn anything about it now.''

And Mrs. Sibly put away the paper, not even reading it to herself, but devoting her attention to Agnes.

When Mallaby took his place that day at the bar, he kept his eyes down for some seconds. He feared to raise them lest he should turn them to the place opposite, and find it again vacant. But, at length, he lifted them quickly, and threw a frightened glance across the sea of heads that intervened. Thank God! she was there, and as she met that sad, tender, and unutterably wistful look, something within her, despite herself, responded to it. She smiled at him, mournfully, it is true, but still, it was a smile that caused her pale features to light for a moment, and that brought to his heart a brief renewal of courage and hope.

The witness who was to be the last for the state, was called—Nanno Kelpley—and an old, and poorly, but cleanly dressed woman responded. It was evident from her manner that she had never been in a court of justice before, and that she regarded her presence there now, as somewhat derogatory to her self-respect. Her wrinkled face bore as bright a blush as though her years were sixteen, instead of sixty, and her eyes conveying an unusual degree of intelligence, sought the ground with a modest timidity, as often as she involuntarily raised them.

The prisoner gasped when he heard her name, and as he saw her ascend to the witness-stand, he half started from his seat. His counsel, Fullerton, with knit brows and flashing eyes stooped and whispered to him:

"No wonder *we* could not find her; from the first *they* have had her in secret keeping."

Nanno Kelpley, in a cracked, but strangely pathetic voice, deposed to having been a servant in the house of Mr. Reuben Turner; a servant, but one whose position also embraced the duties of house-

keeper, and in some measure elderly companion to
Reuben Turner's daughter when the mother of the
latter died.   The time to which she referred was in
the early, pioneer days of San Francisco, when houses
were built solely for shelter, and were destitute of
the modern appliances of luxury, or even convenience.
Reuben Turner kept a sort of general store in which
everybody dealt, and the witness, with growing volubility seemed inclined to linger in her account of
the day on which Mr. Forrester, with two other men
came for the first time to Reuben Turner's store.
Forrester seemed to have the most money and
promptly paid the bill of his companions. They were
on their way to the mines, but were nothing loath to
accept Turner's hospitality for a day, or two, while
they looked about San Francisco.

At that time, Turner's family consisted besides himself, of his daughter then eighteen years of age, and
Nanno Kelpley.   His young brother, a lad of nine-
teen, was employed some distance out of San Francisco, and only visited them at intervals.   During the
sojourn of the three strangers, Forrester became
sick, and his companions went on to the mines
leaving him in the house of Reuben Turner.   Then
Turner and Forrester seemed to become great friends
to the surprise and annoyance of Miss Turner who
had a sort of contempt for Forrester, holding up to
ridicule his odd dress and old-fashioned ways, until he helped her father with loans of money; then,
in her gratitude, she seemed to get to like Mr. Forrester, and finally in accordance with the wish of her
father she married him, and they lived happily until Mr. Forrester and his father-in-law went to the
mines.

Thence, letters came from Reuben Turner to his
daughter, which the latter used to read to Nanno
Kelpley, and they were filled with complaints of
his son-in-law, accusing the latter of unfairness, and

even dishonesty. These letters changed the regard of the wife to bitter hatred for her husband, a hatred that she even communicated to her young uncle, John Turner.

To this point of her evidence neither the prisoner, nor Miss Hammond had turned their eyes from her. The prisoner was looking with such emotions in his soul as seemed to tear it to pieces. Would no question of the council elicit from her what she ought to tell in common justice to him, in mercy to his ward? Would she step down from the stand, leaving still about him all the doubt distrust, and suspicion that enveloped him in the eyes of Agnes? And he could not open his lips. Oh God! it was hard.

To Agnes though her eyes were fixed quietly on the prisoner, and her form betrayed no movement of agitation, her heart was beating with wilder throbs that it had ever beat before. Mallaby, during all the years she had known him, had not so much as hinted that he had ever been married; now, to find that the murder with which he was charged was that of his own father-in-law, made her gasp and shiver inwardly, but without making an outward emotion, until it flashed upon her mind that, according to Mr. Mallaby's statement, it was not he who was guilty, but, her father; that Mallaby was but suffering the charge to be imputed to him. She gasped outwardly then, and turned her attention once more to the witness.

"Did you see Mr. Forrester after the reputed suicide of his father-in-law?" asked the counsel for the state.

"I did see him," replied the witness, "he came home with the body, he and the two men that came to the house first with him—I forget their names now —and his grief was terrible.

"The grief of his wife," she went on, without giving an opportunity to the counsel to continue his questions, "was as much because her father had taken his own life, as because of his death; she thought his soul could not be saved, and she used to say that if he had only died any other way she would be satisfied."

The counsel interrupted her; her evidence was out of form with the pointed questions he had prepared but which she gave him no opportunity to ask.

"You are here, Mrs. Kelpley, to testify to your knowledge of the bad feeling which existed between Reuben Turner and his son-in-law, during their stay together in the mines; that knowledge, as you learned it, from the letters read to you by Mrs. Forrester and to testify to the conduct of Mr. Forrester after his return from the mines."

The witness dropped a courtesy, answering at the same time with touching, but firm simplicity:

"Ah, sir; I must be allowed to tell me story in me own way, and if I'm a little roundabout or mixed in things I'm trying to tell, you must have patience."

"But, remember, woman, you are on oath, and you must be particular as to the facts.'

"It is because I am on me oath that I must tell me story in me own way. I was told when they brought me a few days ago to Mr. Turner's house, that it was found out how Mr. Forrester had killed his father-in-law, and that I was only wanted to tell in the court, what I knew of their bad feelings for each other, and how Miss Millicent disliked her husband for his treatment to her father. And I said nothing, one way, or the other then, but I made up my mind that if I was put on oath to tell one thing I'd tell another. I'd tell something that I never told before to mortal creature and that'll maybe surprise Mr. John Turner himself."

Up to that point there had been no stopping her, and it was evident from the strained attention of everybody, that her testimony out of order as it was,

was intensely interesting. Into the prisoner's face were coming repeated changes of color and expression. and he leaned forward and looked at the witness as if by the piercing and longing earnestness of his gaze he must force her to look at him; but her eyes seemed only to see the questioning attorney, or modestly to seek the floor.

The counsel, evidently annoyed at the woman's persistency, would—when at length she did stop with that strange innuendo to John Turner,—have forced her to give just the answers to his questions and nothing further, but the Judge interposed, and Nanno Kelpley was asked to continue her evidence in her own way, which she did in her former, simple manner, looking only at the counsel.

"When Mr. Turner was buried, Mr. Forrester's two friends that had come home with him from the mines, went away, and the lad, Mr. John Turner was taken away sick by the man that he worked for.

There was no one in the house but Mr. and Mrs. Forrester and me, and Mrs. Forrester was like to go out of her mind with grieving for her father's soul because he killed himself. Her baby was born a few days after, and her grief seemed to get worse; it was so bad, that Mr. Forrester came to me in his trouble about it, and he said, taking my hand:

"Nanno, I am going to tell my wife something, and you must come and hear it too."

"And I went with him, and he told us both, how *he* shot Mr. Reuben Turner, not meaning to do it, and how his friends advised him not to tell that, but to let it be thought the way it was, so that there would be no trouble made for him that might keep him away from his poor young wife; but that seeing her feel so badly, thinking that her father had killed himself, Mr. Forrester thought it might ease her to know the truth.

"But it did not ease her; of anything it made her

wilder. She said her father's blood was on her husband's hands, and neither of us could quiet her.
She would not let her husband touch the baby; and
then, when Mr. Forrester, nearly out of his mind
himself, asked her what he should do that would
satisfy her saying he would give himself up and
stand his trial if she wished, she got quiet all of a
sudden, and she asked him if he had loved her.

"To show her that he did, he got down on his
knees beside the bed and said he would prove his
love in any way she wanted.

"Then she asked him if he would take the most
solemn oath, never to make known to the child that
he was its father; that should she, its mother, die,
he might be the guardian of the child, but never
to let himself by word, or sign show to the child or
anybody else, that he was a drop's blood to her.
And he swore, calling to witness the heavenly names
she made him say, and then she said to me:

"'That was to avenge my murdered father, Nanno;
as my husband caused *his* death away from me, his
only child, so shall he, my husband, never be permitted the caress of this, his child. He has sworn
to be the cold, watchful guardian, nothing more,
and I know his affectionate nature. Nanno; it will
wring him to the soul.'

"And then she told him a name to call the child
by. She did not ask me to take any oath, and an
hour after that, she was out of her mind, screaming
the words of the oath she had made her husband
take, and making him say the dreadful words again
after her. The next day she died quietly, but without getting back her senses, and the people who
came to her funeral thought that her baby had died
too, and was lying in the coffin with her.

"Mr. Forrester shut up the house then till Mr.
John Turner could look after it, and he and I with
the baby went away at night; we went away to an-

other part, and I stayed with him until he found a
nurse for the baby. Then he went east, but saying
to me before he went:

" 'You are the only one, Nanno, who knows that I
am the father of this child, and who knows of my
oath to the dead. I do not ask you to take any
pledge to keep the secret, but I trust in you because
of your love for my poor wife.'

"And I kept the secret. When I went back to
San Francisco and I saw Mr. John Turner, and he
asked me about his niece, I told him only that she
was dead, and her husband had gone away. And
in all the years after that, I still kept the secret,
though I sometimes saw Mr. Turner, and knew how
rich he was getting, and I wondered if Mr. Forrester
were living and if he knew how rich his brother-in-
law was, and how Mr. Turner, having no near kin
would feel if he knew his niece had a child, and
that perhaps that child was living.

"I kept the secret until now when it wouldn't
seem right to keep it longer."

She stopped suddenly, and a sort of awe seemed
to have fallen upon the audience; not a motion was
made and hardly a breath drawn, until the counsel
asked softly, as if the awe had fallen even upon him:

"The name of this child whom the prisoner swore
to regard only as his ward?"

"The mother said it should be called Agnes Hammond."

"Look at the prisoner and tell us if you recognize
in him Mr. Forrester whom you knew as the husband
of Reuben Turner's daughter."

She turned and faced the prisoner, hearing at the
same time a sort of commotion behind her, but not
noticing it.

"I *do* recognize him. He is older, to be sure,
but he has the same features; he is the same person."

The commotion behind her was caused by Agnes

Hammond. She had started from her place not well knowing what she was doing, and looking wildly from the prisoner to the witness, and seeing, as one sees sometimes in the fantastical back-ground of a dream, another face looking at her from the rear rank of the jury. Even in that wild, awful moment, when every emotion of her being seemed to center in the certainty of that utterly unexpected revelation, she felt the stare of its piercing eyes, but she looked beyond it to Mallaby. He, seeing her forward movement, had arisen, and she, regardless of everything but that trembling figure fain to support itself against the side of the dock, rushed on, flinging herself as it were, through the people who affrightedly made way for her, until she reached the elevated railing that inclosed him. There, confronting him with a face, so pale and set it seemed more like that of a corpse, she stood, extending her arms to him.

"*And you are my father!*"

The concentrated reproach, the bitter amazement, the struggling affection in her tones, made them wild, and high, and thrilling, and they pierced the ears and the hearts of everybody in the court-room. But, after that, the room swam about her, and there seemed to be two Mallabys struggling to reach her, both being withheld by the grasp of powerful men, and she heard as if it came from a distance, a hoarse, quivering voice say:

"For God's sake, gentlemen, let me go to her. She is my daughter."

The rest was a blank.

XLI.

THAT dramatic and unexpected scene made it necessary to adjourn the court; but it was difficult to
clear the court-room. People *would* linger either to
see, or hear further of Mallaby's ward, so startlingly
proved to be his own child.

She had been borne to one of the waiting-rooms,
and it was reported that she was still in an insensible
condition, attended by the lady who always accompanied her, and a physician; that the prisoner had
been remanded to his cell, and that Mr. John Turner
—to whom the revelation of *his* relationship to Mallaby's ward had come with startling astonishment—
had given orders that everything should be done for
the young lady. Some people wondered why he had
not waited to see her, and if he would call upon her
or have her brought to his palatial home, at which
the more knowing ones shook their heads, and said
that John Turner was not that sort of a man. Hating his brother-in-law as he did, and being as determined to bring him to justice as he had avowed himself to be, it was not probable that he would permit
himself to be affected by any sentiment toward his
grand-niece; out of a sort of dutiful benevolence he
might assist her immediate wants, but further than
that, authoritative opinion felt assured he would not
go. She was the daughter of his own niece, it is true,
but she was also the daughter of a man whom, from
the opinions of others he had learned to abhor long
ago, and who he now fully believed to be the murderer of his brother.

Within the waiting-room slowly recovering from

her swoon, Agnes was lying, partially supported by Mrs. Sibly. Her first glance was into the kind face of the widow, and then she remembered. Her strength seemed to return with marvelous rapidity. She sat up, putting back the arms that still would have enfolded her, and taking her bonnet that lay on a chair beside her, she put it on her head. But all the time her face retained its ghastly expression, and her eyes seemed to look strangely into the blank space before them.

The physician shook his head somewhat ominously at Mrs. Sibly, and then he attempted to take Miss Hammond's hand while he told her to refrain a little from any exertion. Instead of obeying him she sprang to her feet, removing her hand far from his touch, and saying in such a changed voice, Mrs. Sibly hardly recognized it:

"I must go to Mr. Mallaby."

Her companions wondered if, having no memory of the revelation in the court-room, she still thought that Mr. Mallaby was only her guardian, but, at the same time, the physician felt that it would not be well to keep her from the prisoner, and securing the necessary permission, he with Mrs. Sibly, accompanied the young lady to the door of the cell. There they left her, the doctor doubtful of the effect of the interview, remaining in the corridor, in order to be within call, and Mrs. Sibly waiting in one of the warden's apartments.

The prisoner, finding that his entreaties to be permitted to see Agnes were ineffectual, on his return to his cell, had relapsed into a sort of bitter silence. The officials had assured him of the attention she was receiving, and one had told him also of Mr. John Turner's charitable offer. But all that assuaged little his agonized longing to know how *she* regarded her startlingly discovered relationship to *him*—did she blame him for his course of seeming deceit, and be-

lieving him to be guilty of the crime of which he
was accused, abhor him? did she shrink from a relationship that imposed upon her so much obloquy,
and giving full credit to the evidence thus far adduced against his character, hate and despise him?
or, most harrowing thought of all, would she sink
beneath the strain of her terrible feelings, and die as
her mother had done, a shrieking maniac? Her face
while borne past him in her swoon, had seemed to be
in its set, marble whiteness, an exact reproduction of
that of his dead wife.

Some one was opening the door. There was the
slight click of the lock, a sound that slight and ordinary as it was, never failed to give him a peculiar
thrill. On this occasion it was like an electric shock,
going out to the very ends of his fingers, and he
rose from his stool, looking as if the whole of his
poor, struggling soul were in his eyes.

The door opened wide, unusually wide, it seemed
to him, before any one appeared in sight; then, Agnes stood there, not advancing for a moment, but
looking at him.

As persons drowning are said sometimes to see in in-
stantaneous review the most minute instances of their
past lives, so Agnes, in the moment that she stood
as if wanting the power to advance, seemed to recall
every action, word, and sign, that puzzling her in the
past regarding her guardian, were now such strong and
touching confirmation of his paternal relation to herself. From what else could have sprung his
gentle kindness, and watchful regard? what but a
father's affection could have made him so unselfishly
content with the meagre compensation of a ward's
attachment? And how much he must have suffered
in earlier years from her indifference and ill-concealed contempt; how much she now knew that he had
suffered in recent years from his struggle to keep his
painful secret. Guilty he might be; friendless, odd

and contemned, he certainly seemed to be, but he was *her* father — her broken down, imprisoned, suffering father.

She nerved herself out of the paralysis that had seemed to have settled upon her limbs, and the blood came back to her heart and her face.   With arms that opened wider to him every step she took, she bounded across the floor of the cell.   He caught her upon his bosom, and even the official, feeling that sight too sacred for human witnesses, softly withdrew, closing the cell-door behind him.

XLII.

Since that to which the prisoner's oath bound him, had been disclosed in open court, there need be no more secrecy on his part; he could tell everything to his daughter; and he did, giving her the history of his life from his boyhood.

Born and educated in England he was the only child of parents in comparatively affluent circumstances. His mother died when he was a boy, his father just as he was entering manhood. Their death put him into possession of a moderate fortune, and partly from a spirit of adventure, and partly to increase his means, he went to New York, meeting there Kellar and Kellar's cousin. Kellar made the first advance to acquaintance, and Forrester being young, knowing little of the world, and having a generous, trusting, unsuspicious nature, was attracted by the cordial, affable manners of Kellar; Kellar's cousin was equally affable, but less demonstrative. Forrester was easily induced to go to the West with the cousins, and when taken ill in Reuben Turner's house, he was so grateful for the kindness of Turner and his daughter, that he felt it would be little to repay his debt of gratitude by the gift of his whole fortune. He had also learned to love Millicent Turner, but feeling that she did not return his affection, he was careful to betray no warm regard. He was painfully aware that she ridiculed his appearance, and his odd ways; his shyness in her presence made him all the odder. But her father liked him, and when an opportunity came in which Forrester could assist Turner out of a sudden and very serious financial difficulty, it delighted him to do so. That seemed to change Miss Turner's feelings to him: she began to show a pleasure in his attentions which encouraged him, and being further encouraged by her father who eagerly desired that his daughter should marry their guest, he proposed, and was accepted, and for months there was not a cloud upon their happiness. Then, financial difficulty again came, and both Turner and his son-in-law, thought of the mines as a very possible way not alone to retrieve, but to make their fortune. The fact of having friends there as Forrester considered Kellar and his cousin to be, was an additional inducement.

But, their advent in the mines was the beginning of the unpleasantness for Forrester. He was immediately asked for a large loan by Kellar; he gave it, being assured that he should be shortly repaid. Instead, however, of any repayment, he was asked again and again for smaller sums until he finally refused. The refusal did not seem to make any change in Kellar's cordial, and even confidential manner; he continued to seek the companionship of Forrester as he had done, and was always pleasant and affable.

Suddenly, Turner became distant and moody with his son-in-law, and at length, on occasions, gave vent to angry innuendoes of the unfairness of the latter's superior luck. At the same time, Forrester was in the receipt of very strange letters from his wife— short, cold, and containing an undercurrent of dislike and irony that he could not understand, but that he could not mistake. Kellar, seeing the ill feeling which Turner manifested more and more every day, used in private to sympathize with Forrester, and Forrester believing in and trusting him, was grateful for his sympathy.

On one occasion, when Forrester happened on an unusually lucky find, Turner became violently excited, and in a burst of passion accused his son-in-law of dishonesty appropriating it. Forrester, knowing how honestly he had on every occasion fulfilled the terms of the compact regarding division of their finds, was stung into bitter words of retaliation; the bitterness increased by his secret intention at the end of their stay in the mines, to make a further generous division of his gains with his father-in-law.

But, Turner, angered beyond all bounds, sprang upon his son-in-law, and Kellar and his cousin who were present, caught him and pulled him away.

Then Forrester said:

"I shall fix him some day."

He meant, as he explained afterward to Kellar and his cousin, to fix him by surprising him with a totally unexpected and generous gift when they should both return to San Francisco.

After that, Turner's ill feeling seemed to become more bitter, and the letters from the young wife shorter and colder. In vain Forrester sought an explanation; he could get none further than what his own judgment told him; a blind, unreasonably jealousy and suspicion on the part of Turner, and which he must have communicated to his daughter. To add to Turner's unhappiness he received an angry letter from his young brother-in-law, John Turner, but it explained nothing, and Forrester returned an indignant reply denouncing the causeless dislike of his father-in-law, and ending with the words, "but I shall fix him some day," meaning as he had meant when he had spoken the threat, to fix him by heaping coals of fire on his head, for his love for his wife made him able to forgive any injury done by her kindred.

At lenght, Forrester could endure the situation no longer. He announced his intention to throw up mining and return to San Francisco. That was an occasion for the manifestation of more bitter feeling on the part of his father-in-law, and on the night before his intended departure being asked by Kellar to join him in the game of cards he and his cousin were playing, he had hardly seated himself when Turner, whom he had left in moody silence a moment before rushed in, and was down upon him.

During the struggle to defend himself, he felt Turner draw a pistol, and in self-defence Forrester wrested the pistol from him, but in striving to put it beyond Turner's reach it went off, and Turner fell, exclaiming:

"Forrester has killed me."

Everley had come upon the scene only in time to witness that to which he had testified, and Forrester dazed and horror-stricken was dragged away by the cousins. Knowing his guiltlessness of intention to kill he never thought that any suspicion could attach to him, and he was surprised at the proposition to have it supposed that Turner had committed suicide; but when it was represented to him that in any other case he might be held until an investigation could be made, and so be detained from his unprotected and friendless wife, he consented, gladly permitting Kellar, who seemed to be more of a sympathizing friend than ever, to make all the arrangements.

Then occurred all that Nanno Kelpley had told save that she had not depicted the extreme bitterness with which Mrs. Forrester received her husband, nor his frigid reception by her young uncle, John Turner. The unjust feelings of Reuben Turner toward his son-in-law, had been but too successfully imparted to his daughter and his brother, and though neither of them doubted the story of the suicide, they seemed to feel that it was due in a great degree to the unfair conduct of Forrester. Kellar was everywhere, trying to soothe the wife and uncle, and to impart courage and hope to the wretched husband, while his cousin was as silent as though he had been a mute; and Forrester was so grateful to Kellar, that, after the interment, when young John Turner was carried back ill to the home of his employer, and Kellar announcing his intention to return to the East, hinted his impoverished condition, Forrester made him a generous gift of money. Then he was left alone with his wife and Nanno Kelpley, and the only time that his wife showed any return of the tenderness she had once given him was when he took the oath she demanded. That seemed to be a proof of a love too great to be resisted, and her embrace of him he never forgot; the memory of it seemed to be a constant help in the keeping of his oath.

In one of the suburban villages of New York he found a nursery in which to place the babe, and at the earliest age possible he transferred her to the Convent of the Sacred Heart. His thoughts, his hopes were all for her, and his last gift to Kellar having well-nigh exhausted what had been left of his early fortune, it was necessary to work hard to accumulate the wealth he desired for his daughter. Bred to no trade, and unable to secure a higher position than that of collector of bills, he turned all his energies to that, hoping by the means of great personal economy to be very successful to a degree that exceeded his expectations. His great struggle was to conceal his wild affection for his ward. He dreamed of her, and lived upon the visits he was permitted to make to the Convent. Having secured an eligible boarding place with Mrs. Denner, and finding her to be a kind, motherly woman, he brought his little ward there for a few days during her summer vacation; that was when she was seven years old. A little after her next birthday, and when she had made a second vacation visit of three days to Mrs. Denner, and had returned again to the convent, Forrester was suddenly confronted on the street one day by Kellar. Little dreaming of Kellar's object, and confident of his friendship, Forrester welcomed him, taking him to his office, and talking to him freely of his business, his circumstances, and everything save his daughter: and when Kellar asked him about his wife, he answered simply that she died a few days after Kellar's departure from California. He explained his assumption of the name Matthias Mallaby, by his wish to obliterate from his memory every circumstance of the harrowing past, and Kellar seemed to agree with him, and was very particular never to forget himself and use the name of Forrester.

One day in the office, Kellar saw by accident an open letter addressed to Mallaby, in a child's hand, and beginning:

"Dear Guardian."

He interrogated Mallaby about it, and was answered with admirable composure that Mallaby *was* guardian to a little girl, in obedience to the request of her dying mother, and Kellar seemed satisfied with the reply.

For one whole week Kellar acted the part of a pleasant, confidential friend. Then, he suddenly disclosed himself. His object in returning to New York from Australia was to extort from Mallaby a large sum of money. It was no accidental meeting on the street as Mallaby had supposed it to be; Kellar had simply made it appear so, though how, or where he had learned to find Mallaby, he would not tell.

Did Mallaby refuse to accede to his demand, both he and his cousin whom he had left in Australia were prepared to swear that Mallaby with deliberate intention had killed his father-in-law, Reuben Turner. That he, Kellar, would communicate with the brother of the murdered man, John Turner, who as Mallaby knew from newspaper paragraphs was already rising into wealth and prominence: that pains would be taken to hunt up Everley who could testify to Reuben Turner's last words; that the very fact of Forrester having assumed an alias would prove the

fear in which he lived, a fear that could only be induced by a consciousness of his guilt; and altogether,
Kellar placed before Mallaby so systematic and well
laid a plan of proving the murder of Reuben Turner
by Forrester, that the latter was aghast. He thought
of his child, and what to her would be the consequences of his arrest on this charge; that anxiety
was greater even than his bitter detestation of Kellar. But it would be impossible to pay the large
sum demanded, and Kellar substituted the payment
of certain remittances four times a year, to which
Mallaby consented. Then began Mallaby's torture,
for, after Kellar's departure every letter with which
he acknowledged the receipt of the remittance, contained cunning, but harrowing reference to the murder. After a little, finding that the reading of them
caused him so much anguish, he wrote to have Kel-
tar send them to his boarding-house rather than to
the office; he could conceal his torture better in his
room in the boarding-house, than in the office where
he could not be always sure there would be no eye
upon him.

It was owing to the payment of those remittances
that Mallaby had been unable to give his ward a
larger income, and that had caused him to hesitate
when she spoke of going to Italy.

The letter which had fallen so strangely into Miss
Liscome's hands and which had been sent to his office
instead of to his boarding-house, he could not explain, unless by believing that Jared had written it.
The fact that it had come to the office, and that it had
been directed in unfamiliar penmanship, had caused
Mallaby greater fear, always dreading as he did,
since Kellar's first visit, that something of the past
would be disclosed to his employers, or even to his
ward, and that it would be disclosed in a manner
which would disgracefully criminate him. In that
way Miss Liscome had him at her mercy when she

mentioned the name of Jared; Jared was the Christian name of Kellar's cousin, and Mallaby did not know but that Jared had communicated the facts of the past to Miss Liscome, causing that lady to believe that he, Mallaby, was really a murderer. He did not mention her visits to his ward because he felt that he could not do so without betraying something of his fear, and through that, breaking in some way his oath to his dying wife. Nor could he bring himself to ask Miss Liscome what she meant by her use of the name; he felt that if she did not know the whole of the dreadful story he feared she had been told, his very agitation must betray it to her; and when he thought to write to Kellar, demanding why the pledge that Kellar had given for his cousin's silence as well as for his own, had been broken, he was deterred by the little satisfaction he would gain. Kellar might reply, utterly disbelieving Mallaby, or saying, as he was already beginning to hint, that the remittance was too small to purchase the absolute secrecy of two witnesses.

Conscious of his entire innocence of the crime threatened to be so fiendishly imputed to him, Mallaby would have defied all threats, and willingly, gladly, have submitted to be tried but for his daughter. Circumstantial evidence would be so strongly against him, that she might believe *him* guilty, and abhor him accordingly. Not dreaming that Kellar suspected she was Forrester's own offspring, instead of Mallaby's ward, he did not think there would be any means of showing his paternity, unless he himself were to break his oath; and that, with the vivid memory of the satisfaction the taking of that oath had given his idolized, and dying wife, he was resolved not to do. Thus, did he submit to a trial the evidence would show that he had shot his own father-in-law, but not that he had shot the grandfather of his ward; and, even though by some means evidence were obtained to reveal that, it might cause in Agnes, since his innocence of any intention to kill could not be proved, emotions alone of aversion and horror. In this way was poor Mallaby tortured by his fears, and secretly idolizing his daughter, he was torn by his perpetual struggle to betray for her no more than the respectful regard of a guardian.

Then, Kellar came again with a business scheme proposed by a certain company in Australia; but the coöperation of some New York firm was desirable, and he came to Mallaby for the coöperation of the firm with which he was connected. He knew that Mallaby by his exceptional integrity had won the esteem and confidence of the firm, and Kellar knew also that if he were introduced to the firm by Mallaby, his reliability guaranteed by Mallaby, the firm would accept his proposal without further question. But, Mallaby insisted upon knowing everything connected with the basis of the scheme, and Kellar had at length to admit that it only presented a fair showing long enough to enrich its promoters, and then would collapse involving Mallaby's firm in absolute loss. But Mallaby himself would be safe with thousands of dollars in his pocket. Mallaby scouted the proposal with horror. Kellar coaxed, promising to take back every threat he had ever made instituting the charge of the murder, and offering to make a deposition before witnesses, that he knew Mallaby to be innocent, so that the latter might feel assured of being no longer threatened with the charge. It was a grievous temptation, and it became more so when at its height, Wilbur appeared as a suitor for Miss Hammond.

Mallaby still did not think Kellar suspected his paternity, but beset, as he was by all sorts of fears and suspicions, he began at length even to suspect that, and he was wildly anxious for Miss Hammond's marriage. Kellar was still giving him time to reconsider his refusal to introduce him to the firm, and if only the marriage could take place before Kellar should set about the vengeance he promised, Agnes would be secure. The honesty of Mallaby's conscience was such, that he could not even pretend to Kellar that he would consider the matter, and so gain sufficient delay for the marriage to be consummated.

He felt that were his daughter as well and happily married as he was confident she would be, from what he knew of Wilbur, he could give her up, and submit to any fate, only praying Heaven to guard his secret, and she, believing him to be only her guardian could not grieve very much. But, when he found that a shadow from his own haunted life had come between the lovers, and found his ward pressing him for information which he could not give without breaking his oath, he answered, preserving his secrecy, and retaining even such outlines of truth as it was possible for him to do, and he thought at the same time of seeing Wilbur. But what could he tell without violating his pledge, that would satisfy the young man; that might not even cause greater suspicion and discredit to come to his mind. When again he found that the engagement had been broken, and as he had strong reasons to suspect, broken by Kellar's revelations to Wilbur he determined to see the latter. He was certain that Kellar had revealed the shooting affray, making it a strong case of murder on the part of Mallaby. But what had he told regarding Agnes? Did he, suspecting her to be a daughter, instead of a ward, tell his suspicion as if he knew it to be a fact, and what reason did he assign for Mallaby's concealment of his paternity? He meant to demand from Wilbur what he had been told, and then he would tell *his* story of the shooting, and that he was prepared directly after the marriage to go away. Should Wilbur ask him about his paternity he would demand by what knowledge Kellar could have made such an assertion, and in that he would avoid breaking his oath. But he was unable to find Wilbur, and then feeling from the absence of Kellar that the latter must have set about his vengeance, the most harrowing part of his life began.

Every day made his ward dearer to him, and every day intensified his desire to keep from her all knowledge of the past.

Her tender regard brought out by his troubled life, and never experienced by him before made him all the more fearful that when she knew the past she would despise him. Her indifference to his odd dress, gave him exquisite pleasure, just as her ill-concealed contempt for it in earlier days used to give him pain; it recalled her mother's ridicule; but, somehow it was part of the odd tastes that he inherited from his father, and which he could not seem to change.

Then his pride in Agnes; how he had to struggle to conceal that; his pride in her beauty, her queen-like air, her accomplishments. Often the struggle combined with his longing to clasp her to him, and his fear that one day he would be torn ignominiously from her, sent such a look into his face as he felt attracted attention; it was so on the evening when Agnes, and Florence, and he, stood on the stoop of the house on Hubert Street; it was so on the frequent occasions on which Agnes alone saw it.

Yielding to his fear he kept changing his office quarters, and his abode, yet knowing that the change was useless; but his fear was combined with a restlessness which he could not control. He felt that he was tracked, felt it even before the day on which he saw Malliflower Mallary, for his fears made him fancy that he had many proofs of it. He would have gone abroad with his ward, but he knew it would be useless; he could not hide himself from the doom

that Kellar's vengeance was making, and then, also
he was too poor.

When at lenght he *was* seized it was a most unexpected relief; the strain of fear of just *that*, had been
so great, and could he have told Agnes that which
he was bound by oath not to tell her, he would have
been resigned to his fate. He fancied that she
might not have despised him.

But, when the evidence began, criminating him as
it seemed to do, all his fear that she would be-
live in his guilt, and despise him, returned. He
wondered a little, why, if Kellar felt that Miss Hammond were a daughter, instead of a ward, he did
not include that in some way in his testimony, and
he wished he had, for the simple, cold fact of proving Forrester to be guilty of the murder of his own
father-in-law, without showing that the murderer
was of near kin to herself, must repel her sympathies; knowing the prisoner to be her own father,
wretched murderer though he were, must surely in
the natural order of things win her sympathy.
Thus, at least, reasoned the poor prisoner at first,
until she remained away from the court-room and
the prison: then, he feared that somebody had told
her, and that she hated him the more for being her
father.

The relief that he experienced when he saw her again
in the court was tempered by his anguish lest no evidence would be adduced to show that she was his
child. His one hope had been that his counsel would
find Nanno Kelpley, and when the latter appeared in
the witness-stand, seemingly to testify against him,
he was hardly concerned about that fact: she might
give the most criminating testimony, providing she
told what she alone could tell; and when it seemed
that no question was to be put, which would elicit
that, the poor prisoner, trying to transfix her with
his eyes felt as if he must shriek to her. But she
did tell it, and Agnes knew it all at last.

XLIII.

THE prisoner's story told with such pathos as a father's feelings could alone give, carried entire conviction to his daughter's heart long before he had finished it, and long before he had finished it she had clasped his head to her throbbing bosom, and poured upon his grizzled locks burning tears of self-reproach. Not all his loving comfort could stop them until they had quite spent themselves. How she thanked God for not having accepted Wilbur's proposition; all his love could never repay her had she added her ungrateful abandonment to the other horrors of her father's fate, and what would have been her feelings when she should learn who it was she had thus deserted. As she kissed the wrinkled forehead, and fondled the large, white, freckled hands, she felt a sort of shuddering indignation against Wilbur for having wished her to leave her guardian. And the poor prisoner, knowing now, that not alone was he not despised, but loved with more intense filial affection than he had dreamed could be his, felt as if Heaven had rewarded him for his fidelity to his oath; the phantom of his dead wife which so often in the past had seemed to be near him in reproach and condemnation, now appeared to merge itself into the face of his daughter, and to look upon him with an expression of unutterable love. In his intense happiness, no fate that might result from the unjust charge against him, had any horror, or anxiety; even his bitter feelings against Kellar were absorbed, and for the time he forgot to be anxious about

the future fate of his daughter, should the evidence
sustain the jury in finding a severe verdict.

*   *   *   *   *   *   *   *

To the interested public they were no longer guardian and ward, but father and daughter; nor was
his alias of Matthias Mallaby suffered to cling to
him; everybody spoke of him as Frank Forrester,
and it was astonishing how many people suddenly
seemed to appear who knew, or pretended to have
known Forrester when he lived in Reuben Turner's
house.   A number of persons remembered Reuben
Turner's reported suicide, and though from Nanno
Kelpley's evidence, some sympathy was felt for the
prisoner, the prevailing opinion,—an opinion largely
contributed to by the opinion firmly held by John
Turner,—was, that he was guilty.

Nothing, however, disturbed the affection existing
between father and daughter; her devotion to him
was intense and unintermitting, and his happiness
in that devotion superseded every feeling save that
of anxiety for her future, and even her present circumstances.

He had won from her, how Mrs. Sibly had not a-
lone refused all compensation for board, but had insisted upon giving her at different times sums of
money more than sufficient to defray her current expenses , and that when she had refused and remonstrated. protesting that she might never be able to
repay them, Mrs. Sibly had responded, that it was
no money of her own she was giving, but that which
had been placed in her hands for charitable purposes, and she knew of no worthier charitable purpose
than supplying Miss Hammond.

"And I have accepted it," Agnes said, tearfully,
"intending when your trial is over to work and repay it."

He knew also, that John Turner had made overtures of aid to his daughter, sending a messenger to

Mrs. Sibly with an invitation to make his house her home; but the invitation was not accompanied by a single reference to her father, and to it Agnes returned a polite but spirited refusal, on reading which John Turner looked darker than ever and ground his teeth a little.

Agnes firmly believed in her father's innocence; not the testimony of a hundred Kellars could cause her a doubt of it; neither did she credit the evidence that gave so unfavorable a shade to his early character; the unvarying gentleness and kindness with which she was so familiar could hardly be traits of a temperament not distinguished by the same virtues in youthful manhood.

XLIV.

THE court had granted a long adjournment in the case of Forrester, in order to give time to his counsel to secure such evidence as he might for the accused. Not one witness could be found in California who knew sufficient to testify in his favor, and an order was issued by the court, to take testimony by commission of the prisoner's character during his long residence in New York. In that way, was adduced the sworn evidence of the members of the firm which had employed Mallaby — an evidence that showed not a flaw in his character for exceptional honesty, and for prompt and unintermitting attention to his business until within the last two years, when his frequent change of office quarters, and lack of his wonted energy, made it seem that his mental, or physical health was not what it had been.

Mrs. Denner had been also summoned, and never was there delivered a more eulogistic testimony. She could speak of the prisoner by no other terms than "that blessed man," and her praise took such extravagant flights that she had to be called repeatedly to the point. Nor did she give the most remote hint that there ever had seemed to be any trouble upon his mind, or that mysterious letters came to him, causing him to show strange emotions. She would have torn her tongue out by the roots rather than give such testimony.

Fullerton, distrusting Kellar's evidence as to the death of his cousin, since in all his intercourse with Mallaby in New York, he had not hinted at such a thing, caused notices asking for information of the cousin to be inserted in the Australian, and even in all the prominent European papers. To be sure, the lawyer was smart enough to divine how necessary to the promotion of Kellar's fiendish scheme, it was, that the prisoner should suppose the cousin to be alive, at the time that Kellar was threatening to execute his vengeance. But, to leave nothing undone, he caused the notices to be inserted; it might be, that if the cousin were not dead, and could be found his testimony might differ from that of Kellar.

Fullerton regretted that the prisoner had burned Kellar's letters, despite the fact that in every one of them Kellar had so disguised his hand as to make it difficult to prove his penmanship, and also the fact that Kellar probably would swear without hesitation that he had never written them. He had been careful never to sign his name to one of them. The lawyer hoped, however, by his vigorous and searching cross-examination, to be able to break down, or at least, to confuse the testimony of the witnesses examined for the state, and he said to the prisoner on the day before the cross-examination was to begin:

"I think we can make Kellar show himself to be a thorough villain."

The prisoner did not answer.

XLV.

ALL San Francisco was excited about this murder case brought to light after such a lapse of years. Even ladies clamored and struggled for places in the court-room, and men of every profession jostled and push-ed each other in their efforts to obtain even standing room within auditing distance of the counsel.

Public opinion tended almost unanimously to the conviction of the prisoner, and though it was min-gled with pity for the devoted daughter, that fact did not cause it to lose any of its severity in the interest of justice.

Agnes, accompanied by Mrs. Sibly, sat nearer to the prisoner than she had done on any previous day of the trial. She kept her veil up that she might smile at him at intervals, and that he might read continually in her face, her unutterable affection and sympathy. Her eyes rarely turned from his coun-tenance, but on the few occasions on which they did, she saw, a little in the rear of the prosecuting-attor-ney, the face that had seemed to look at her so mys-teriously on the day on which she fainted. It was looking at her now, with a look that thrillingly re-called the face of Wilbur; but this face was so much older, having deep lines in the features, and it was heavily bearded. With a wildly beating heart, she at length quietly drew Mrs. Sibly's attention to it, asking if she knew the name of the gentleman, and Mrs. Sibly whispered:

"That is Mr. Dawson, a rich Californian."

Agnes, with a sigh, possibly of disappointment, withdrew her eyes, and looked no more in his direc-tion.

Her uncle, John Turner, watched her; watched her more, than he did the prisoner, and as he saw with what intense affection she was occupied with the prisoner, his beetling brows seemed to grow heavier, and his strong, determined-looking face to take on an expression that was akin to cruelty.

As Nathan Kellar had been the first witness to give testimony, so he was the first to be subjected to the fire of Fullerton's cross examination. His flashy dress, and fine physique, caused a little sensation as he took his place; the sensation being increased by the bold manner in which, before facing the dignitaries of the court, he turned and surveyed the audience, bowing with exasperating effrontery to Agnes. She crimsoned with indignation and turned her head quickly away.

Fullerton seemed in no hurry to get beyond the questions that only brought out in repetition the main points of Kellar's evidence, and the witness smiled with a sort of scornful satisfaction, and those in the audience who knew the methods of the lawyer hardly stirred themselves to listen; but, when Fullerton, drawing a long breath like one preparing to make a spring, suddenly straightened himself, and darted a question at the witness with an unexpected rapidity and strength of tone, then, nearly every man in the audience straightened himself too, and leaned forward with strained attention, for it was whispered that was the way in which the clever lawyer always opened the fire of his battery. And that he knew how to charge and time his volleys was quickly apparent, for every question was a leading one and put in a skillful manner. But Kellar was equally smart. He might have been a lawyer himself for the way in which he knew how and when to evade, and when he need not answer; and when he could do neither, he made flat and decisive denials.

When he was asked what he knew of the person named Jared, he answered that Jared was the Christian name of his cousin, but he denied any knowledge of the letter signed with that name, and which had caused the prisoner to betray so much agitation. He admitted, however, that the prisoner had told him, without referring to any letter, of Miss Liscome's mysterious use of the name, and that he himself making Miss Liscome's acquaintance in the office of the prisoner was surprised at her use of it. But he thought it probable that his cousin had written it, and had not thought it necessary to say anything to the witness about it.

"Did you learn how Miss Liscome obtained the knowledge which enabled her to use the name of Jared in the manner that she did?" asked Fullerton.

"I did," was the reply emphatically given.

"From whom did you learn it?"

"From herself."

"What means did you take to learn it?"

"I cultivated an acquaintance with her."

"And she voluntarily told you?"

"She did."

"State what she told you."

"That a letter intended for Mr. Mallaby, but apparently addressed to her nephew, Malliflower Mallary, was opened by the latter; in his inability to understand the contents, he brought the letter to her. She read it and was able to guess that the letter must be for Mr. Mallaby."

"Did she tell you what motive prompted her to mention this name of Jared to the prisoner?"

"Yes; having learned from her nephew of the agitation betrayed by Mr. Mallaby in receiving the letter, she, from a spirit of mischief and curiosity thought herself to test Mr. Mallaby with it."

"Did she tell you the result of her test?"

"Yes; manisfestation of such agitation as was described by her nephew."

"Did the prisoner ever lead you to think directly, or indirectly, that he knew, or suspected whence Miss Liscome derived her mysterious knowledge?"

"Never; he was not able to obtain an opinion as to its source."

"On your acquiring this knowledge, did you enlighten the prisoner?

"I do not remember."

"Did Miss Liscome tell you the contents of this letter?"

"Only that the writer, Jared, referred to the laying of some spectre of the past."

"Did Miss Liscome ask you for an explanation of the letter?"

"No."

Did you give her any explanation?"

"No."

"Was your cousin, Jared, in the habit of writing to the prisoner?"

"Not to my knowledge."

"Were you in the habit of writing to the prisoner?"

"I wrote to him sometimes."

"What was the character of the contents of your letter?"

"A friendly character."

"Particularize some of the contents."

"I do not remember them."

"Why should your cousin, Jared, if he were not in the habit of writing to the prisoner, write the letter that caused the prisoner's agitation?"

"I do not know."

"Did *your* letters cause the prisoner agitation?"

"I do not know."

"Were they of a character to cause him agitation?"

"No."

"What was the date of the letter to the prisoner that fell into Miss Liscome's hands?"

"I do not know."

"On what date, or about what time of the year, and in what year, did *you* learn about that letter?"

To the latter part of that question the witness gave a prompt answer.

"Now tell the date of your cousin Jared's death."

For reply he produced from his pocket-book a paragraph from an Italian newspaper. Interpreted, it was found to contain the notice of his cousin's death from a railroad accident in Italy; the date was six months subsequent to the date he had given in his previous answer.

"Was this letter from your cousin written in Italy?"

"I presume it must have been written in Australia."

"Why do you presume?"

"Miss Liscome told me it had an Australian postmark."

"Did you ask Miss Liscome to come to California to testify on this trial?"

"I did not."

"Do you know by what means she was led to come?"

"Mr. John Turner wrote to her."

"Having obtained his knowledge of her through you?"

"Yes; Mr. Turner requested me to tell him everything that had any connection with the prisoner."

"That will do, Mr. Kellar," said Fullerton shortly, and the witness stepped from the stand with the triumphant consciousness that his previous testimony had not been shaken in a single point.

Miss Liscome was summoned, and she tripped to the stand, holding her head on one side, and smirking, and bowing, and looking so ridiculous in her

jaunty attire, that some people laughed outright.
Fullerton adopted a different tone with her; he
was gentle, flattering, insinuating, and it would almost seem confidential. The spinster, in her wretched
vanity, imagined that his manner was due to her
graceful appearance, and she replied to his questions
with great sweetness, and an amusing frankness
that more than once destroyed the decorum of the
court. The decorum was more especially destroyed
when his cross-examination turned upon the extent
of her acquaintance with Mallaby.

"You met him, you say, my dear young lady, for
the first time, at the house of an acquaintance ?"

The audible titter of some of the ladies in the court
at the juvenile term, had no effect upon Prudence.
She imagined it was her youthful appearance had
called it forth, and she was so delighted with both
herself and with him, that she was in danger of forgetting the object of her presence on the witness-
stand.

"Yes;" she simpered. "I met him first at Mr. Wilbur's home on Hubert Street in New York."

"Your impression of Mr. Forrester, or Mr. Mallaby, then ?"

"I thought he was a very delightful and honor-
able gentleman, and he paid me a great deal of attention."

"Had you occasion after that, to change your
impression, to retract your opinion regarding his
honor ?"

The lawyer's voice had sunk to a tone soft and
gentle enough for a woman; it was almost as if his
own heart were aching for the disappointment of the
witness in finding that Mr. Mallaby was not worthy
of her regard. And the poor, shallow-minded, vain
witness was caught by the bait, and she leaned toward the lawyer as if she were talking alone to him,
and were trying to show how much she appreciated
and was grateful for his sympathy.

"Yes, sir; I found out that Mr. Mallaby was not the pleasant, and high-minded gentleman I thought him to be. He had an insinuating way at first, but it meant just nothing, nothing at all."

And Miss Liscome shook her head in a way that set all the flowers in her bonnet quivering, while the audience laughed.

"Give one instance of your disappointment in him."

The lawyer's tone seemed to indicate that he was as confidential as circumstances permitted him to be.

Miss Liscome smiled and imagined that she blushed but she answered without any hesitation.

"I went to him to ask his advice about investing some money."

"Your esteem for him was so great that you selected him rather than any other of your male friends or acquaintances, to give you this advice?" interrupted the lawyer.

"Yes, and—"

"One moment, my dear young lady," he interrupted again, and Prudence not annoyed at the interruption since it was accompanied by so flattering a term beamed upon him with a smile—"in order to have a very clear understanding of the ungallantry of Mr. Mallaby, the name by which you know the prisoner, please inform the court whether you had ever seen him from the time of your first meeting at a friend's house in New York, until you applied to him for financial advice."

"No! "

"And it was owing entirely to his attentions to you on that first meeting that you conceived so high and warm a regard for him?"

"Yes!"

"A regard that, as I said, was not only high, but warm, my dear young lady; so warm, that you would probably, would you not, had he given you the opportunity to do so, have reciprocated the tender feelings which seemed to have prompted his attention to you on the occasion of your first meeting?"

"Yes," replied Prudence, being for the first time dimly aware that her answer had something to do with the burst of laughter which succeeded it. But the lawyer was more softly persuasive and confidential than ever; and fixing his black, lustrous eyes on the face of the witness with a look so kindly it was almost tender, she became indifferent to everything but the impression she fancied she was making on the heart of the handsome counsel.

"On the occasion on which you solicited this advice from the prisoner, how did he respond?"

"He refused until I mentioned that name of Jared."

"The name obtained from the letter opened by your nephew in mistake?"

"Yes, sir."

"What motive had you in mentioning to the prisoner, the name of Jared?"

"Oh, just a spirit of mischief and curiosity," tossing her head in a jaunty way that again set the flowers in her bonnet quivering. "My nephew told me Mr. Mallaby was so agitated on receiving the letter. I just thought I'd try him myself, by mentioning the name."

"Were you not afraid of being asked for an explanation?"

"Oh, no; and if I had I needn't have given any."

"What were the contents of that mysterious letter?"

"I don't remember them."

"Did you take particular note of them at the time that you read them?"

"Only in a general way."

"Can you not then, my dear young lady, call to

mind some of the contents now, or in a general way give us some idea of them?"

"Oh," with a ludicrous affectation of girlish impatience, "there was something about laying a spectre—that is all I remember."

"Did you wonder what that phrase 'laying a spectre' meant?"

"In a kind of a way, but I didn't trouble myself much about it."

"Did you ask Mr. Kellar to explain it?'

"No, sir."

"Did Mr. Kellar give you any explanation?"

"No, sir."

"What emotion did Mr. Kellar show when you described to him Mr. Mallaby's agitation caused by your mention of the name Jared?"

"I don't remember. I only know that Mr. Kellar seemed to be very much interested in me."

The audience laughed.

"Now, my dear young lady, did Mr. Kellar approach you at all on the subject of coming here to San Francisco, to testify on this trial?"

"No, sir."

"What led you to think of coming to California?"

"I received a letter from Mr. Turner offering to pay my expenses and those of my nephew, if we would come and give our testimony. He said that he had heard all about us from Mr. Kellar."

" In your former testimony you referred to another instance of the prisoner's want of gallantry, something pertaining to a *souvenir*. Please inform the court about that."

" Oh, yes, sir! " simpered the witness, " in my gratitude for the service Mr. Mallaby did me, I desired to give him a little token. I offered him a heart."

" In your gratitude, my dear young lady, you offered him *your* heart?"

The audience were silent only because they waited in a state of suppressed mirth for her answer, and the moment that she had replied:

" It wasn't exactly that, but it was a little golden heart that I prized very much! " everybody laughed even to the jurors, and the merriment was repeated when Fullerton said:

" Your little gift was symbolical, no doubt—symbolical of the grateful attachment you had formed for this strangely ungallant and unresponsive man."

When silence was restored, he continued:

" Did the prisoner absolutely refuse your little gift? "

" Yes, sir."

" And his refusal, as it is natural to suppose, turned the current of your youthful and impulsive affections—you felt a dislike of this unimpressionable man—to a young lady of your strong, clever mind, it was impossible not to have a very great aversion for him: you hated him, did you not? "

"Yes, sir, I hated him," replied Prudence, utterly unsuspicious how directly her answers led to the points Fullerton intended to make in his summing up.

" What was your impression of Mr. Kellar, when you met him first? "

" I had the very highest opinion of him. He was different from Mr. Mallaby; so kind, and gentle and confiding."

" Did you on Mr. Kellar's departure from New York, keep him informed of the prisoner's movements? "

Fullerton's eyes, more than his question drew the frank admission:

"Yes, sir."

" Was it at his request that you did so? "

" Yes, sir."

" For all this valuable service on your part, my

dear young lady, is Mr. Kellar sufficiently grateful—
does he appreciate you—will he reward you?"

Prudence looked down with affected bashfulness,
and toyed ludicrously with her watch-charm; her
action seemed to give the lawyer a cue for another
question:

"Did you, my dear young lady, test *his* gratitude by giving him a little token as you did to the
prisoner?"

Prudence affected to be very much abashed; so
much so that it was fully three minutes before she
answered, but the court patiently waited, and everybody was rewarded by hearing her say:

"I did."

"Was this little token the heart that was so ungallantry refused by the prisoner?"

"Yes, sir."

"Only two more questions, my dear young lady;
did Mr. Kellar take the heart you in your gushing
ingenuousness offered, and does he retain that heart
yet?"

"Yes, sir."

Every neck in the audience had been craned for
her answer, and the laughter that succeeded it was
loud and long from every part of the court-room, and
when it had ceased some one renewed it by remark-
ing what a fishing time the witness must have had
with her heart.

Even across the pale face of Agnes there had flitted the shadow of a smile, but that was for the
moment that her eyes had turned from the prisoner
to the witness. The prisoner had given no sign of
amusement at the evidence of the witness; not even
when the mirth was loudest and most general; the
only time *he* smiled was when he responded to his
daughter's look of affectionate encouragement.

Malliflower Mallary was the next witness, and
most of the people remembering the amusement oc-

casioned by his former appearance, prepared themselves for a renewal of their mirth. His response to
the summons was marked by the same ludicrous
haste that had caused a laugh before, and his appearance was distinguished by the identical bright
blue suit, only his proportions seemed taller and
more attenuated.

Fullerton adopted a stern manner in order to awe
the witness out of his propensity to preface his remarks; but his method had the opposite effect. It
awed the witness, it is true, but at the same time it
disconcerted and confused him to the extent of prefacing his answers much more frequently than he
might otherwise have done. To the very first question of the lawyer, "How long have you known
Mr. Nathan Kellar?"

Mallary replied:

"I shall preface my answer to your question, boss,
by saying, that my desire for the acquaintance of Mr.
Kellar was not from any idle curiosity."

"Keep to the point—how long have you known
Mr. Kellar?" thundered the counsel.

"How long?" repeated the witness, frightened by
the stentorian tones of the questioner, "since the
night Aunt Prudence upset the teapot."

Even the grim face of the judge relaxed a little
while everybody in the court-room laughed as loud
and long as everybody had done during the cross-examination of Aunt Prudence.

Fullerton waited with visible impatience for the
restoration of order; then, he tried to get at the date
of the first meeting of the witness with Kellar, or
about what length of time had elapsed since then.

But the mind of the witness was utterly befogged
and all that he could do after prefacing his remarks
with exasperating frequency, was to give a ludicrous
account of Kellar's first visit, and the desire of Aunt
Prudence to have Kellar all to herself after supper.

Fullerton, finding there was little use of keeping at that point, attacked another.

"Were you not employed in New York to be a spy on Mr. Mallaby—to watch his daily movements?"

The eyes of the witness seemed to grow as large as bullets, and the decorum of the court was again destroyed, as he answered:

"Say, boss, how did *you* hear that? Aunt Prudence said not a living soul beyond herself and Mr. Kellar knew it: and I always ran away so fast when I found Mr. Mallaby, or that young lady that was with him looking, that nobody on earth could tell I was a-watching them."

"Were you, or were you not employed by Mr. Kellar to be a spy on Mr. Mallaby's movements?" fairly roared the counsel, and Mallary actually jumped in his fright, and looked around him as if he contemplated some sort of an escape, at which Fullerton realizing the mistake he had made in the adoption of such a severe manner, attempted to rectify it by repeating his question in a soft, reassuring tone.

Mallaby seemed to take fresh heart, and he drew up his stiff shirt collar until it touched his ears, and straightened himself until he looked as if his back were kept in its rigid position by an iron bolt through its center. Then he answered, speaking very loud and rapidly:

"I'll just preface my remarks by saying that Mr. Kellar's a gentleman of the sort that a fellow likes to know; and I'd have been glad to do that, or anything else he'd a-asked, but Aunt Prudence was so sweet on him herself she didn't give me any chance."

"Then perhaps it was—" began Fullerton in the same gentle tone he had used before, but he was interrupted by the witness:

"Hold up, boss, I ain't finished yet—I was a-going to tell you how Aunt Prudence asked me to watch that ere Mallaby, but when I told her how keerful I was to run every time I saw him, or the girl looking, why she took the whole business right out of my hands, and gave it to my father.''

"And did your father continue the watch upon the prisoner that you had begun?" asked the counsel, very softly.

"Well, I can't calkerlate about continuing it—he never continues anything so far as I know; and I'll just preface my remarks by telling you what Aunt Prudence says. She says he ain't got the head to continue anything, and I'm as certain as that apples don't grow on cranberry bushes, that he wouldn't a-had the head to run off as I did when he found they were looking. He'd a-sneaked out of sight."

"Were you aware that it was at Mr. Kellar's instance you were employed to watch the prisoner?" persisted the counsel.

Mallary shook his head.

"I can't say as to that. Aunt Prudence told me to watch that ere Mallaby, and I'll just preface my remarks by saying, I didn't know what in thunder she wanted him watched for. Any more questions, boss?"

But Fullerton had no more questions to ask. He had gained for his summing up what few points it was possible to gain, from the witness, and the latter was suffered to leave the stand which he did with the same bound that had marked his exit on the former occasion.

The cross-examination of the other witnesses elicited nothing in favor of the prisoner ; excepting that of Nanno Kelpley. She testified to the kindness she had always experienced from him.

XLVI.

THE summing up by the prosecuting-attorney riveted the popular conviction of the guilt of the prisoner. The summing up by Fullerton, which followed, though eloquent and masterly was unable to shake that conviction.

He sought to show from Kellar's own evasive replies on the witness-stand, as well as his refusal to answer some of his questions, that his motive for telling John Turner of the shooting of his brother so many years after the deed, was revenge, and not the conscientious motives to which he had sworn; and he tried to show also from Kellar's evasive and as the lawyer believed it to be, perjured evidence, that the witness had taken "hush money" from the prisoner but, lacking proofs to sustain his statements, and not being able as in those days to have the testimony of the prisoner taken, all went for naught. He defended the prisoner's course in permitting the death of the victim to seem to be a suicide, on the plea of the protection needed by his poor, young, friendless wife—had he, confiding in his innocence of any intention to kill, proclaimed the truth, there might have been in those early, lawless times in California but scant justice done him, though many should believe his story. Then he gave a pathetic account of the meeting of the young husband and wife, and the oath she expected, after which he drew a picture of the prisoner's struggles for a score of years to seem to be only the guardian of his child, when his heart was bursting to tell her that he was her own father.

"But such, gentlemen of the jury, was the remark-

able character of the prisoner; his regard for his oath
shows an exceptional conscientiousness, and his integrity during the many years of his residence in
New York, an integrity that has been fully proved
by the evidence obtained thence, shows a character
that it would be inconsistent to believe could be
guilty of murder. And this singular honesty of the
prisoner was no match for the conspiracy formed
against him by the witnesses Mr. Kellar and Miss ·
Liscome.

"Mr. Kellar, in his evidence, elicited by cross-examination, denies all knowledge of the letter written
by his cousin to the prisoner—a letter containing
mysterious allusion to the laying of a spectre, and
which is signed alone with his cousin's Christian
name—until he is told of it by Miss Liscome, and at
the same time made acquainted by that lady with
the agitation which the mere utterance of the name
Jared, caused the prisoner to show.

"Mr. Kellar admits that while he is silent on the
subject of the prisoner's mysterious agitation to Miss
Liscome, he thinks nevertheless that his cousin *was*
the author of the letter which gave to Miss Liscome
her knowledge of the name that she used with such
singular and sinister purpose.

"It is evident that Mr. Kellar, despite his sworn
evidence to the fact that he was actuated alone by
conscientious motives, managed his points so well,
that not only were Miss Liscome and her nephew
brought to California, but that Miss Liscome was ad-
mirably coached with regard to her testimony of the
prisoner's agitation as witnessed by herself, since that
lady could remember no more of the contents of the
remarkable letter than the phrase already quoted,
and the signature.

"It is also evident that revenge is no small part of
the motive which has induced Miss Liscome to testify. Had the prisoner in the interview so graphically

described by her, accepted the heart, both symbolical and literal, that she offered him, she would not
have transferred her maidenly regard to Mr. Kellar,
and consequently she would not have given that
gentleman the opportunity to make of her so willing
a tool.

"When these facts are well considered, and when
the exceptionally honest and conscientious character
of the prisoner is remembered, the conviction of his
guilt at least in impartial minds, must yield to the
belief that the killing of Reuben Turner was done
in self-defence."

But that speech had little power against the
proofs of guilt ably marshalled and reviewed by
the prosecuting-attorney. It seemed almost farcical
to oppose it to the prisoner's letter to John Turner,
containing the criminating threat, to the evidence of
Wildred Everley who had come upon the scene of
the shooting in time to see the pistol in the grasp of
the prisoner, to hear its report, to see Reuben Turner
fall, and to hear his dying exclamation, beside the
testimony of the other witnesses. And as there was
no proof of the charges made by Fullerton against
Kellar's evidence, no proof of anything favorable to
the prisoner, beside the testimony of Nanno Kelpley
save the integrity of his character while in New
York, there was no prospect of an acquittal for him,
and but little that his sentence might not be the extreme penalty of the law. The faint, forlorn hope
of finding Jared, to which Fullerton had clung, had
also vanished: not a line of reply had he received to
any of his numerous notices.

In the shadow of that gloomy outlook, neither the
prisoner nor his daughter, when they were again together in his cell, had any disposition to speak
even to each other. On the morrow the case would
be given to the jury, and then would come the verdict and the sentence. Father and daughter were

thinking of the sentence, but each in a different way; she was dwelling upon the ignominy for him, and her heart-broken grief of her parting with him; he was picturing the lonely, unprotected condition in which it would leave her. In the intensity of their thoughts they drew closer to each other, and at length to conceal emotions against which she could no longer struggle, she dropped her head upon his shoulder, lifting it almost immediately, however, for the door of the cell was opening. It was not Mr. Fullerton, as both she and her father expected to be, but the warden accompanied by the gentleman whose name she had one day in the court-room inquired of Mrs. Sibly. Though knowing that it could not be, still, he was so like Wilbur in form, gait, expression, everything, save his heavy beard and the lines in his face, that she sprang to her feet, her countenance flushing and paling, and her heart beating as if it would burst.

The gentleman advanced slowly, seeming to keep in the rear of the warden, while at the same time he drew his handkerchief from his breast-pocket, it might be to conceal with it some emotion showing in his face; but with it he had drawn forth also something that fell with a little metallic ring, and that glistened almost at her feet. With a sort of involuntary motion she picked it up, and seeing upon it her own Christian name, she recognized the case of her long lost rosary, and looking from it to the stranger it did not need that he should extend his hands, for her to know him at last.

Mallaby also recognizing him, had arisen, and the warden, feeling that it was not necessary for him to remain to introduce Mr. Dawson, as he had expected to do, and divining that it was not quite an ordinary meeting of friends, silently withdrew.

Alas! for the strength of a woman's indignation against the object that she once has fondly loved, when that object seems to approach her with its old affection. It was so with Agnes; she forgot for the moment everything but the delight of being again in the presence of one who was once, and it must be written, was still so dear, and when he took her hands and pressed upon them kiss after kiss, she did not withdraw them.

The prisoner, never having considered that there was any just cause for indignation, and delighted because of his daughter's delight was smiling his own welcome to Wilbur.

It was some time before the lovers could compose themselves. Wilbur to tell his story, and Agnes to listen to it. But, at length, he told rapidly how Kellar had informed him that Mallaby was a murderer; that Miss Hammond was his, Mallaby's own child, and that she probably knew that fact, but thought it well for some purpose to conceal it. He depicted the anguish it had cost him to give her up, and how when he had compromised with his pride by asking her to leave her guardian, her refusal to to do so had confirmed him in the belief of Kellar's suspicion, that he knew Mallaby was her father. He described his flight to California to claim the fortune left by his uncle's peculiar will, and his assumption of the name of Dawson in accordance with that will. His vain efforts to distract his thoughts from his betrothed; his presence in the court-room from the very beginning of the trial, and his belief in the prisoner's guilt, and that Miss Hammond was but acting a part until the day of the revelation of her relationship to the prisoner. The startling manner in which she received that disclosure compelled him to believe in *her* innocence, and though he could not conquer his pride sufficiently to see her and resume his severed relation to her, his love for her prompted him to ascertain if there were no way in which he might be of secret assistance to her. Learning Mrs. Sibly's address he contrived to see that lady and without revealing his entire story to enlist her sympathy and confidence, giving to her the money with which she so liberally supplied Miss Hammond. "I would not tell you this now," he continued, "but that it may serve as a little extenuation of conduct that seemed, and that *was* heartless.

"To-day at the close of the speech of the prosecuting-attorney, when I saw how utterly hope seemed to have died out of the hearts of you both, I would listen to my pride no longer. Criminal, though you were," turning to the prisoner who stood as if he were transfixed, "your sacred regard for your oath, your upright character during those years of struggle and suffering, were expiation sufficient to wipe from your character every stain, and your daughter, she who sacrificed everything in the interest of the duty she felt to be hers, what manhood clinging to such a wretched pride as was mine, would not before the nobility of such a character have felt itself ashamed and wretched. It was so with me. I hated myself for the course I had pursued, and I could not rest until I came as I have done to ask the pardon of you both, and, should I not be permitted, as I do not deserve to be, to resume my former relation to your daughter, that, at least, I may have the mournful satisfaction of being to her a brother and a protector."

He drooped his head a little at the last words as if in accordance with the humility of his speech, while into the prisoner's eyes came an unwonted and unbidden mist. He turned to his daughter. Her tears were already flowing; tears of gratitude and joy. Her father took her hand and placed it in that of Wilbur.

"This is the best answer I can make," he said, "except to add that God is very good!"

And then a silence fell upon the three for a few moments; the emotions in the heart of each were too sacred and too thrilling for speech to break upon them by a word.

Wilbur accompanied his betrothed when she went home from the prison, and when Mrs. Sibly met them at the door on their entrance she seemed very joyfully surprised.

"I know it all," Agnes hastened to say, "the cunning plot between you both to supply me with money. It is a consolation to know you considered me a charitable object."

The widow laughed.

What a lenghty conversation the lovers held; there were no reserves now, and as Agnes frankly depicted her sufferings from the mysterious fear, doubt and suspicion that marked every day since her last farewell to Wilbur, over two years before, he was mentally calling himself a brute, a monster, and other equally hard names. Then, he told of his constant love for her which he could neither forget nor subdue; how it flamed with an ardor that drove him day and night to his law book for distraction; and how it made hateful the very fortune he had gained by giving her up.

"But I can atone for that," he continued, "for to-morrow morning I shall set about resigning it."

This sacrifice of fortune which he had been so willing to make in the past and which he was now ready to renew, to her mind, more than atoned for his conduct in having sacrificed her to his pride, and she said half tearfully:

"It is too much, far too much, that you should lose so large an amount of money for my sake."

He silenced her with a look even before he answered:

"Never speak to me like that again."

He told her that Deborah kept house for him, and

that, when she would have commented on the trial accounts of which she carefully read in the paper, he sternly commanded her not to make the slightest allusion to it; also, when he learned of the presence of Miss Liscome in San Francisco, that he forbade his sister to give her any invitation to the house.

Then he expressed his opinion of Kellar, an unmitigated scoundrel— and he cheered Agnes's heart by saying that he was convinced of her father's innocence so far as regarded any premeditation of the crime. At that point, Agnes feeling that she had cruelly permitted herself to forget in her present happiness the poor prisoner, burst into tears, telling as soon as her emotion would suffer her to speak the cause of her distress, her anxiety about the verdict of the morrow.

Wilbur's face also grew very grave and sad. He knew how little there was to inspire hope; still he must say something to comfort the weeping girl.

"Where is your trust in God which has sustained you so far, and so well? Can he not work miracles to aid us, and will he let the innocent perish unjustly?"

The words seemed to have a strange and prophetic significance; she dried her eyes and looked up with a smile, and a little after when they parted, it was with singularly renewed hope in her heart.

The prisoner on the departure of his daughter and Wilbur, had dropped to his knees. His gratitude to God who had so singularly come to his succor must have fervent expression and he clasped his hands and raised his eyes. He uttered no form of prayer, but his grateful soul looked through every lineament of his raptured countenance.

His one thought, his one anxiety had been his daughter; her want of means, her unprotected, friendless condition should the verdict insure for him either death or a long imprisonment; now that his anxiety in that respect was removed, confident that in Wilbur she would have all he could desire, he was cheerfully resigned to any fate.   He could even forgive Kellar, and smile at the poor vengeance the latter had gained.

Later in the evening when there called the Catholic clergyman who visited him at regular intervals, the prisoner seemed strangely happy.

"Thank God for me, Father," he said, shaking the priest's hands, " for he has relieved me of every anxiety."

XLVII.

THERE was many an angry struggle for places in the court-room on the day that the verdict was expected, and by the time that influence, or main force had succeeded in effecting an entrance, despite the fact that there seemed to be not an inch of room, the place was so densely crowded some of the ladies fainted, and not a few of the sterner sex contemplated with some dismay their packed quarters.

Agnes and Mrs. Sibly were attended by Wilbur, and his betrothed, feeling his strong arm near her, seemed to have renewed within her the strange hope with which he had inspired her the evening before. The prisoner had never looked as he did on that morning; he seemed to be so perfectly at peace, and with even something like a constant smile about his lips. The wonted restlessness of his hands—that restlessness which always seemed to suggest that he missed his umbrella—was entirely gone; they reposed without a motion upon his knees. His eyes turned nowhere from his daughter; no commotion in the crowd, no stir in his own vicinity took them for an instant from her face, until his counsel coming in hurried to him and whispered something. The whisper seemed to be like an electric shock, for the prisoner started in his seat, then he turned and faced Fullerton; that gentleman nodded as if in confirmation of what he had said, and then the prisoner looked again at his daughter.

The witnesses were all there each in his or her accustomed place. Kellar in his flashy dress and with his triumphant air—it was all the more triumph-

ant this morning because he at length succeeded
by arts best known to himself in winning John
Turner's warm friendship, and that friendship like
every other friendship of Kellar's meant money to
him.

Miss Liscome looked crestfallen and sad; even her
dress gave evidence of her dejected feelings; it had
neither the ornament, nor the jauntiness of former occasions, and the rouge on her cheeks seemed short in
quantity. She was seated beside her nephew and between the frequent sighs to which she gave vent she
looked with piteous appeal at Kellar. But her looks
met no response; his eyes never wandered even in her
direction. The cause of her sadness lay in the little
paper parcel which was in her pocket, and that, accompanied by a note had been left at her residence
the evening before.

It was the return of her golden heart from Kellar,
and the note, also from him, said, that as she had
chosen to parade the delicate affairs of her life before a public court, he could not without violating
his self-respect, retain longer her present to him, nor
continue any acquaintance with her. He had been
careful to give in the note no hint that he had retained her gift until he was assured she could not be
of further use in the trial. Vain and shallow as she
was, she *had* experienced a little misgiving about
the effect upon Kellar of some of her answers during
the cross-examination.

Though Kellar prepared many of her answers for
her, he was not able to forecast all the whole of Fullerton's cross-examination and Miss Liscome had not
the skill to evade the questions, nor could she resist
the flattery that accompanied them. But her misgiving had been allayed by Kellar's own manner to her
on the evening of that day; he had called upon her at
her boarding-house, and treated her with his flattering attention, wearing as he had done from the time

of its presentation, the little gold heart as a charm on his watch-chain. Such conduct made the cause assigned for the return of his gift inexplicable, and the more frequent were her failures to attract a look from him the more direfully woe-begone became the expression of her face. At length in her utter dejection, she seized the arm of her nephew and whispered: "Why does not Mr. Kellar ever look this way like he used to do, Malliflower?"

But Malliflower holding himself rigidly upright, and looking over his stiff shirt collar for any stray speck on his bright blue suit, either did not hear the question, or was incapable of giving an answer, and his aunt had not even the spirit to repeat her inquiry.

It was evident that something unusual was pending. Instead of the wonted preliminaries of giving the case to the jury there were proceedings that made people whisper, and crane their necks, and in some cases even rise from their seats. Papers were rustling in the hands of each counsel, and being exchanged between the assistant attorneys; the Judge seemed to be studying voluminous documents, and the faces of the jury were expressive of puzzled surprise. Wilbur and his companions became affected by it; the eager, concentrated expression of his face showed that, though he did not speak, and Agnes almost breathless from a sort of wild, mysterious hope, not however unmixed with fear, felt unable to say a word. The prisoner sat as he had done at first; calm, motionless, almost smiling, and constantly looking at his daughter.

The cause of the unusual proceedings was announced—the trial was to be reopened in order to take the testimony of an important witness who had just arrived from a distance. Then the name Jared Hale was called. Kellar bounded from his seat, his action causing as many eyes to be turned upon him as

there were upon the witness; his eyes protruding until they seemed likely to burst from their sockets,
and his face pale to ghastliness, changed his appearance in such a manner that Miss Liscome who had
been so absorbed in watching him as even not to
have heard the name of the witness, said in a loud,
frightened whisper to her nephew:

"What on earth's the matter with Mr. Kellar,
Malliflower?"

But Malliflower still engaged in looking for specks
on his clothes, only answered, indifferently:

"Nothing, I reckon."

Some one pulled Kellar down into his seat, and
then every eye was turned upon the witness, Jared
Hale, who by this time had taken his place in the
witness stand—a tall, slim man beyond middle age,
with a certain odd looseness about his dress, and a
face with a kind though somewhat weak expression.

It was Wilbur's turn to start. The witness was
his old college professor with whom he had sojourned
in the little French town. With the suddenness of
a flash he remembered the explanation given to him
of so many American papers being in the little bachelor household — in case that some one should be
brought to trial that he, the professor, should learn
it in order to testify to the innocence of the accused.
And the prisoner was the accused, and the professor
had come to testify his innocence.

Thrilling with delight he stooped and whispered
to Agnes:

"Your father is saved."

He was right. The evidence of Jared Hale, own
cousin to Nathan Kellar, and supposed by the latter to have been killed, proved conclusively, that
not only was Kellar's testimony false in every particular, but that he had been the means of breeding
the emnity between Forrester and his father-in-law,
Reuben Turner.

Hale's testimony given in full was to the effect that he and Kellar were brought up by an uncle in one of the New England States, both receiving the same advantages of education, but the witness, Jared, seemed to be more the favorite of the widowed, childless, and wealthy uncle. The favor to Jared was further increased when the latter at an early age was offered and accepted a professorship in Yale College. That professorship he retained for two years, then home to spend a vacation, and succumbing to the fascinating influence of his cousin, he stole a thousand dollars from his uncle. The amount in some way was not missed for a long time and then it was supposed to have been a miscalculation. But Kellar used the theft as a rod over his cousin, threatening whenever the latter seemed reluctant to yield in any matter, to reveal it to his uncle, and as the uncle had unusual confidence in Jared and seemed disposed to make him largely his heir, the threat always had the desired effect.

Kellar, thirsting for novelty and excitement induced his cousin when the California gold fever broke out to consent to accompany him to the mines. On their way thither they met Frank Forrester, and reading at once his trustful, generous disposition Kellar exerted his blandishments upon him. The result was Forrester's consent to accompany them to the mines, and his generous defrayal of expenses on frequent occasions. In San Francisco, stopping to make purchases at Reuben Turner's store, all three fraternized with Turner, and Forrester becoming ill was urged by Turner to remain. He did so, marrying Turner's daughter as had been told in the former evidence, and eventually coming out to the mines with his father-in-law.

Thus far both Kellar and Jared's luck in the mines had been poor; and the former had become moody and despondent, but from the time of Forrester's arrival his spirits brightened, one reason being that he was able to strike Forrester immediately for a loan. And Forrester seemed to have unusual luck, better than any of them, thus exciting Kellar's secret envy and rage; often he vented his feelings in private to Jared, calling Forrester hard names, and saying that he would yet compel him to give up the greater part of his lucky finds. But that which most excited his malicious anger was the final refusal of Forrester to continue his loans of money to Kellar: they might better have been called gifts, for they were never repayed; and to further his revengeful ends he set deliberately but secretly to work to make Reuben Turner hate his son-in-law. He made insinuations; he told willful lies; he created distrust of his fairness in dividing his finds according to mutual compact, but all under the pledge of secrecy, and Reuben Turner, being naturally of a suspicious nature, and lacking both penetration and judgment, imbibed it all. At the same time, Kellar pretended to be Forrester's friend, deploring the growing dislike of Forrester that was so apparent on the part of Turner, and Forrester too frank, unsuspicious and generous to divine the truth of matters, seemed to think at first it was but a trifling misunderstanding which time would explain.

So much had Kellar wormed himself into old Turner's confidence, that the latter on more than one occasion showed him the letter he was about to send to his daughter, and it always contained bitter statements of his son-in-law's deceitful, and even dishonest character; he also showed to Kellar his daughter's replies in which she said how her marriage to such a man had been due alone to her gratitude to him for saving her father from financial ruin, that she should have trusted to her first instincts of dislike for him owing to his odd dress and ways, and now, because of the accounts in her father's letters every feeling of love that had been born both of her gratitude to

him and his tender regard for herself, had given way
to hate and loathing: that she had imparted her feelings to her young uncle, John Turner, so that his
hatred of Forrester was as strong as her own. Kellar when confiding all these things to his cousin, exulted, and when the latter, repelling in his heart
such utter baseness, ventured to remonstrate, he was
silenced by the old threat, for the uncle though not
altogether pleased with Jared's departure to the
mines still somewhat sympathized with the ambition
it evinced, and he continued to write encouragingly,
if not affectionately.

On one day, that Forrester was in high spirits about
his luck, his father-in-law excited by recent insinuations of Kellar, could not contain himself from making some scathing insinuations as to Forrester's fairness and honesty. Forrester hotly repelled them,
and then, Turner's blood becoming roused he sprang
toward Forrester but was caught and held back before he reached him, while Forrester looking at him
indignantly said that he would fix him one day,
meaning as he afterward averred to both the cousins
to make at the end of their stay in the mines, such a
generous division of his gains with his father-in-law
as must surprise and shame the latter.

After that there were other occasions on which
Turner seemed to want to assuage his feelings by descending to brute force, and it required all Forrester's
self-control to prevent himself from yielding to his
own instinct in that respect. And all this time Forrester never suspected the underhand work of Kellar; he even confided in him to the degree of deploring the utter unreasonableness of his father-in-
law's strange dislike, and referring to his agony at
the brief, cold letters written to him by his wife.
She did not state in them that her father told her
anything, but too well Forrester divined that he
did, and at length unable to endure the situation

longer he determined to leave the mine and return
to San Francisco. That was the signal for unusually
bitter feelings on the part of Turner; influenced by
Kellar he believed the resolution to depart was owing to a desire to cover up his dishonesty, and in-
flamed both by passion and the liquor with which he
had been plied by Kellar, he, on the last night that
Forrester was to spend with the miners, rushed suddenly upon Forrester as the latter sat at play with
Kellar and Hale. Forrester was obliged to struggle
to defend himself, and when Hale would have gone
to his assistance he was withheld by Kellar. During the struggle he saw Turner draw his pistol, but
it was wrested from his grasp by Forrester, and immediately after went off, the ball piercing Turner's
head. Everley coming upon the scene at that instant beheld what might very well seem to him to
be the murder of Turner by Forrester, and his opinion was further corroborated by the dying man's
exclamation.

That his cousin and he had taken Forrester away
from the fallen man. That Forrester seemed dazed,
and declared on recovering himself that the shooting was purely accidental; he had no intention of
firing the pistol when in self-defence he had wrested
it from Turner. Kellar pretending the utmost sympathy for Forrester, held hurried consultation with
his cousin, advising that it were better to give out
that Turner had committed suicide. Hale, seeing
no necessity for that, as he and his cousin were
sufficient witnesses that the shooting was done in
self-defence, objected, but Kellar silenced him. And
then Kellar worked upon Everley's sympathies, picturing the destitute condition of Forrester's young
wife and how if anything were said about the shooting other than to make it appear a suicide, Forrester would be held, and perhaps summarily punished.
Everley consented to say nothing about the matter.

When told of the plan, Forrester at first, neither assented nor objected; he seemed to be unable to realize that he had really killed Turner, and he returned to the corpse, and felt in a wild way its face and limbs as if to assure himself that death had really taken place. Owing to the lawlessness and excitement of the times the event did not attract much notice among the miners, nor was the report of suicide doubted. In their rough way a few were sorry for the mournful task of Forrester — to have to bear back to his young wife the body of her father, dead by his own hand—but the majority had neither time, nor thought for the event.

Kellar, on the pretence of taking temporary charge of Turner's effects, helped himself to what he fancied would not be missed immediately, and before setting forth with the corpse to San Francisco, he exulted in secret to Jared, boasting, that not alone would he contrive to keep some of the dead man's property, but he even intended to get a handsome bonus from Forrester. He succeeded, for having with his cousin and Forrester accompanied the remains to Turner's home, and having waited their interment, he managed when announcing his intention of going East, to make Forrester understand that he would not be averse to some compensation for his services. And he was liberally compensated, Forrester being grateful for Kellar's sympathy and assistance.

Kellar and Hale went East; both sojourning for a time in their uncle's house, and Kellar pretending that he had been very successful, and was eager to cement his success by speculations in Australia where there seemed just then to be a field for such, he gained his uncle's confidence to the extent of an advance of money, and his consent to have Jared accompany him. They went to Australia, and Kellar engaged in speculations which involved all his money and which lost it. Then he began to think of taking part in a questionable scheme formed by some new acquaintances he had made: the scheme proposed dishonest operations with a firm in New York, and in looking over a New York paper for the advertisement of this firm, he saw a paragraph relating to a man named Mallaby. Not knowing that Forrester had left California, and that he had changed his name, Kellar did not dream the paragraph had any interest for him. He read indifferently how a man named Matthias Mallaby had a sharp chase after some one who was a heavy debtor to the firm by which he, Mallaby, was engaged, and how outdoing detectives employed in the case, he had caught him and brought the fugitive to justice. Then followed remarks on the clever manner in which Mallaby had done his work, and a full description of his own odd appearance. From that description Kellar became convinced that Mallaby was Forrester and a new idea entered his mind. It was to return to New York, seek Forrester, or Mallaby, and endeavor to obtain a price for his silence on the manner of Reuben Turner's death. He might acquire as large an amount from Mallaby as he could do by being connected with the proposed dishonest scheme, and certainly with much less risk. Evidently, Mallaby was doing well, and rather than be disturbed he would be willing to pay liberally.

To Jared's remonstrances he replied that it was nothing to bleed Mallaby a little and that as Jared could not help matters he had better be silent, for he, Kellar, had only to tell their uncle of Jared's theft to destroy at once, and entirely, all hope of Jared's inheritance, knowing as both nephews knew, the utter abhorrence entertained for all forms of dishonesty by their rigid old uncle. As it was, Jared's prospects were very good, for the uncle, led to believe that both of his nephews were doing finely in Australia, wrote with great affection to Jared, encouraging him to remain, until he had made a fortune, and too weak to resist, and too fearful of losing his inheritance he yielded as he always did. He remained in Sydney while his cousin returned to New York, found Mallaby, and boldly told him his errand; he had come to be paid for his silence. His plan for enforcing his demand was so well arranged that Mallaby had no alternative but to consent to it.

On Kellar's return to Sydney he told it all to Hale, exulting in his success as a fair and clever piece of work, and to the sworn knowledge of Hale, Kellar received three or four times every year sums of money from the prisoner which Kellar admitted to the witness were paid in order to prevent him, Kellar, from telling John Turner that the latter's brother was killed by Forrester. That Kellar always acknowledged the receipt of those amounts by letters written in a disguised hand, and never signed with his own name. That never had the witness written a line to the prisoner. That during all this time the witness was very unhappy; that he wanted to get away from his cousin, but he was too morally weak, friendless, and destitute of means. That he both feared and detested his cousin. That his own hope of separation was his uncle's death; did that give to him the fortune he expected, he could defy his cousin and put a long distance between them.

That, before that event happened a letter came from the prisoner to Kellar, stating that, owing to business difficulties he was obliged for the present to lessen the amount of the remittances. That Kellar swore on reading that letter, and then being again approached by parties with inducements of the large and rapid gains to be made by coöperation with them to entrap the firm with which the prisoner was connected he declared that if the prisoner continued to send a decreased amount, he would return to New

York, and compel the prisoner himself to manage the matter of involving the firm.

That, to further his plan he took into his confidence Samuel Wylie, one of the company who was anxious to enlist his, Kellar's services. That Kellar told Wylie of the sword which he, Kellar, held over the prisoner in the shape of exposing the facts of the shooting of Reuben Turner, at the same time unguardedly admitting to Wylie, that the prisoner was a fool for permitting himself to be terrorized when he knew he had shot his father-in-law in self-defence. That Wylie was not quite the unscrupulous villain Kellar thought him to be, for though from the force of circumstances and evil association, he had been led to make one of a dishonest company, he secretly recoiled from the base scheme of compelling another to promote swindling operations as the price of forbearance to make an unjust charge of murder.

That said Wylie and the witness finding in each other more congenial qualities than either found in Kellar, they grew to fraternize in secret, and to exchange confidence that enlightened each as to the opinion of Kellar held by the other.

That Hale's uncle died, leaving to him not the fortune he had expected, but a moderate annuity, and to his cousin, what the latter considered a very paltry sum of a thousand dollars.

That Hale determined to separate from Kellar; that he proposed to Wylie for the latter to leave his trickster friends, and accompany him, Hale, to Europe. That Wylie consented, and Kellar was furious until Hale appeased him, and at the same time somewhat quieted his own conscience, by offering to raise for Kellar on his annuity a large amount, providing that he, Kellar, would pledge himself to threaten the prisoner no more. That, Kellar, always eager to get money, gave the pledge, but at the same declared that he was not going to lose sight of his cousin, a declaration which Hale felt would be fulfilled, and with regard to frequent occasions of begging money, and otherwise annoying him, unpleasantly kept. That, parting with his cousin with assumed grace, he and Wylie went to Rome, Italy. That, when there but a single week, a railroad accident happened in which there was killed a tourist, by singular coincidence bearing the name of Hale, and being of the same age. That, the coincidence suggested to Hale an entire escape from his cousin. He sent Wylie back to Sydney with the Italian newspaper containing an account of the accidental killing of the tourist, Hale, and he also sent by Wylie such personal effects as might tend to corroborate the story. That, about the annuity Kellar could not trouble himself, as he knew in accordance with the terms of the will it was at the death of Hale to revert to the institutions to which the bulk of his uncle's wealth had been bequeathed.

That Wylie, to insure Kellar's conviction of the death of his cousin, remained some time in Australia. That, during that time he learned that Kellar regardless of his pledge to Hale, was again contemplating extorting a consent from the prisoner to coöperate with the dishonest company of which Wylie had once been a member. This company had begun its operations in Sydney, and it was eager to be affiliated with some reputable and wealthy firm in New York.

That, Wylie having learned that, left Australia, joined Hale who had gone to Paris where he lived under an assumed name. That, the two repaired to Annecy where they made a permanent home. That, in order to learn if Kellar should execute his threats regarding the prisoner, Hale became a constant subscriber to the leading New York and California daily papers, that in such an event he might be ready to rebut the false evidence of his cousin.

That, the delay in his present appearance as a witness, was due to illness which had caused him and Wylie to spend several weeks at some German baths; that it was only at the end of their stay there he happened upon the notice in a German paper requiring information of himself. That, though the notice was not explicit as to the direct object of the information required, he suspected it, and without waiting to return to Annecy, he and Wylie had come with all possible speed to San Francisco. That, they had only arrived the evening before, and had gone directly to the address given in the newspaper notice.

The subsequent events had been arranged by Mr. Fullerton who had not an opportunity of acquainting the prisoner with the good news until that morning in court.

That evidence turned the scale at once in favor of the prisoner, and it was whisperingly reported and fully believed that Wylie's testimony which was about to be taken, would criminate Kellar to the extent of not alone having given perjured evidence, but of having been an accomplice in a business scheme intended to defraud and swindle.

But Kellar gave no opportunity to convict him. Reading in the face of everyone about him convicting testimony of the entire and indignant change each one's feelings had undergone regarding his testimony, his resolution was quickly formed. Taking a note-book out of his pocket he tore a leaf from it and wrote a few lines rapidly in lead pencil; folding it he addressed it to the prisoner, and passing it to his counsel, he whispered:

"Don't give this for five minutes."

Then he put his hand into his breast-pocket and drew forth some small, dark object; he raised it quickly to his head, and before a hand could interpose, he had fired and fallen, shot through the brain.

XLVIII.

Forrester was acquitted; not only acquitted by the unanimous verdict of the jury, but entirely acquitted in the mind of everybody; even John Turner knowing at last how utterly wronged had been his brother-in-law, and as full of admiration for his self-denying, patient, generous character, as he had been before of hatred for his supposed baseness, hastened to tender his congratulations, to ask pardon for his own misguided conduct, and to insist that his niece and her father and even Mrs. Sibly should make their home with him; but Agnes and her father, grateful though they were for his offer, and freely forgiving him, preferred to remain with Mrs. Sibly for the short time that was to elapse before Agnes's marriage to Wilbur, Wilbur insisting that their union should take place as speedily as possible.

He had already resigned his fortune to the utter horror and dismay of his sister, and had declared his intention of returning East directly after his marriage where people need not know that he had ever borne any name than Wilbur, and where he intended after a voyage to Europe with his bride, to begin the practice of law. Regarding Deborah, he would provide for her anywhere she chose to reside only he stipulated that her choice was not to fall upon the abode he and his wife should select; and then he suggested that she might throw her lot with her friend, Miss Liscome; probably the latter would return to New York, and if Deborah were so inclined she could go in her company to all of which

Deborah having already exhausted tears and hysterics, vouchsafed only a scowling look.

But, when she heard that the very day was appointed for the wedding and that a magnificent entertainment was to be given directly after by John Turner at his palatial residence, she acted upon her brother's suggestion, and actually returned to New York in the company of disconsolate Miss Liscome, and her queer, ridiculous nephew.

In the preparation for the wedding there was but one cloud on the happiness of Agnes; the memory of Florence; and telling everything about that last letter to Sydney he also thought it strange; neither had he heard from her, since he had parted with her and her mother in Italy, and not having the heart to tell her of the cloud again upon his happiness, he had not written to her.

"But we shall seek her," he said by way of comforting his betrothed; "we three, your father, you and I. A little after our return to New York, we shall go to Europe for a few months. I need a rest before beginning my practice."

Agnes answered with a smile of delight, and her happy father smiled also; indeed, his face might be said never to be without a smile now, and the smile seemed to have worn away many of the lines, produced by his past suffering, and to give a glow of youth to his features on which his daughter was never tired of fondly commenting.

The contents of the paper that Kellar had given to his counsel, for the prisoner, Agnes never knew. Neither her father, nor her betrothed would breathe a word of it to her. It ran:

"Did Wilbur tell you my revelation to him concerning *your daughter* that she was your illegitimate offspring, and that she probably knew that fact? I honestly thought so, not having your guardianship satisfactorily explained to me. It gave him a healthy shock, which added to my revelation of your cold-blooded murder, would tend, I did not doubt, to break his engagement. I fancy that it did, although to-day I behold him with Miss Hammond—pardon me, Miss Forrester.

"To clear your mind with regard to the letter that husband-seeking spinster used with such terrorizing effect over yourself, I wrote it just previously to Jared's departure for Italy. I wanted to show you, that he was waking up to the fact of his silence being worth something, and to imply that I had been wont to share with him what I had received from you. But I did not tell him about that letter, and I sent it to your office in order to scare you more effectually. The effort to disguise my hand anew sent it I suppose into the possession of that fool Mallary.

"With your old luck in the mines, the cards in this game have turned in your favor, but, in order not to let you euchre me this time, in five minutes I shall be dead.

                                  Your *old* friend,
                                          KELLAR."

At the wedding entertainment there were Jared Hale, his companion, Samuel Wylie, and the old nurse, Nanno Kelpley, not to mention the bridesmaid, Mrs. Sibly. Hale was groomsman; he and Wilbur having warmly renewed the friendship begun so many years before at college, and resumed for a brief period at Annecy. The entertainment was much more simple than John Turner had intended it to be; but he could not withstand the wish of his beautiful niece.

Immediately after the wedding the bride and groom accompanied by the father of the bride, departed for New York, while Hale and Wylie, to gratify a desire both had for oriental travel, took passage in a steamer for Yokahama. Mr. Turner being a bachelor, and seeming to have conceived a very friendly interest in pretty Mrs. Sibly it was hardly difficult to predict what might happen. Nor was Nanno Kelpley forgotten; in addition to Turner's promise to provide for her, Wilbur made her a munificent present, so that the poor old creature was quite bewildered with her good fortune.

Mrs. Wilbur, having requested that on their arrival in New York, the little party should go to Mrs.

Denner, instead of to a hotel for the brief time of their stay before departing to Europe, a telegram to that effect was dispatched to that good woman. Never were preparations for guests made with such unmixed delight. Everybody was pressed into the service, and everybody was informed that the parlor was to be given up to the exclusive use of Mr. and Mrs. Wilbur, so that if anyone should want to receive company during the time of the stay of the distinguished guests, that person must either receive his, or her company in his or her own room, or find a place outside for such reception.

And what a meeting it was when the little party arrived; Mrs. Denner was not restrained into proper decorum by even the presence of handsome, stately Mr. Wilbur, but having kissed and hugged the bride she actually threw her arms around Mallaby, or Forrester's, neck, and kissed him, saying through her tears of joy:

"You dear, blessed man."

And the "dear, blessed man" took the caress with a pleasant grace, knowing how warm and true were the feelings that prompted it. And when the excitement of the meeting was over, including the extravagant welcome of all of what used to be the little Denners, but, having grown so much might now be called the big Denners, how much Mrs. Denner had to say about the events that had occurred to Mr. Mallaby, the name by which she still called him.

And in the preparations for the voyage to Europe she took so active a part it threatened to interfere with the interest which duty demanded she should take in her boarders. Indeed, that large-hearted woman was in such a high and perpetual state of exhilaration that her vivacious spirits infected the boarders, and they all, even to the two deaf old ladies acted as if they expected some very great good

to come to themselves from this visit of the distinguished Mr. and Mrs. Wilbur. Of course everybody had heard of the singular story from Mrs. Denner; but the part upon which she loved most to dilate was the evidence that *she* had been summoned to
give. In telling that she was wont to become so interested, and so particular to impress upon her hear-
er, or hearers, that no judge nor jury were going to
get out of her anything derogatory to "that blessed
man," that the most imperative summons to attend
to some domestic affair was entirely unheeded.

The universal interest continued to the very last
day of their stay, as well as the universal desire to
contribute in every possible way to the happiness,
or accommodation of the distinguished guests.

To Mallaby, as everybody in the house still called
him, no one being able to get used to the name of
Forrester, it all seemed to be a delightful dream; he
could hardly realize that he was free from the old
haunting fear of the past, and sometimes, when he
was alone and the memory of it became so strong
that it was almost like renewed reality, he was obliged to hurry into the presence of his daughter, or
his son-in-law, to dispel the delusion. And never was
a father the recipient of more tender attentions—it
seemed to be a sort of rivalry between the husband
and wife as to who should maintain the most constant and affectionate watchfulness of the gentle old
man.

Sometimes, when Agnes fondled the large, white,
freckled hands—hands that she would not now have
changed for the most beautiful ones in the world—
there came to her even through all her joy, a pang
of remorse for the mortification those same hands
had so often caused her in her school days, and she
kissed them the more passionately for her self-reproach.

Every one of the Denners went down to the steam-

er to see the departure of their guests. It required
four carriages to convey the party, not including the
carriage in which the guests themselves went and
the way in which Mrs. Denner lingered over her own
leave of " that blessed man," and the way in which
she compelled her numerous offspring to linger over
his, or her leave of "that blessed man departing for
a foreign shore," was exceedingly amusing and would
have been trying, did not he and Agnes and Sydney
know how it was prompted by the very warmest affection.

To London the travelers turned their faces in order
to obtain information of Florence.   London was the
home of her mother's kindred, and thither would
be the most likely place for knowledge of Mrs. Wilbur's whereabouts.

What was the dismay and self-reproach of Agnes
to learn that Florence's mother had died three months
before in an insane retreat in the northern part of
Italy being devotedly attended by her daughter to
the last.   That Florence had then repaired to a convent of the Order of the Perpetual Adoration in Paris
where she was now a postulant.

It seemed to Agnes as if every mode of travel were
too slow to take her to Paris; she wanted to flee
there, to clasp Florence at once in her arms, confess
her selfish, unkind, unjust neglect, and beg forgiv-
ness.   Sydney also reproached himself, and he was
as anxious as Agnes was to lose no time in seeing
his niece.

How little fear they need have had of any reproach,
was dispelled on the first sight of the pale, young novice who flew to greet them, but who in her eagerness
to embrace Agnes seemed almost to ignore the latter's
companions.   Again and again she pressed Agnes
to her, unable to speak for tears of joy, while Will
bur and his father-in-law retreated to a respectfu-
distance.   It was Agnes who at length half bore her

to the gentlemen, saying with a strange mingling of playfulness and tears:

"Your uncle, Florence, and my husband; and this is my father."

The last words were uttered with a tone of pathetic gravity, and the astonishment they caused Florence who had not heard a word of the wonderful events of the past three years, stopped the greeting she was extending to her uncle.

"*Your father!*" she repeated, and then in a sort of dazed silence she looked up at the odd figure which she so well remembered. It was as odd now, and save that its hair was entirely gray, and its face much older, it was the same veritable figure even to the umbrella, only that the latter was black silk with a sterling silver handle, and not the green cotton one with its knotted horn handle. But the brown eyes wore the expression which had so won her that evening in Hubert Street, and while the tears that her astonishment had stopped for the moment, began again to flow, she put both her hands into those of Mallaby that were already extended, and said:

"I am so glad; it always seemed as if you ought to be more to Agnes than her guardian."

After that the wonderful story was told, and then mutual explanations were given of the neglect of everybody to write. Florence, generous, self-sacrificing Florence, at the time that she received Agnes's last letter, had just been made aware by the physician attending her mother that the latter's mind was giving way, and that the best course to be pursued was to take her to a retreat which he could recommend in the northern part of Italy, and his opinion was corroborated and his advice endorsed by other physicians.

Forence could not, would not cloud the happiness of either Agnes, or her uncle, by writing such sad news, and having obtained permission to attend her mother in her retreat, she thought it was better since Agnes's happiness was assured, to write in a way that might stop for a time all correspondence. Since her beloved friend was so happy she could bear a little wound like that better than the sorrow of knowing that Florence was immured with her insane mother. And the generous girl, not dreaming that the insanity was to continue and finally end in death still forbore to write, until she could have brighter news to tell. And when the end came that released the troubled spirit of Mrs. Wilbur, and left her daughter free to gratify the longing for a cloistered life which had seemed to grow steadily during her residence in Italy, she still refrained from writing to America, only because she waited to tell them of her religious profession.

That she had chosen well and happily for herself every word that fell from her lips, every expression that crossed her face seemed to tell. She was the same cheerful Florence that Agnes had ever known only that her cheerfulness now, seemed to spring from something much higher than its sources in the past.

To Agnes, and even to Wilbur, the plain features seemed to have assumed an inexplicable beauty; as if the pure, peaceful, generous soul shone through them, and informed every lineament with its own spiritual loveliness. Mallaby felt while looking at and listening to her, as if he were in the presence of an angel.

They parted at length, the happy-hearted novice to add a *Te Deum* to her prayers of praise and gratitude for the reward which God had given to sacrifice and devotion to duty, and Agnes, and her husband and father to feel as if that interview had brought upon them a very special blessing.

XLIX.

THERE is little more to tell that would interest the reader. Wilbur, and his wife and father-in-law, after the absence of a half year returned to New York where Wilbur began the practice of law, and Mallaby,— as it seems more natural to call him—declared that he felt as if his youth was wondrously renewed, insisted on resuming his old avocation; he stipulated that it was necessary for his health, and his son and daughter had at length to give a reluctant consent. The three lived in a very pretty, but modest suburban residence, and thither Mrs. Denner visited as frequently as she could be spared from her domestic duties, and she always received a warm welcome. Thither also, came letters from Florence, signed, after her religious profession, "Sister Mary Agnes," and breathing the happy, peaceful, heavenly spirit that had seemed to emanate from her on their meeting in Paris. And thither came one day, announcements of the marriage of John Turner to Mrs. Sibly; the announcements accompanied by magnificent presents to everybody, each member of the numerous Denner family being remembered individually, and a promise to come East on their wedding trip which promise was duly and delightfully fulfilled.

Deborah Wilbur and Miss Liscome took up house together, the latter severing entirely all relations with her sister and her sister's family; the only occasion upon which she ever visited them being to attend the funeral of her nephew, Malliflower, who had met his death prefacing his remarks one day at dinner, while at the same time he was attempting to greedily swallow an unusually large mouthful of meat. His parents, thinking that his efforts to relieve himself were only part of the eccentricities in which he sometimes indulged, did not go to his assistance soon enough, and the unfortunate youth was choked to death.

As the time wore on, and little ones blessed the charming home of the Wilburs, Agnes, in her own happiness compassionating the lonely and isolated life led by the two spinsters, prevailed upon her husband not only to tender them a warm invitation, but when it was rejected, to repeat it, and to keep repeating it at stated intervals, until at length, time and disappointment having softened the feelings of the two maiden ladies, the invitation was accepted.

Agnes treated them both with such cordial grace, Wilbur was so delightfully affable, and Mallaby—as if he did not have a single thought of the past—was so gentle and gracious, that the suburban visit speedily grew to be a longed for occurrence by the two old creatures; indeed, Miss Liscome after her first shyness had worn off, was so exceedingly affable to Mr. Mallaby, that both Sydney and his wife could not refrain from making jocular comment upon it to the old gentleman, and begging him to be on his guard lest he might again be put to the painful task of refusing the proffer of her heart.

Of Hale and his companion, Wylie, Wilbur occasionally heard; they had concluded their oriental travel and had resumed their bachelor existence in Annecy, but the latter threatened to be broken, for Wylie was contemplating matrimony.

For Wilbur himself, happy in the possession of his noble and beautiful wife, and of children whom she trained to that strict conscientiousness which swerves from no duty, he never failed to thank God for it all, and also, to unite with her in instilling into the minds of his children such a respect for worth of character that no oddity of costume or manner could detract from it. Thus, the close of "Mr Mallaby's" life was rich in affection, and honor, and happiness.

"Deo Gratias."

So. WOODBURY, VT.,
Aug. 25, '86.

FINIS.